School Safety in the United States

School Safety in the United States

A Reasoned Look at the Rhetoric

David C. May
Associate Professor of Sociology
Mississippi State University

Carolina Academic Press
Durham, North Carolina

Library of Congress Cataloging-in-Publication Data

May, David C., 1966-
School safety in the United States : a reasoned look at the rhetoric / David C. May.
pages cm
Includes bibliographical references and index.
ISBN 978-1-61163-021-3 (ali. paper)
1. School violence--United States. 2. School discipline--United States. 3. Schools--Safety measures--United States. 4. Behavior modification--United States. 5. Classroom management--United States. I. Title.

LB3013.32.M39 2014
371.7'82--dc23

2014031419

Carolina Academic Press
700 Kent Street
Durham, North Carolina 27701
Telephone (919) 489-7486
Fax (919) 493-5668
www.cap-press.com

Printed in the United States of America

This book is dedicated to my wife, Natalie, and my children, James, Will, and Grace May. The main reason I care so deeply about school safety (and thus the topics in this book) is because of these incredible people and my desire for them to be safe when I'm not around to protect them. They are my reasons for living and, without them, nothing I've accomplished or hope to accomplish really matters.

Contents

Acknowledgements

This book, and the research included herein, would never have been possible without the guidance, assistance, knowledge, and friendship of Mr. Jon Akers, Executive Director of the Kentucky Center for School Safety. Although I had dabbled in school safety research prior to my position as School Safety Research Fellow at the Kentucky Center for School Safety (KCSS), it was in that position that I truly begin to understand the complexities of school safety. Much of that understanding is due to his own knowledge and experience and to discussions, experiences, and research that Jon and I shared over the decade we worked together at KCSS. Jon allowed me the flexibility to conduct research about school safety in a wide variety of areas. He and I didn't always see eye-to-eye but, in every discussion, our mutual respect for one another and our friendship was not damaged by the sometimes heated disagreements we had about how school safety research should be conducted. In the time since I have left the KCSS, I have continued to rely on Jon's guidance and friendship to help my family as we have dealt with more personal issues. I treasure the time I've spent with Jon and all the things I have learned from him. His impact in my life and the lives of my family is one that will truly never be forgotten.

In addition to Jon, there were numerous KCSS staff that helped me in my research over the years. I'd like to thank Kristie Blevins, Yanfen Chen, Barbara Gateskill, Nadine Johnson, Shannon Means, Ashlee Oliver, and a number of other current and/or former KCSS employees that tolerated my impatience and crazy requests that shaped my research agenda over the years. I would also like to send a special thanks to Lee Ann Morrison, my replacement as KCSS research fellow, whose desire to use this book in her class was the final push that I needed to put this project together. Without that decision, the book certainly wouldn't be in print in 2014 (and might not ever have made it to print).

Next, I'd like to thank the numerous coauthors that I worked with in conducting the research included in this book. Without exception, each of them was a joy to work with and I'm happy to count them as coauthors, colleagues, and friends. Each of the chapters where coauthors are listed are better products because of their contribution.

Next, I'd like to send a special note of gratitude to Ethan Stokes and Brianna Wright, graduate students that worked with me in preparing this book. Although both are listed as coauthors for one or more chapters, their contributions went far beyond those chapters. Ethan assisted in updating the literature reviews in a number of areas and I'm thankful to him for that. Brianna served as my copy editor, peer reviewer, and guide; without her skills and quick responses to requests, this book would have been delayed for weeks and perhaps even months.

Finally, I'd like to thank Beth Hall and her coworkers with Carolina Academic Press. Working with them has always been a joy; their easygoing nature and their attention to detail makes any work I've done with them much better (and much more pleasant) than an author could expect from a publisher. I look forward to continuing my work with them in the future.

School Safety in the United States

Chapter 1

Introducing the Critical Study of School Safety

This book took over a decade for me to complete. No, I did not begin writing this book in 2004; that process actually began in earnest (with some extended breaks that followed) on August 16, 2011. On that day, I was sitting in a lawn chair under a portable pop-up shelter in Powell County, Kentucky. As I began this book, I heard the birds, a bee, and crickets chirping as the wind rustled through the trees. On that day, a wild turkey walked within 10 feet of my chair and three deer ran within 50 yards of where I sat. In this idyllic setting, I found it difficult to even conceive that such a thing as school violence could ever exist. Yet I knew that this topic was important and that this book needed to be written. Furthermore, given my own life and research experiences in this area, it made sense that I would be the author.

In fact, one of the reasons I began writing this book in the peaceful, relaxing setting was because I had to go to a rural setting with limited cell phone and no Internet service to escape the daily needs and activities of my job as the Kentucky Center for School Safety Research Fellow and criminal justice professor at Eastern Kentucky University. At that time, I had been in that position (in some fashion) for over a decade. In the 11 years I spent in that role, I was immersed in a world of research around School Resource Officers (SROs), safe school assessments, cyber-harassment of teachers by parents, parental aggression against parents, school-level crisis response plans, mentoring of at-risk youth, and weapons in schools.

Three hours after I penned the first paragraph of this book, I was reminded of the need for continued attention to school safety. My wife called me and interrupted my serene, peaceful environment to inform me that the middle school where my eldest son attended was in lockdown because of a bank robbery within two blocks of their school (McDonald, 2011). While I commend the school administrators for their quick response and their attention to the protocol that we developed collaboratively as part of their crisis response plan, that phone call reminded me that, no matter how we try to escape the issue of school safety, it is one that everyone hears about, cares about, and has an opinion about.

In 1998, the Kentucky General Assembly passed House Bill 330. This bill, among other things, established the Kentucky Center for School Safety (KCSS) and required that school districts report data about the disciplinary actions in their districts annually to the KCSS. The mission of the KCSS is to serve as a central point for data analysis, research, and dissemination of information on successful safety strategies, and technical assistance for safe schools. Through the KCSS, each year the General Assembly distributes over 10 million dollars to public schools throughout the state to be used to help with efforts designed to promote school safety. Part of that money is used to support the KCSS operations, which are housed at Eastern Kentucky University.

House Bill 330 is generally considered to be a result of the school shooting that occurred at Heath High School in West Paducah, Kentucky, on December 1, 1997. At 7:45 a.m., 14-year-old Michael Carneal walked on campus carrying two rifles, two shotguns, and one .22 pistol wrapped in a blanket. He then proceeded to the school's lobby where about 40 students were holding an informal prayer group before classes began. Carneal opened fire on the group, killing three students and wounding five others. The media followed the small-town, rural American shooting closely, focusing on the fact that the victims were primarily from a prayer group meeting at the time of the shooting (CNN Library, 2014). From this tragedy, and the Kentucky state legislature's response to it, emerged the KCSS and my job as research fellow.

From 2003–2012, I was the lead author on a report submitted to the Kentucky Department of Education and the Kentucky state legislature (May & Chen, 2011). This report provided a portrait of disciplinary actions against students in Kentucky. Many of these disciplinary actions were used to ensure the "safety" of the school environment and the students that attend that school. Yet, despite the time and energy involved in the analysis of the data and report writing for that report, I'm the first to admit that (a) I have little faith the report presents an entirely accurate picture of behaviors in public schools in Kentucky (the reasons for that skepticism are outlined later) and (b) the report had little impact in Kentucky and even less nationally and internationally in terms of truly impacting school safety. At best, it gives a fuzzy picture of what is going on in public schools in Kentucky.

Nevertheless, my decade of experience and research as a criminal justice professor and as the Kentucky Center for School Safety research fellow convinced me of several things. First, and most importantly, schools are the safest, most positive environment many adolescents have in their lives. In a typical week, I join my two sons at a Boy Scout troop meeting where I serve as their scoutmaster and all three of my children attend mid-week Bible study on Wednesday nights. At least one night each week, one or more of my children are involved in band, play practice, Tae Kwon Do, or some other extracurricular or community event. Most weekends, I either attend a scout outing in the outdoors with one or both of my sons or go horse riding on my children's horses. We spend Saturday night together as a family where both parents eat supper with their children in a suburban house that they own. For my kids, the public schools that they attend are places where both mom and dad have great relationships with the teachers and administrators and are generally positive environments.

However, my family's experience is the exception, not the rule, in many towns in the United States. I have often said "I hope my kids never know how blessed they are until they become adults and look back on their childhood." I say this because my work with disadvantaged youths has exposed me to the dark, seamy underside in which many kids survive. Not long ago, I was at a Teen Center where my 12-year-old and I had gone to deliver some school supplies for the kids attending the center. While we were there, I saw a 14-year-old youth named Tejon (not his real name, but a pseudonym I've given him to protect his identity). When I think of discussions of school safety, and hear parents, the media, and some legislators portray our schools as dens of crime and iniquity, where children are lucky to come home each day alive, Tejon (and many others like him that I have met over the years) are the children that I wish they knew.

In the spring semester, Tejon was involved in an incident at that teen center that the director felt warranted his suspension from the teen center. I personally knew Tejon because of my work with kids at the center. Because of that relationship, and my role as one of the Board members for the Teen Center board of directors, I was asked to go to the middle school (which both Tejon and my son attended) and inform him that he could no longer attend the Teen Center. While we were waiting for Tejon to be summoned from his class, both the guidance counselor and the assistant principal in charge of discipline asked if there was another way to handle the situation that did not involve Tejon being denied participation in Teen Center activities. Both of them knew Tejon well and knew that their school and the Teen Center were the most stable and rewarding experiences in Tejon's life. Given that it was not my decision to make, I told them we had to abide by the director's decision but would try to get Tejon back on track in whatever way we could. When I informed Tejon that he was suspended, there was no angry outburst, no violent reaction. Tejon mumbled that he understood, dropped his head, and walked out of the room.

That was about six months prior to the beginning of this book. In those six months, Tejon changed middle schools, then ended up back in the middle school my son attended. Tejon was back at the Teen Center and, by all accounts, was behaving better in school and at the Teen Center, although he was on probation for some activities he chose to engage in outside of those environments. I was happy to see him and proud to see that he was doing better. My son was also happy to see him and greeted him warmly whenever they saw one another.

Yet, the story I hope my son never knows is what has happened to Tejon in the six months prior to the time I penned the first words of this book. During the summer months, Tejon was homeless, because his mother was strung out on various drugs, hopping from boyfriend to boyfriend, and either didn't care to or was unable to provide a place for Tejon to stay. If not for the summer feeding program through the schools, Tejon wouldn't have eaten many days. The guidance counselor and the Teen Center director and volunteers were strong advocates for Tejon (in fact, he spent some nights in the home of one of the directors during the week); without them, I have no doubt that Tejon would have been in a residential facility for juveniles or, even worse, dead.

I share the stories of my kids and Tejon with you to give you a backdrop for this book and the context in which it is written. I know schools (whether public or private) have problems. I know schools have crime and criminals in them. I know unsafe actions occur at schools. But I also know that, without our schools, our society would be in much worse shape than it currently is. You see, I know that the "safest" place some kids go to during the school year is the school. When they leave the school, they return to abusive and addicted parents, grandparents, or guardians; on the way to their homes, or when they step outside those homes, they see gang members, drug dealers, and other criminogenic role models and peers. Schools are these kids' refuge from an otherwise tragic life.

That knowledge has shaped my research around school safety and every article, book, meeting, or presentation that has come from that work. You see, 30–35 years ago, I was Tejon. Despite the fact that I was regularly in trouble for my behavior at school, school was the only sanity I had in an otherwise insane life. My mom left my dad when I was nine because his abuse of my family had escalated to the point where she was afraid we wouldn't survive another year. School was my safe haven. I'm convinced it is the safe haven of many kids today. But "schools as safe havens" is a topic you rarely hear discussed (unless you're in a discussion about natural disasters); in fact, when that term is used in discussions of school violence (see Denmark, Gielen, Krauss, Midlarsky, & Wesner, 2005), it is often used as a statement to be refuted by the sentences and statistics immediately followed by the statement.

I'm convinced the reason for this lack of understanding about the important safe haven schools offer to many students is the misinformation around this topic. This book is an effort to cast a critical eye on the issue of school safety. My hope is that the readers of this book, if they find the wherewithal to complete it, will walk away with a better understanding of school safety, its causes, and its consequences. But, most importantly, my hope is that the reader walks away with a knowledge of the facts around school safety that the untrained eye often doesn't see. As the saying goes, each journey begins with the first step. The first step in this journey is to understand exactly what is meant by the term "school safety"; the second step is to understand the data around school safety and the context from which they come. In the first chapter, these two steps of the journey will begin.

Definition of School Safety

In reviewing a wide variety of texts and articles for this book, I was struck with the pessimistic tone of many of the works. Titles such as "Violence in Schools," "School Violence," "Preventing Violence and Crime in America's Schools," among many others, reflect the strategy of publishers and/or authors to draw attention to this topic from a definite direction. In fact, the title of this book also reflects that strategy of "eye-catching titles" that make the reader want to look inside. Additionally, many of the authors chose similar strategies in organizing their works about school violence. They began with a definition of school violence and then moved on to a discussion of the prevalence and incidence of violence in the schools.

Nevertheless, I was unable to find any text that began their discussion with a definition of *school safety*. Given that there are a wide variety of ways to define both "school" and "safety," combining the two words into one concept has the potential to confuse readers and researchers even further. This fact was vividly reinforced for me several years ago when I was asked to collaborate with professors in our university's college of education to develop a graduate certificate in school safety. At the time these discussions occurred, I was in an academic department entitled "Safety, Security, and Emergency Management," a department with diverse interests (e.g., fire safety, occupational safety, homeland security, assets protection), none of which appear in the "typical" criminal justice department. My research and interests have always been in preventing crime and delinquency in school; in other words, keeping students "safe" from criminal victimization. My discussions around school safety with my colleagues in safety, security, and emergency management opened my eyes to a definition of "school safety" that I had previously ignored. In at least the early discussions around this topic, some colleagues' definition of school included the university setting; my own definition had always included only K-12 settings. Their definition of "safety" encompassed bus safety (e.g., should children wear seat belts on the bus, do drivers have proper operator's training), occupational safety (e.g., preventing hazards in buildings and on grounds), and fire safety (e.g., removing and/or controlling locations of flammable objects in the school setting). Each of these definitions was important in its own right and caused me to realize both my naiveté and lack of knowledge about school safety.

Given that experience, I want to begin the discussion of school safety by providing an operational definition of school safety that will be used throughout this book. According to the U.S. Department of Education Office of Safe and Drug Free Schools, as part of a request for proposals from Statewide Educational Agencies to fund school safety programs, school safety is defined as "the safety of school settings, such as the incidence of harassment, bullying, violence, and substance use, as supported by relevant research and an assessment of validity" (National Archives and Records Administration, 2011, p. 4).

The first part of that definition is familiar to most readers. When the typical person thinks of school safety, however, they do not think in terms of safe actions; they think of unsafe actions such as bullying, assault, drug use, or even sexual harassment. Thus, when most people think about activities other than education that take place in a school setting, what they think about would be better termed as "school unsafety," not school safety. They don't think about (or are unaware) of the strong relationships forged between teachers and students, the mentoring that takes part in those relationships and in other parts of the student's typical day. They often ignore the strong friendships that are forged between students that last a month, a year, or even a lifetime. The typical person can name at least one relatively recent school shooting (Sandy Hook would be the one that came to most people's mind at the time of this writing) but generally couldn't identify even one situation where a student told a trusted adult in the school setting about their own experience as an abused child or their knowledge that one of their fellow students intended to do harm to themselves or others, even though reports such as these occur daily throughout the United States. Thus, most citizens in the United States are very familiar with the unsafe part of the school environment but know relatively little about school safety.

To have a good understanding of school safety requires close attention to the second part of that definition " ... as supported by relevant research and an assessment of validity" (National Archives and Records Administration, 2011, p. 4). This second part of the definition is the primary focus of this book and, ideally, what sets this book apart from many other books around this topic. With one exception (the chapter on School-Specific Crisis Response Planning, where almost no scientific research exists), the chapters in this book are data-driven. In other words, each chapter begins with a literature review around the topic of that chapter, then closes with data analysis on that topic and recommendations based on those analyses. Some of the research presented in the following chapters is a result of data collection and analysis done through my role as the Kentucky Center for School Safety Research Fellow; some either predates that work or is derived from more recent data. In those chapters where the data analysis is based on previously published work, I provide the citation for that previous work, update the literature around that topic, then explore the data in the chapter and make recommendations based on those analyses. Thus, in each chapter, I strive to provide recommendations based on data gathered through the scientific method. While the recommendations from those analyses are tempered with my own experiences, they are not driven by my own experiences. Again, my hope is that distinction sets this book apart. By the time you complete this book, you will have a good idea about whether or not I met that goal.

School Safety Statistics

Cornell (2006) provides a lengthy discussion about part of the rhetoric around school violence in the late 20th and early 21st centuries. Cornell correctly points out that any discussion of crime and violence in schools must also consider youth crime and violence outside of schools. He suggests that the focus on school violence in the latter 20th century thus did not begin with Columbine but began with an article by Professor John J. DiIulio, Jr. that appeared in *The Weekly Standard* entitled "The Coming of the Super-predator." In that article, DiIulio predicted that an emerging group of violent young people termed "super-predators," young males engaged in serious, repeated violence, would increase dramatically at the end of the 20th century, thus creating a youth crime explosion by 2010. Coupled with Columbine and other school shootings that occurred at the end of the 20th century, the widespread attention given to this article over the next five years (despite the fact that his predictions never were realized) brought the issue of youth crime, and particularly youth crime in schools, to everyone's attention.

Cornell also provides evidence of how little effort is often given to sort myths about school violence from facts about violence. Cornell provides an account of a widely reported story on school violence that compared perceptions of teachers in 1940 with perceptions of teachers in more recent times. According to the report, teachers in the 1940s listed talking, gum chewing, making noise, and running in the halls as the top four problems they faced, while modern teachers listed drug abuse, alcohol abuse, pregnancy, and suicide as the most serious problems they faced. A "skeptical" professor from Yale traced the origin of the story to a Texan named T. Cullen Davis, who admitted he fabricated the lists based on his own experience as a student in school in the 1940s and his reading of newspaper accounts of school violence as an adult. Despite the fact that Davis's story was found to be incorrect, and a number of subsequent publications refuted the story, this story continued to be cited as evidence that schools were less safe at the end of the 20th century than they were in the mid-20th century.

Thus, the reader should begin this "story" with a review of current data about school safety in the United States. Fortunately, in 2014, this is much easier to accomplish than at any point in our history. The most comprehensive report about school safety is free and publicly available. Thus, rather than bore the reader with a plethora of tables about the incidence, prevalence, and types of crime that occur on school grounds, I will simply refer you to that report entitled *Indicators of School Crime and Safety, 2013*, available for free download from the National Center for Education Statistics and the Bureau of Justice Statistics at http://nces.ed.gov/pubs2014/2014042.pdf. Data from this report will be used in a number of chapters throughout this book. However, before the reader begins Chapter 2 of this book, I would encourage them to digest that report, as it is the most comprehensive descriptive analysis of school safety in public schools that is available.

Outline of This Book

In the following chapters, I provide an in-depth analysis of a variety of topics in the area of school safety from a scholarly perspective. This book is designed so that each chapter can be used as a stand-alone chapter; thus, instructors using this book can "cherry-pick" those topics they find most relevant for their course or use the entire book as a resource for a number of contemporary issues in school safety. While the topics covered in this book are not a comprehensive picture of all areas of school safety (for example, there is no chapter on bus safety or weapons in school, although these are certainly topics worthy of study), I believe that the depth provided around each topic covered here makes an important contribution. In Chapters 2 through 11, my coauthors and I review the current research around the topic addressed in that chapter, then offer a number of recommendations for research and policy at the conclusion of the chapter. Our hope is that the reader can digest each chapter in one sitting and then consider the implications of the chapter prior to delving further into the book. I close the book with a concluding chapter that attempts to tie together the recommendations from each of the previous chapters in a cogent, comprehensive, and considered manner. I close this chapter by providing brief summary of each chapter so the reader can have an idea about the journey to come.

In Chapter 2, Erin Henry, Steve Kimberling, and I examine 40 years of school homicides by expanding and updating an article that we wrote that appeared in the *International Journal of Sociological Research*. In this chapter, we use newspaper reports from the *Chicago Tribune* and the *New York Times* to track school shootings over the past 40 years. In addition to presenting the fact that the actual incidents of school shootings has not increased dramatically (but the number of victims involved in those shootings has), we review the research in this area that suggests there is no profile of a school shooter, but there are factors that can discourage them. We then make recommendations for societal change that might reduce school shootings in the United States.

In Chapter 3, Preston Elrod, Nate Lowe, and I look at the predictors of what makes students more or less likely to report the presence of a weapon at school. We use data collected from a middle school and a high school to determine that, despite the continuum of reporters that exists, the likelihood of reporting depends on both the relationship of the student with the weapon carrier and the type of weapon at school. We close by presenting implication for school policies and future research in this area.

In Chapter 4, Jerry Johnson, Yanfen Chen, Lisa Hutchinson, Melissa Ricketts and I analyze data collected from over 7,000 public school teachers to examine the prevalence and incidence of parental aggression against teachers. The data suggest that very few teachers have been victims of physical violence but many have been victims of electronic and verbal aggression. We close the chapter by providing recommendations to teachers and school administrators for strategies to reduce the likelihood of these aggressive confrontations.

In Chapter 5, I use data collected from middle and high schools in two states to discuss what makes students fearful of violence at school. The results suggest that females, those who perceive themselves most at risk, and those who feel less integrated in the school setting are most likely to be fearful. I close the chapter by providing recommendations for policies to reduce fear of crime in the school setting.

In Chapter 6, Timothy McClure and I revise an article published in *Youth and Society* to examine the prevalence of corporal punishment in schools and who is most likely to receive it. We begin by presenting arguments for and against the use of corporal punishment in schools, then analyze data collected in Kentucky to determine that a community's culture outside the school setting has an important impact on a school's decision to use corporal punishment. We suggest that, consequently, any decisions regarding corporal punishment should consider that culture as well.

In Chapter 7, Carly Cornelius, Ethan Stokes, Christy Rogers, April Walters, and I use data from a control and experimental school to examine the effectiveness of a bullying prevention program in reducing bullying and increasing student intervention in bullying incidents. We determine that, while the program increased the likelihood of bystander intervention in bullying situations, it did little to encourage bullying victims to take steps to decrease their own victimization. We close by discussing the implications of these findings, and the importance of program efficacy for effective treatment, in reducing bullying in the United States.

In Chapter 8, Ethan Stokes and I use national data and Kentucky data to examine the causes, consequences, and possible solutions to the disproportionate representation of black students in disciplinary actions in schools. We determine that Blacks, more than any other ethnicity, are disproportionately punished in the public school setting, and this disproportionality has serious implications for these students' success later in life. We close the chapter by offering a number of recommendations to reduce the disproportionate use of punishment for black students.

In Chapter 9, Ethan Stokes, Ashlee Oliver, Tim McClure and I review the literature around the negative consequences of out-of-school suspensions, then examine the impact of community service works in reducing suspensions in public schools in Kentucky. We analyze data collected from a quasi-experimental project where we implemented community service works in a number of schools to reduce out-of-school suspensions. The data suggest that alternatives to suspension reduce out-of-school suspensions for both the individual student and the entire school. Consequently, we recommend expanded use of alternatives to out-of-school suspension in general, but community service works in particular.

In Chapter 10, Brianna Wright, Gary Cordner, Stephen Fessel, and I use surveys from over 100 School Resource Officers (SROs) in Kentucky to examine the various roles that SROs fulfill in the school setting, along with their challenges and conquests in reducing violence in schools. I close by making recommendations for hiring, training, and supervision of these officers.

In Chapter 11, I review the literature around crisis response planning in schools and couple that literature with my own experiences in developing school-specific crisis response plans to discuss the need for these plans and the most effective means to create those plans. In the appendix to the chapter, I present portions of a model crisis response plan to the reader that can be used in their own local schools.

In Chapter 12, I close this book by utilizing a "lessons learned" format to summarize the conclusions of the previous chapters. I begin by discussing what the data have shown in each chapter of the book and close by using those findings to make recommendations to the reader on how to more effectively control misbehavior in schools. These ideas include:

1. The necessity to build a positive reporting climate at the school
2. The necessity of building a climate of "student ownership" in the local school building
3. The necessity of using alternatives to suspension to deter misbehavior
4. The necessity of having a local crisis response plan for each school
5. The importance of collecting and using meaningful data for schools, rather than avoiding data collection to avoid potential negative media attention.

This book is a compilation of my work with a variety of coauthors in the area of school safety over the past 15 years. My hope is that the knowledge and recommendations provided around these topics, colored through my own lens as a school safety researcher, will allow readers to explore school safety in a way that they had never previously considered. By the end of this book, I hope you share my opinion that, despite the rhetoric and negative attention given to school safety, schools remain one of the safest places many children have in their lives. Even with that assurance, I hope this book gives each reader at least one strategy or recommendation that they can use to make the schools where their children, or their neighbor's children, safer and more positive environments for children.

References

CNN Library. (2014, April 18). *Columbine high school shootings fast facts.* Retrieved June 30, 2014 from http://www.cnn.com/2013/09/18/us/columbine-high-school-shootings-fast-facts/.

Cornell, D. G. (2006). *School violence: Fears vs facts.* Mahwah, NJ: Lawrence Erlbaum.

Denmark, F., Gielen, U., Krauss, H.H., Midlarsky, E., & Wesner, R. (2005). *Violence in schools: Cross-national and cross-cultural perspectives.* New York: Springer.

May, D.C., & Chen, Y. (2011). *Kentucky 2010: Eleventh annual safe schools data project.* Richmond, KY: Kentucky Center for School Safety and Kentucky Department of Education. Retrieved June 30, 2014 from http://www.kycss.org/data10.php.

McDonald, A. (2011, August 16). Schools locked down after Richmond bank robbery. *KYNEWS.org.* Retrieved June 29, 2014 from http://www.kynews.org/articles/show/2390.

National Archives and Records Administration. (2011). Department of Education funding priorities, requirements, and definitions. *Federal Register, 76*(69), Monday, April 11, 2011.

Robers, S., Kemp, J., Rathbun, A., and Morgan, R.E. (2014). *Indicators of School Crime and Safety: 2013* (NCES 2014-042/NCJ 243299). National Center for Education Statistics, U.S. Department of Education, and Bureau of Justice Statistics, Office of Justice Programs, U.S. Department of Justice. Washington, DC.

Chapter 2

Forty Years of School Homicides: Are Our Kids Really More at Risk in the 21st Century?

*David C. May, Erin Henry, and Steve Kimberling**

Well-Known School Shootings

As mentioned in the first chapter, recent media frenzy about school violence has led many people to believe their children are at risk of being a homicide victim each time they walk through the school doors. This perception is fueled by media accounts of firearm-related homicides on school grounds (hereafter referred to as school shootings). Partly because of this attention, school shootings that occur on elementary and secondary school grounds have become familiar events in the United States. Schools such as, Heath High School in West Paducah, Kentucky, Columbine High School in Littleton, Colorado, Westside Middle School in Jonesboro, Arkansas, and Sandy Hook Elementary in Newtown, Connecticut have become infamous sites of lethal school violence. Nevertheless, despite the intense media scrutiny surrounding these murders and the impact they have, relatively little scientific information has been collected regarding school shootings (Anderson et al., 2001; Muschert, 2007) and no scientific database currently exists that captures all the school shootings each year. Of the more recent school shootings occurring at K–12 institutions, four major events stand out above the others. These are described below.

Heath High School: Paducah, Kentucky

The first in a series of infamous school shootings in the late 1990s occurred on December 1, 1997, in West Paducah, Kentucky at Heath High School. At 7:45 a.m., 14-year-old Michael Carneal walked onto the campus carrying two rifles, two shotguns, and one .22 pistol wrapped in a blanket. He then proceeded to the school's lobby where about 40 students were holding an informal prayer group before classes began. Carneal opened fire on the group, killing three students and wounding five others. The media followed the small-town, rural American shooting closely, focusing on the fact that the

---

* The information presented in this chapter is largely drawn from articles I have coauthored with two colleagues that have appeared in print elsewhere. Citations for these articles are included below:

Kelley, Erin, and David C. May. (2011). Increases in School Shootings: Reality or Myth? Forthcoming in the *International Journal of Sociological Research, 4*(1), 45–57.

May, David C., & Kimberling, S. (2007). School shooters: Research unveils 10 myths regarding perpetrators. *Kentucky School Leader*, Fall, 10–13.

victims were primarily from a prayer group meeting at the time of the shooting (Cabell, 1998; CNN, 1997).

Westside Middle School: Jonesboro, Arkansas

A second notorious school shooting that occurred in the late 1990s took place in Jonesboro, Arkansas at Westside Middle School. On March 24, 1998, cousins Mitchell Johnson, 13, and Andrew Golden, 11, ambushed and killed four students and a teacher, injuring 10 others in the event. Dressed in military-style camouflage clothing, the boys stole a van from Johnson's home and drove it into the woods near their school, loaded with seven weapons that included two semi-automatic rifles, one bolt-action rifle and four handguns. Upon arrival, they activated the school's fire alarm to get students and teachers outside and then began shooting into the crowd (Flock, 1998).

Because of their age, under Arkansas state law, the shooters could not be prosecuted as adults or held in custody beyond their 21st birthday. The case, and the intense media coverage surrounding it, led to public outcry for harsher sentencing laws for juvenile offenders. In fact, the Jonesboro prosecutor assigned to the case later stated that if it were not for the boys' age, he would have sought a death sentence for the pair. Johnson and Golden were later charged with murder, making them among the youngest ever charged with murder in American history. They were both sentenced to confinement until 21 years of age, the maximum penalty under Arkansas law. As a result of the shootings and the media coverage surrounding them, changes in Arkansas state law now allow juveniles to be tried as adults and sentenced to life in prison (Flock, 1998).

Columbine High School: Littleton, Colorado

Perhaps the most notorious of the school shootings that occurred in the 20th century was the Columbine High School shooting that occurred on April 20, 1999, in Littleton, Colorado. On this day, two students, Eric Harris and Dylan Klebold, killed 12 students and a teacher before ending the massacre with their own suicides (CNN, 2000).

The aftermath of the Columbine shooting created media frenzy. Intense debate in both print and television media outlets surrounded the killers' motivation and whether or not anything could have prevented the crime. Many believed that the pressure of social cliques in high school and bullying lead Harris and Klebold to snap. Others felt it was the influence of violent video games and music the pair enjoyed. Still others believed the shooters to be suffering from depression and other mental disorders. Further media attention focused on the shooters' apparent hostility towards religion; victims Rachel Scott and Cassie Burnell were hailed in the press as Christian martyrs for standing up for their beliefs (CNN.com, 2000).

Sandy Hook Elementary School: Newtown, Connecticut

The long-term impact from these shootings led to new nationwide anti-bullying and "zero tolerance" policies in regards to weapons and threatening behavior. New safety measures such as see-through backpacks, metal detectors, and security guards added to the so-called "Columbine effect" of increased security across in the U.S following the shooting (CNN.com, 2000). Nevertheless, as the December 2012 shooting at Sandy Hook Elementary school in Newtown, Connecticut, where 20 students and 6 adults were shot and killed by Adam Lanza, suggests, the post-Columbine safety measures cannot completely prevent further school shootings such as these described above. After the Sandy Hook shooting, there were renewed calls for additional gun control measures from President Obama and numerous other political leaders. Despite this public outcry, relatively few gun control measures were actually adopted, although Connecticut did ban assault weapons and large capacity magazines (Dolmetsch & Pettersson, 2014).

Despite the host of changes brought about because of these shootings, there is little evidence that supports the popular notion that school shootings have increased in recent years (Muschert, 2013; Anderson et al., 2001). Until 2010, there was only one database of which we are aware (compiled by the National School Safety Center) that sought to document the school shootings in the United States for an extended period of time and that database is no longer current. However, this database had a number of weaknesses, the primary weakness being that it only covered school shootings back to 1992, an inadequate amount of time when one is looking at long-term trends in school shootings. The NSSC also highlighted the fact that they may have missed certain school shootings due to their collection methods and lack of reporting from local newspapers. Furthermore, the media articles that report on school shootings that do exist are often skewed, leading us to believe we are living in a more dangerous and crazed society than we actually are (Herda-Rapp, 2003; Lundman, 2003; McCombs & Shaw, 1972; Muschert, 2013; Muschert & Carr, 2006; Potter & Kappeler, 2006; Schildkraut, 2012).

In this chapter, we attempt to add some clarity to the topic of school shootings in the United States. Using databases from two of the largest newspapers in the United States, we trace a 45-year history of school shootings in the United States. By doing so, we hope to add some reality to what may well be an "ill-conceived myth" of increased school shootings in the United States.

The Facts about School Shootings

A common public perception surrounding school shootings is that they are currently at an all-time high, with schools being dangerous places for children and adolescents (Borum et al., 2010; CDC, 2001; Cornell & Mayer, 2010; Elliot, Hamburg, & Williams, 1998; Halikias, 2004; Ryan-Arredondo et al., 2001). Recent research, however, indicates that this is not the case, as school shootings, while tragic, are in fact only rarely occurring events (Anderson et al., 2001; Borum et al., 2010; CDC, 2008; Kimberling & May, 2007; U.S. Department of Education, 2001; Vossekuil, Fein, Reddy, Borum, & Modzeleski, 2002). Surette (1998) perhaps best describes this phenomenon of rare events receiving massive amounts of news coverage by stating that the "relative infrequency of violent crime in the real world heightens its newsworthiness and leads to its frequent appearance in the crime news. Crime news thus takes the rare crime event and turns it into the common crime image" (p. 68).

The evidence reviewed in *Indicators of School Crime and Safety* highlights the fact that, while children are at risk for violence at school, the chances that they will fall victim to homicide while on school grounds are remote. Children are at a far greater risk of homicide in their own communities than at school. From 1997–1999, 100 students were murdered on or around school grounds, while during those same years, more than 6,000 people under the age of 18 were murdered in their communities (Gillespie, 2000).

In regards to yearly trends of school shootings, again contradicting popular beliefs that school shootings are increasing, from 1992–1999 there was a steady decrease in homicide rates per year (Anderson, 2001; CDC, 2001). However, during this time frame, there was an increase in the amount of multiple-victim homicide rates. Recently updated figures by the CDC (2008) report that overall and single-victim school-associated student homicide rates decreased significantly from July 1992 to June 2006, decreasing from 0.07/100,000 students to 0.03/100,000 students. However, during a more recent timeframe (July 1999 to June 2006), these rates did not change significantly. Also during this timeframe, multiple-victim homicide rates remained stable.

Although school shootings may not be common events, it is still important to understand the characteristics surrounding them. In their 1999 paper, McGee and DeBernardo separate school shootings into two distinct groups, traditional and non-traditional school shootings. In their view, traditional school shootings involve juvenile gangs, inner-city problems, minority or ethnic status, turf warfare, drugs, or other criminal activity. Non-traditional school shootings involve more than one victim and are similar to episodes of workplace violence, described as workplace vengeance. Most of the media attention, especially since 1998, has focused on non-traditional school shootings (McGee & DeBernardo, 1999).

When it comes to understanding the attacker in school shootings, it is also important to note that there are no clear-cut profiles to use or signs to look for when attempting to identify a potential attacker (Kimberling & May, 2007; Linder, 2014; Mulvey & Cauffman, 2001; Vossekuil, Fein, Reddy, Borum, & Modzeleski, 2002). Vossekuil et al.'s (2002) in-depth report of 37 school-homicide attacks in the United States failed to reveal a common profile amongst attackers. Although all of the offenders were males, there were no common set of traits that described all or even most of them. The attackers ranged in age from 11 to 21. While three in four were white, the others were from a variety of ethnic groups. The attackers came from a wide variety of family backgrounds, ranging from youths from wealthy intact families with numerous social ties to those who were in foster care with histories of neglect. While some of the students were considered "loners," the majority of the attackers was involved with their classmates and involved in extracurricular activities.

In 2002, the United States Secret Service and the U.S. Department of Education released a report in which researchers reviewed case files of 37 attacks by current or former students and interviewed 10 of the perpetrators (Vossekuil, Fein, Reddy, Borum, & Modzeleski, 2002). The authors identified 10 myths about school shootings based on those interviews and case files. These reported myths are reviewed below:

1) **"He didn't fit the profile."**—In the study, it was concluded that there are no useful profiles or profile tools to effectively identify individuals that could possibly initiate a school shooting. Within the 37 cases, the personality and social characteristics

of these individuals varied greatly. The shooters' ages ranged from 11 to 21 and they came from various racial and ethnic backgrounds.

2) **"He just snapped."**—It is rare that a case of "targeted violence" is an impulsive act. More often than not, these actions had been well thought out, sometimes up to two weeks (or more) in advance.

3) **"No one knew."**—This is a disturbing finding in that in virtually all the studied cases, someone else knew about the idea or plan. In the majority of these cases, the other people knowing about the plan were students, friends and/or siblings. This knowledge rarely made its way outside the "code of silence" (to school officials prior to the attack). The reasons why students choose to report knowledge of weapons on campus is covered in the next chapter; nevertheless, in two-thirds of the cases studied, the perpetrator acted alone, but friends or fellow students encouraged or influenced the attacker to take action in almost half of them.

4) **"He hadn't threatened anyone."**—The study takes the position that too much emphasis is placed upon actual threats. The research indicates that most attackers did not threaten. Further, most people who actually threatened did not carry out an attack.

5) **"He was a loner."**—In many cases, the students who actually carried out the attack(s) were considered to be in the mainstream of the student population and were active in sports, school clubs, or other activities. Only a quarter of the students hung out with a peer group that was considered to be a "fringe group." Advanced knowledge of the attacks by other students contradicts the notion that "school shooters" are loners and that they just "snap."

6) **"He was crazy."**—The only mental health themes that emerged were a history of suicide attempts or suicidal thoughts and a history of feeling extreme depression and/or desperation. Most of the attackers in the study had difficulty dealing with significant losses or personal failures.

7) **"If only we'd had a SWAT team or metal detectors."**—Most incidents were not resolved by law enforcement intervention. In fact, all of the shootings studied were quick and of short duration. Most of these incidents were stopped by school staff or by the shooter's choice to stop shooting or commit suicide.

8) **"He had never touched a gun."**—The research study revealed that most of the attackers had access to weapons and had used them prior to the attack. The weapons utilized in the attacks were usually obtained from the shooters' homes or the home of a friend or relative.

9) **"We did everything we could to help him."**—Continual harassment and bullying behaviors were common themes throughout the study. While not all students bullied will resort to this severe form of retaliation, this was a factor in some of the school-based attacks.

10) **"School violence is rampant."**—The media attention that gravitates to these high profile incidents makes it seem like school violence is at an all-time high, when it actually is not. While there are homicides and targeted attacks on school grounds, this number has actually decreased by nearly half over the past decade. The fact is the number of children and youth victimized by school-related homicides makes up less than one percent of the total number of murders of children and youth in the United States each year.

Although the report's findings highlighted the fact that there is little common ground surrounding the perpetrators of school shootings, the research is more cohesive regarding the causes behind the murders. While there is no clear answer as to why shooters decide to shoot, many studies cite prior bullying and continual harassment from peers as a common cause of school shootings (Beane, 2005; Bender, Shubert, & McLaughlin, 2001; Burgess, Garbarino, & Carlson; Kimberling & May, 2007; Kimmel & Mahler, 2003; Klein, 2012; Vossekuil et al., 2002). In Vossekuil et al.'s report (2002), 71% of the attackers felt persecuted, bullied, threatened, attacked, or injured by others prior to the attack. Other commonly cited causes for school shootings consist of the aforementioned reasons behind traditional school shootings, including gang-related and ethnic issues, violent music, video games, the availability of guns in schools, and mental disorders amongst the attackers (Elliot, Hamburg, & Williams, 1998; Kimmel & Mahler, 2003; McGee & DeBernardo, 1999).

The Fiction of Rampant School Shootings and Its Causes

As mentioned earlier, the most common public perception surrounding school shootings is that they are currently at an all-time high, with schools being dangerous places for children and adolescents (Borum et al., 2010; CDC, 2001; Cornell & Mayer, 2010; Elliot, Hamburg, & Williams, 1998; Halikias, 2004; Ryan-Arredondo et al., 2001). Many believe this public perception and increase in fear over school violence is a result of extensive media coverage of school shootings (Arnette & Walsleben, 1998; Brooks, Schiraldi, & Ziedenberg, 2000; Chiricos, 2000; Glassner, 1999; Lawrence & Mueller, 2003; Reddy et al., 2001). For example, in 1999 alone, major television networks aired 296 stories on school shootings (Halikias, 2004; Reddy et al., 2001). In a Gallup poll conducted one year after the Columbine High School shooting, 63% of parents of students in kindergarten through 12th grade believed that a similar tragedy was very or somewhat likely to occur in their community. Furthermore, 70% of these parents agreed that the Columbine shooting made them more concerned about their own child's safety at school (Gillespie, 2000).

The research presented above reveals large gaps in the existing research. One glaring gap is the lack of research regarding the prevalence of school shootings in decades prior to the 1990s. There is little research examining these types of homicides in the 1960s, 1970s, and even 1980s in any systematic way. Thus, in the following pages, we examined school shootings in two of the most widely circulated national newspapers in the United States from 1966–2013, gaining knowledge on the prevalence, trends, and characteristics of school homicides from the earlier decades to the current one.

Because of the dearth of research examining long-term trends in school shootings in the United States, coupled with the popular perception that school shootings have increased over time, we examine the following hypotheses:

H_1 Following popular perceptions (CDC, 2001; Elliot, Hamburg, & Williams, 1998; Halikias, 2004; Ryan-Arredondo et al., 2001), there will be a significant increase in the number of incidents of school shootings per year when comparing the 1966–1996 time period with the 1997–2013 time period (Cabell, 1998; CNN, 1997; CNN.com, 2000; Flock, 1998).

H_2 In line with popular beliefs (CDC, 2001; Elliot, Hamburg, & Williams, 1998; Halikias, 2004; Ryan-Arredondo et al., 2001), there will be a significant increase in the number of total victims from school shootings per year when comparing the 1966–1996 time period to the 1997–2013 time period (Cabell, 1998; CNN, 1997; CNN.com, 2000; Flock, 1998).

Data Source

For these analyses, a school shooting was considered any firearm-related homicide that took place in the United States on the property of a functioning public or private elementary or secondary school or at a school-related event. The articles used in this study were drawn from two national newspapers with wide circulations in the U.S., *The New York Times* and the *Chicago Tribune*. Online archives and databases were used to obtain the articles.[1] These two newspapers were chosen primarily because (a) their wide circulation and coverage of events throughout the United States arguably offer the most thorough coverage of events from all parts of the United States and (b) our database searches revealed that, among the national newspapers with the widest circulations, the newspaper archives of these two papers offered the most comprehensive coverage over the 40-year period.[2]

Finding Articles: The Search Process

The online archives were searched a year at a time, beginning in 1966, exhausting each year before moving on to the next year. Truncations were utilized in the search process in order to maximize search results. Each search began with the word "school" and then continued with a combination of other relevant keywords such as "shoot*," "shot*," "gun*," "kill*," and "murder*." After the word "school" and the list of keywords were exhausted, the words "student," "teacher," and "principal" were combined with the keywords in order to complete the search.

After performing a search with keywords, the relevant articles displayed in the search results were then analyzed and recorded. An article was deemed relevant to the study if it documented a firearm-related murder that occurred on school grounds or at a school-related event. The variables for which data were entered included the year, date of the article, date of the incident, time, and location of the shooting.

Results

The results presented in Table 2.1 and Figure 2.1 illustrate the breakdown of 47 years of school shootings (we included 2013 as the last year because that was the last year for which an entire year of data were available at this writing). Interestingly, despite the fact that school shootings began receiving an increased amount of press in 1997, the total number of incidents in which school shootings occurred did not increase dramatically after 1997. In fact, the number of incidents of school shootings remained relatively stable over the 47-year period. Despite the fact that the number of incidents did not increase dramatically over the 47-year period, the number of school shooting victims did increase considerably after 1997. The three years in which the number of homicides at schools was highest were all after 1997. The years with the greatest number of school homicides were 2013 (36), 1999 (15), and 2007 (11).

H_1 Results—Number of Incidents

To examine the hypothesis regarding the number of incidents of school shootings, we first documented the number of incidents per year from all 47 years. We then recoded the year of each incident into a dichotomous variable where the incidents occurring from 1966–1996 were coded (0) and the incidents occurring from 1997–2013 were coded (1). We then conducted an independent samples t-test to determine whether the hypothesis was correct. The results demonstrate that the mean number of incidents per year for the earlier years was 2.52 and the mean number of incidents for the latter years was 3.24. This difference was not statistically significant ($t = -1.46$; $p = .076$, one-tailed). As such, H_1, which stated that there would be a significant increase in the number of incidents of school shootings per year from 1966–1996 to 1997–2013, was not supported.

H_2 Results—Number of Victims

To examine the hypothesis regarding the number of victims of school shootings, we first documented the number of victims per year from all 47 years. We then recoded the year of each incident into a dichotomous variable using the same strategy outlined above and conducted an independent samples t-test to determine whether the hypothesis was correct. The results demonstrate that the mean number of victims per year for the earlier years (4.68) was much lower than the mean number of victims for the later years (7.47). Although this difference was not statistically significant at the $p < .05$ level, it was very close to that level ($t = -2.83$; $p = .055$, one-tailed). Thus, we argue that H_2, which states that there will be a significant increase in the number of victims of school shootings per year from 1966–1996 to 1997–2013, was partially supported.

Discussion

The purpose of this chapter was to examine trends in school shootings from the perspective of writers in two national newspapers from 1966–2013. Below we discuss the findings uncovered in this research.

Our first hypothesis (H_1) stated that, following popular beliefs (CDC, 2001; Elliot, Hamburg, & Williams, 1998; Halikias, 2004; Ryan-Arredondo et al., 2001), there would be a significant increase when comparing the number of incidents of school shootings occurring per year from 1966–1996 to the time period when school shootings were more publicized, in the years 1997–2013 (Cabell, 1998; CNN, 1997; CNN.com, 2000;

Flock, 1998). The results presented earlier demonstrate that, although the number of school homicides did increase slightly between the two time periods, this difference was not statistically significant.

This important finding suggests that, despite the general public's belief that school murders have risen rampantly over the past two decades, the number of incidents of school shootings in the United States have not significantly increased in recent years. In fact, they have remained relatively stable. As mentioned throughout this work, one possible reason for the popular belief that school shootings are on the rise is the influence of the media. By sensationalizing events such as school shootings and flooding newspapers, televisions, radios, and now the Internet with reports of the violence when it occurs, the media are constructing their own reality where school-associated homicides are a frequently occurring and threatening problem to our society. The data collected here disprove this constructed reality, noting that the number of incidents of school shootings occurring now are similar to those that occurred back in the 1960s and 1970s, when there was not a common public perception that school shootings were a major problem.

Our second hypothesis (H_2) stated that, following popular beliefs, (CDC, 2001; Elliot, Hamburg, & Williams, 1998; Halikias, 2004; Ryan-Arredondo et al., 2001), there will be a significant increase in the number of total victims from school shootings occurring from 1966–1996 to those more highly publicized school homicides occurring from 1997–2013 (Cabell, 1998; CNN, 1997; CNN.com, 2000; Flock, 1998). The results presented here demonstrate that there was in fact a significant increase in the number of victims of school shootings from the years 1966–1996 to the years 1997–2013. These findings differ from the findings of the first hypothesis; the number of victims from school shootings in the United States has been increasing in recent years.

Consequently, it appears that the *nature* (but not the prevalence) of school shootings has changed over the past four decades. While the *incidence* of firearm-related homicides on elementary and secondary campuses has not significantly increased, the *number* of victims that have died because of those homicides has. There are several possible reasons for this increase. One possibility is that semiautomatic or handguns or assault rifles may have become more popular firearm choices in recent years than revolvers and shotguns, thus enabling the shooter to quickly fire more rounds, resulting in a higher number of victims. In the articles we reviewed for this chapter, the majority of newspaper articles did not elaborate on the type of gun used in the shooting, so further research into this topic is warranted.

Another possible reason for the increase in victims could be the "copycat effect." As mentioned earlier, the media often focus on high-profile events such as school shootings and spend a great deal of time and effort reporting on the event. Potential offenders who recognize the publicity and attention the shootings that inflict several casualties receive may copy the shooting, aiming for a higher shock value by attempting to kill even more victims than the last school shooter. In the age of the Internet and 24-hour news channels, it is reasonable to anticipate that seeing massive news coverage of school shootings can encourage those who are already isolated and disaffected to commit similar acts (Deppa, 2007; Shenk, 1999). For example, in the aftermath of a 2005 school shooting in Minnesota, numerous copycat threats forced school officials in Waconia, Minnesota, and other schools around the nation to close their doors (Phillips, 2005).

Given this fact, further ways to reduce the likelihood of copycat killings need to be explored as well.

There currently are a variety of strategies that schools can use to reduce the likelihood of school shootings (whether copycat or not) on their campus. The creation of a climate and culture that promotes safety, caring, and a sense of well-being is absolutely essential to any prevention efforts, whether it be weapons, bullying, drugs or alcohol. Consistency is the key to creating this type of atmosphere; therefore the inclusion of all staff, parents, students, and other caregivers in training and information sharing is paramount to achieving these goals. Given the fact that many school shooters announce their intentions to their friends and fellow classmates beforehand, schools should:

1) **Encourage students to report what they see and hear.**—Clearly, this is a culture and climate issue that must be fostered over time in a school. In addition to this, there must be venues for students to report their concerns or findings, such as drop boxes, tip lines, e-mails, etc. There should be multiple venues; some anonymous, others not.

2) **Each student should have an adult in whom they can confide.**—This finding is absolutely essential to an overall safe and caring school environment. Each year, the Kentucky Center for School Safety asks a number of students at sites they visit during their Safe School Assessment process whether they "... have an adult at this school that you can talk to during times of crisis or if you have safety concerns?" In general, one in four students (25%) did not feel comfortable confiding in adult at their school. These students are far less likely to report anything to adults; decreasing this proportion is essential for a proper culture and climate for all students.

3) **Respond aggressively to bullying.**—While interviewing school shooters, the topic of bullying and harassment made its way into the conversation. Many of the shooters indicated that there had been a long history of being harassed or bullied. Sometimes this bullying or harassment continued for years. Schools should take a critical look at their bullying policies and intervention plans, as this type of behavior should not be allowed to go unchecked (see Chapter 7 for a more detailed discussion of this topic).

4) **Avoid profiling students.** As stated, the USSS/USDE research indicates that there is no effective profiling tool that will allow school administrators to effectively narrow down the field. Vossekuil and colleagues (2002) suggest that rather than trying to determine the "type" of student who may be a school shooter, school personnel should focus on a student's behaviors and communications to determine if that student appears to be planning for an attack.

Conclusion

It is important to note the limitations of our research presented here. The most important limitation is that only two (and, from 2006–2013, only one) large, metropolitan newspapers were used to collect the data presented here. It is possible that articles reporting school shootings from 1966–2013 were missed due to not being reported in one of the two newspapers from which the data were drawn. Consequently, it could be that there were other school homicides that occurred during that 45-year period that are not reflected in this study. Further research with other newspapers representing all regions of the United States may uncover further homicides. Nevertheless, given the exploratory nature of this effort, this limitation, while important, does not obviate the findings from this study. It does, however, leave an important area for future research.

School shootings are tragic events with devastating consequences. However, the results presented here suggest that, contrary to popular belief, the number of school shootings has not significantly increased over the past 45 years. This finding contradicts the popular notion that schools are far less safe in 2014 than they were in the 1970s and 1980s. Undoubtedly, the media have played a role in this notion and will continue to do so as long as these tragic events occur.

Nevertheless, while the number of incidents of school shootings has not significantly increased, the number of victims killed in school shootings has increased over the past 45 years. Consequently, this finding needs to be further developed and explored. As mentioned earlier, this finding might be explained by an increase in the availability of semiautomatic handguns and rifles, although a number of authors have suggested that these are not the guns of choice among youth gun carriers (see May & Jarjoura, 2006, for review) or from "copycats" attempting to earn a higher shock value in the press by killing more victims. In either case, more research is needed to delineate causes and responses to those findings.

A number of policy implications can be derived from this research. The most important policy implication revolves around the need to create a complete, comprehensive national database containing information on school shootings that have occurred in the United States. Currently, no such database exists. Until 2010, the best database collecting data about school shootings was the National School Safety Center's school-associated violent deaths database. However, that database has not been updated since 2010 and, even for the years for which they have data, the NSSC admitted that the database may not be complete, a statement we supported during our research when we found articles in national newspapers that were not in their database. Furthermore, the NSSC database only covers the years 1992 to the present. It is important to create a national database, going back as far in time as possible in order to fully understand the scope of school-shootings.

Another important policy implication of these findings concerns the prevalence of school shootings in general. The findings presented here suggest that school shootings, while very rare events, have occurred at some level for over four decades. Consequently, we believe that as long as schools continue to have students between the ages of 5 and 21, there will continue to be the possibility that another school shooting will occur. Given this reality, schools need to develop a systematic approach whereby they can (1) quickly make a determination whether or not threats of shootings at school made by students should be considered to be real and, when evidence is compelling enough, (2) quickly refer that threat to local law enforcement, then (3) initiate crisis response procedures to protect students and staff in the school where the threat is occurring (see Chapter 11 for strategies to do so). School and law enforcement officials need to establish open, routine avenues of communication so that when these threats are referred to law enforcement, everyone involved recognizes the seriousness of those threats and acts accordingly.

Notes

1. The following databases were used to identify shootings from 1966–2006:
Chicago Tribune
Archives http://pqasb.pqarchiver.com/chicagotribune/advancedsearch.html
(Also used the NewsBank database)
New York Times
http://proquest.umi.com/pqdweb?RQT=306&DBId=6861&cfc=1

After 2006, only the *New York Times* database was used because the lead author changed institutions and his current institution only allowed access to the *New York Times* database. Given the convergence of coverage in the previous years, while not ideal, we felt usage of only one database was sufficient for the arguments presented here.

2. As one anonymous reviewer accurately pointed out, limiting the choice of articles examining school shootings over the 40-year period to the *New York Times* and the *Chicago Tribune* may have led to more thorough coverage of the school shootings in the Midwest and Eastern regions of the United States. As such, we acknowledge this choice (which was made in part because of the thorough archives of these two newspapers) necessarily limits the scope of the findings presented here.

References

Anderson, M., Kaufman, J., Simon, T. R., Barrios, L., Paulozzi, L., Ryan, G., Hammond, R., Modzeleski, W., Feucht, T., & Potter, L. (2001). School-associated violent deaths in the United States, 1994–1999. *The Journal of the American Medical Association, 286*(21), 2695–2702.

Arnette, J.L., & Walsleben, M.C. (1998, April). Combating fear and restoring safety in schools. *OJJDP Juvenile Justice Bulletin*. Washington, DC: Office of Juvenile Justice and Delinquency Prevention, U.S. Department of Justice.

Beane, A. (2005). Understanding mass school shootings: Links between personhood and power in the competitive school environment. *The Journal of Primary Prevention, 26*(5), 419–438.

Bender, W. N., Shubert, T. H., & McLaughlin, P. J. (2001). Invisible kids: Preventing school violence by identifying kids in trouble. *Intervention in School and Clinic, 37*(2), 105–112.

Borum, R., Cornell, D. G., Modzeleski, W., & Jimerson, S. R. (2010). What can be done about school shootings? A review of the evidence. *Educational Researcher*, 39(1), 27–37.

Brooks, K., Schiraldi, V., & Ziedenberg, J. (2000). *School house hype: Two years later.* Washington, DC: Justice Policy Institute and Children's Law Center. Retrieved February 9, 2008, from: http://www.cjcj.org/schoolhousehype/shh2.html.

Burgess, A. W., Garbarino, C., & Carlson, M. I. (2006). Pathological teasing and bullying turned deadly: Shooters and suicide. *Victims & Offenders, 1*(1), 1–14.

Cabell, B. (1998, October 5). *Kentucky school shooter "guilty but mentally ill"*. Retrieved June 2, 2008, from: http://www.cnn.com/US/9810/05/paducah.shooting/

Centers for Disease Control and Prevention (CDC). (2008). School-associated student homicides—United States, 1992–2006. *Morbidity and Mortality Weekly Report, 57*(2), 33–36.

Centers for Disease Control and Prevention (CDC). (2001). Temporal variations in school-associated student homicide and suicide events—United States, 1992–1999. *Morbidity and Mortality Weekly Report, 50*(31), 657–660.

Chiricos, T. (2002). The media, moral panics and the politics of crime control. In G. Cole, M. Gertz, & A. Bunger (Eds.), *The criminal justice system: Politics and policies.* Belmont, CA:Wadsworth.

CNN.com. (2000). Columbine Report. Retrieved June 2, 2008, from: http://www.cnn.com/SPECIALS/2000/columbine.cd/frameset.exclude.html.

CNN.com (1997, December 2). *Third student dies in Kentucky school shooting.* Retrieved June 2, 2008 from: http://www.cnn.com/US/9712/02/school.shooting.on/.

Cornell, D. G., & Mayer, M. J. (2010). Why do school order and safety matter? *Educational Researcher*, 39(1), 7–15.

Deppa, J. (2007). Coping with a killer's 'Manifesto'. *Chronicle of Higher Education, 53*(36), 64–65.

Dolmetsch, C., & Pettersson, E. (2014). *Connecticut gun law passed after Sandy Hook ruled legal.* Retrieved January 30, 2014 from http://www.bloomberg.com/news/2014-01-31/connecticut-gun-law-passed-after-sandy-hook-ruled-legal.html.

Donohue, E., Schiraldi, V., & Zeidenberg, J. (1998). *School house hype: School shootings and the real risks kids face in America.* Washington, DC: Justice Policy Institute.

Elliot, D. S., Hamburg, B. A., & Williams, K. R. (1998). *Violence in American schools: An overview.* Cambridge, England: Cambridge University Press.

Flock, J. (1998, March 25). *Hearing today for 2 boys in Arkansas shooting.* Retrieved on June 3, 2008, from: http://www.cnn.com/US/9803/25/school.shooting/.

Gillespie, M. (2000, April). School violence still a worry for American parents. *Gallup Poll Monthly, 415,* 47–50.

Glassner, B. (1999). *The culture of fear: Why Americans are afraid of the wrong things.* New York: Basic Books.

Halikias, W. (2004). School-based risk assessments: A conceptual framework and model for professional practice. *Professional Psychology: Research and Practice, 35*(6), 598–607.

Herda-Rapp, A. (2003). The social construction of local school violence threats by the news media and professional organizations. *Sociological Inquiry, 73*(4), 545–574.

Kimberling, S., & May, D. (2007, Fall). School shooters: Research unveils 10 myths regarding perpetrators. *Kentucky School Leader*, 10–13.

Kimmel, M. S., & Mahler, M. (2003). Adolescent masculinity, homophobia, and violence: Random school shootings, 1982–2001. *American Behavioral Scientist, 46*(10), 1439–1458.

Klein, J. (2012). *The bully society: School shootings and the crisis of bullying in America's schools.* NYU Press.

Lawrence, R., & Mueller, D. (2003). School shootings and the man-bites-dog criterion of newsworthiness. *Youth Violence and Juvenile Justice, 1*(4), 330–345.

Linder, K. E. (2014). *Rampage violence narratives: What fictional accounts of school shootings say about the future of America's youth.* Lanham, MD: Lexington Books.

Lundman, R. (2003). The newsworthiness and selection bias in news about murder: Comparative and relative effects of novelty and race and gender typifications in newspaper coverage of homicide. *Sociological Forum, 18,* 257–286.

May, D.C., & Jarjoura, G.R. (2006). *Illegal guns in the wrong hands: Patterns of gun acquisition and use among serious juvenile delinquents.* Lanham, MD: University Press of America.

McCombs, M. E., & Shaw, D. L. (1972). The agenda-setting function of mass media. *Public Opinion Quarterly, 36,* 176–187.

McGee, J. P., & DeBernardo, C. R. (1999). The classroom avenger: A behavioral profile of school based shootings. *The Forensic Examiner, 8*(5–6), 16–18.

Mulvey, E. P., & Cauffman, E. The inherent limits of predicting school violence. *American Psychologist, 56*(10), 797–802.

Muschert, G. W. (2007). Research in school shootings. *Sociology Compass,* 1(1), 60–80.

Muschert, G. W. (2013). School shootings as mediatized violence. In N. Böckler, P. Sitzer, T. Seeger, & W. Heitmeyer (Eds.), *School Shootings: International research, case studies, and concepts for prevention* (pp. 265–281). New York: Springer.

Muschert, G. W., & Carr, D. (2006). Media salience and frame changing across events: Coverage of nine school shootings, 1997–2001. *Journalism and Mass Communication Quarterly, 83*(4), 747–766.

Phillips, S. (2005, May 20). Copycat threats cancel lessons. *Times Educational Supplement, 4635,* 20.

Potter, G. W. & Kappeler, V. E. (2006). *Constructing crime: Perspectives on making news and social problems.* Long Grove, IL: Waveland Press.

Reddy, M., Borum, R., Berglund, J., Vossekuil, B., Fein, R., & Modzeleski, W. (2001). Evaluating risk for targeted violence in schools: Comparing risk assessment, threat assessment, and other approaches. *Psychology in the Schools, 38*(2), 157–172.

Ryan-Arredondo, K., Renouf, K. Egyed, C., Doxely, M., Dobbins, M., Sanchez, S., & Rakowitz, B. (2001). Threats of violence in schools: The Dallas Independent School District's response. *Psychology in the Schools, 38*(2), 185–196.

Schildkraut, J. (2012). Media and massacre: A comparative analysis of the reporting of the 2007 Virginia Tech shootings. *Fast Capitalism,* 9(1). Retrieved from http://www.uta.edu/huma/agger/fastcapitalism/9_1/schildkraut9_1.html.

Schildkraut, J. (2012). The remote is controlled by the monster: Issues of mediatized violence and school shootings. *Studies in Media and Communications,* 7, 231–254.

Schildkraut, J., & Muschert, G. W. (2013). Violent media, guns, and mental illness: The three ring circus of causal factors for school massacres, as related in media discourse. *Gun Violence and Public Life.* St. Paul, MN: Paradigm Publishing.

Shenk, J. W. (1999). Guns and roses. *Nation, 268*(22), 14–24.

Surette, R. (1998). *Media, crime, and criminal justice: Images and realities* (2nd ed.). Pacific Grove, CA: Brooks/Cole.

U.S. Department of Education. (2001). *Violent deaths in or near schools are rare: Communities and schools must heed threats, Paige says.* FDCH Regulatory Intelligence Database.

U.S. Department of Education & U.S. Department of Justice. (1999). *1999 annual report on school safety.* Washington, DC: Author.

Vossekuil, B., Fein, R., Reddy, M., Borum, R., & Modzeleski, W. (2002). *The final report and findings of the Safe School Initiative: Implications for the prevention of school attacks in the United States.* Washington, DC: U.S. Secret Service and U.S. Department of Education. Retrieved October 3, 2007, from: http://www.treas.gov/usss/ntac/ssi_final report.

Table 2.1: 47 Years of School Shootings

Year	Total Incidents	Total Homicides	Year	Total Incidents	Total Homicides
1966	1	1	1990	1	1
1967	2	1	1991	2	2
1968	2	2	1992	5	8
1969	2	2	1993	9	10
1970	1	1	1994	2	2
1971	3	4	1995	3	4
1972	6	6	1996	2	4
1973	4	4	1997	5	8
1974	3	3	1998	3	7
1975	2	2	1999	3	15
1976	1	1	2000	4	5
1977	3	3	2001	2	3
1978	2	2	2002	1	1
1979	1	1	2003	3	3
1980	1	1	2004	1	1
1981	1	1	2005	2	8
1982	3	3	2006	3	7
1983	4	4	*2007	*4	*11
1984	1	1	*2008	*4	*4
1985	2	2	*2009	*2	*2
1986	2	2	*2010	*3	*3
1987	1	1	*2011	*4	*5
1988	4	5	*2012	*6	*36
1989	2	6	*2013	*5	*7
			Total	**133**	**272**

*2007–2013 results come only from the *New York Times* articles.

Figure 2.1: 47 Years of School Shootings

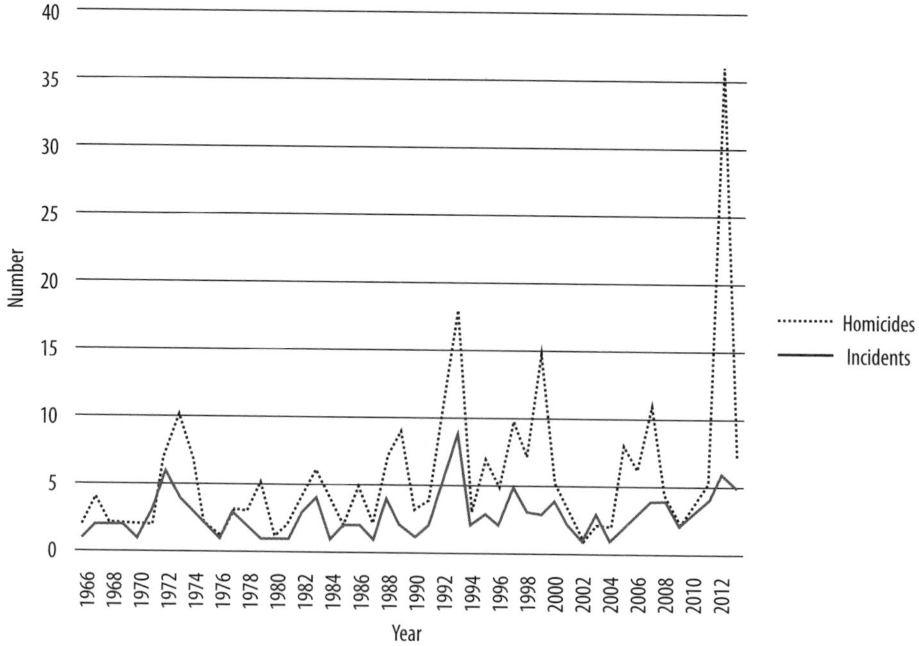

Chapter 3

Predictors of Weapon Reporting Among Students: Who Tells and Why?

*Preston Elrod, David C. May, and Nathan Lowe**

In the previous chapters, I highlighted the fact that, in many of the incidents where school shootings occurred, a number of the shooter's friends and classmates were aware that the shooter(s) were considering perpetrating the shooting before it occurred. I also discussed the fact that my work at the Kentucky Center for School Safety has revealed that a substantial portion of students do not feel comfortable talking to an adult at the school where they attend and thus would be unlikely to report crimes of which they were aware beforehand even if they knew about them. In this chapter, Preston Elrod, Nathan Lowe, and I use data from middle and high school students to examine factors that affect whether or not students would report their knowledge of weapons in the school environment.

Literature Review about Weapon Reporting

Only a few studies to date have examined students' willingness to report weapons possession at school. In this chapter, we add to the small number of studies in this area by examining students' willingness to report weapons possession at school under various conditions. The conditions include: (1) if they heard another student had a gun or another weapon, (2) if they saw another student with a gun or other weapon, and (3) if they knew their best friend had a gun or other weapon. Our hope is that this chapter will inform the reader of a number of considerations they can use in their own school to increase the likelihood that students will report weapons (and various other dangerous situations) at their own school.

According to the *Indicators of School Crime and Safety: 2011*, reviewed earlier, each year about 1 in 20 students indicated that they had carried a weapon at school in the past 30 days (Robers, Zhang, Truman, & Snyder, 2011). Although the percentage of

---

* The information presented in this chapter is largely drawn from an article I coauthored with Preston Elrod and Nathan Lowe. The citation for that article is included below:

Elrod, Preston, David May, and Nathan Lowe

2013 To Tell or Not to Tell: An Analysis of Students' Willingness to Report School Weapons Possession to School Authorities. *Contemporary Issues in Anthropology and Sociology*, 3(1), 7–28.

students carrying weapons to school is thus small, the consequences of this behavior are not. The perception that weapons are present at school can lead to a variety of negative outcomes including: (1) loss of life and serious physical injuries that produce trauma in victims that extends well beyond the school; (2) school avoidance or avoidance of certain places at school (Dinkes, Kemp, Baum, & Snyder, 2009); (3) students' presenting themselves in ways that suggest to others that they are capable of defending themselves (e.g., putting on a "tough front") (Lockwood, 1997); (4) students' carrying weapons to school for protection (May, 1999); (5) development of school "cliques" prone to aggressive actions designed to discourage potential offenders (Welsh, 2000); (6) decreased quality of the learning experiences of students and the work experiences of school staff; (7) a reduction in positive relationships between people in the community and schools; and (8) unfavorable media attention (Cao, Zhang, & He, 2008). Moreover, efforts to respond to the safety concerns of students and staff can produce school environments that alienate students, increase student mistrust, and inhibit learning (Beger, 2003; Farmer, 1999; Verdugo & Schneider, 1999); decrease students' perceptions of safety (Mayer & Leone, 1999); and hamper the development of a positive school environment (Scheckner, Rollins, Kaiser-Ulrey, & Wagner, 2002).

As Cao et al. (2008) have noted, a key limitation in many studies of weapons possession in schools is that researchers have aggregated various types of weapons into a single category (see, for example, Bailey et al., 1997; DuRant, Getts, Candenhead, & Woods, 1995; Forrest, Zychowski, Stuhldreher, & Ryan, 2000; Kulig, Valentine, Griffith, & Ruthazer, 1998; Rountree, 2000; Simon, Crosby, & Dahlberg, 1999; Wilcox & Clayton, 2001). It is important, however, to differentiate between firearms and other weapons, such as knives and razors, because the processes of carrying out violent acts with various types of weapons and the outcomes of their use are different. With less lethal weapons, the act tends to be slow, possibly even preventable depending on the circumstances, and less likely to be fatal. In contrast, with firearms, the act is almost always quick and the potential for serious injury or death is increased.

The possession of various types of weapons at schools poses a variety of threats to students, school staff, and others. As mentioned earlier, however, students' willingness to report weapons possession by their peers could play an important role in preventing serious acts of violence in schools (Vossekuil, Fein, Reddy, Borum, & Modzeleski, 2002).

Although students' willingness to report weapons possession is a critical variable in making schools safe, relatively little research has examined factors related to willingness to report. The current research builds on this small body of literature by examining individual and school variables that influence middle and high school students' willingness to report gun and other weapons possession to a teacher, administrator, or another adult at school.

Students' Willingness to Report Weapons Possession by Other Students

Previous studies on students' willingness to report weapons possession (Brank et al., 2007; Brinkley & Saarino, 2006; Wylie et al., 2010) contained hypotheses derived from three theoretical frameworks rooted in criminology and social development: social bonding, social learning, and rational choice theories. In addition, the research by Wylie and associates (2010) built on the social bonding framework used by Brank and associates (2007) in two ways: (1) they incorporated concepts derived from a social organizational/ecological framework, and (2) they explored the relationship between school climate and the willingness to report weapons possession in school. Brinkley and Saarino (2006) examined the potential impact of school climate on students' willingness to tell adults if other students had brought a gun or knife to school or if they heard a student threaten to hurt someone with a weapon.

The social bonding approach examined by Brank and her colleagues (2007) suggests that delinquency results from weak or attenuated bonds to conventional others and institutions (see Hirschi, 1969), but increases when there are strong bonds to unconventional others (Hindelang, 1973; Samuelson, Hartnagel, & Krahn, 1990). Brank and her colleagues examined "whether exposure to deviant peers and connections to trusted adults differentially affect the likelihood of reporting [among students]" (Brank et al., 2007: 128). Previous studies have determined that although exposure to deviant peers may increase the likelihood a student has knowledge of a weapon in school (Estell, Farmer, Cairns, & Clemmer, 2003), this exposure to deviant peers also indicates a weaker social bond to conventional others (Erikson, Crosnoe, & Dornbusch, 2000). Thus, deviant peer associations are likely to inhibit students' willingness to report weapons possession by other students to school authorities.

Based on the extant research, Brank and her colleagues (2007) predicted students connected to trusted adults at home, at school, or in the community would be more likely to report student weapon possession at school than those without the same bonds. Brank and her colleagues also predicted that students' who associated with delinquent peers and who were involved in delinquency would be less likely to report weapons possession by classmates. Importantly, these predictions were supported by their analysis. These findings, however, would also be predicted by social learning theories because it is through such associations that youths are likely to learn attitudes favorable or unfavorable to reporting weapons possession by other students and to learn nuances related to the appropriateness of reporting different types of weapons under varying circumstances (Akers & Sellers, 2004).[1]

Brank and her colleagues (2007) also borrowed from the literature on tattling or reporting friends contemplating suicide, snitching, and whistle-blowing, which is mostly embedded within a rational choice cost-benefit analysis framework (in other words, people choose behaviors that are most likely to benefit them personally). Previous research on reporting on the behavior of friends and peers in general indicates the social costs of tattling increase with age, and by the time a child reaches adolescence, these costs are substantial (Friman et al., 2004; Greiger, Kauffman, & Greiger, 1976; Ingram & Berring, 2010; Lancellota & Vaughn, 1989). Where this research takes a rational choice cost-benefit analysis approach, researchers argue that the benefits of tattling help the larger unit as well as the individual (e.g., class, school, organization) but the costs are primarily to the individual (e.g., social rejection) (Friman et al., 2004).

Little research has examined the social costs of tattling by adolescents, however (Friman et al., 2004). Those studies that do exist reveal that delinquents are less likely than non-delinquents to report that informing on others is morally wrong (Stein, Sarbin, Chu, & Kulik, 1967), those who tattle are less popular, and youths are generally unwilling to report on peers (Friman et al., 2004). To illustrate, Kalafat and Elias (1992) found that about one-third of their sample of suburban high school students had talked to a peer who was definitely considering suicide but only about 25% reported such information to an adult.

The act of informing carries social costs among other populations as well. In the criminal world, a police informant, or "snitch," is often described as "the worst thing that you can be" (Rosenfeld, Jacobs, & Wright, 2003: 298). Likewise, corporate and government whistle-blowers are typically viewed as being disloyal to the company or agency and their fellow employees (Fitzgerald & Ferrara, 2008; MacNamara, 1991) and may be subjected to blacklisting, dismissal from jobs, work transfers, personal harassment, sexual exploitation (Fitzgerald & Ferrara, 2008; Glazer & Glazer, 1989), and are sometimes denied promotions and the support needed to effectively do their jobs (Fitzgerald & Ferrara, 2008). Loyalty to a friend is noted as the primary factor cited by cadets of the U.S. Naval Academy when they considered whether or not to inform on fellow cadets (Pershing, 2002). Furthermore, lawyers appear to have a general antipathy towards turning in fellow attorneys for misbehavior (Toomey, 2004) and police have a code of silence and are critical of those who inform on fellow officers (Westmarland, 2005).

Based on the knowledge gained from the research reviewed above, Brank and colleagues (2007) hypothesized that students would be more likely to report other students' weapons possession "(a) when their relationship to the target is unspecified versus specified as friendship, (b) under conditions of anonymity rather than giving their name, and (c) when they do not perceive risk of physical or social consequences from the target student or the large peer group" (p. 129). The authors examined these hypotheses using a sample of over 1,900 middle school students in 27 schools across five states in the Northeast, South, and West regions of the United States. Their results indicated that the great majority of students would report weapons possession; however, factors such as anonymity (anonymous reporting was favored over those where the reporter could be identified), gender (females were more willing to report), age (younger students were more willing), and academic performance (those with better grades were more willing to report) influenced reporting. They also found that negative peer associations and greater levels of involvement in delinquency were associated with a decreased likelihood of reporting, while a positive relationship with adults, particularly the presence of a trusted adult in the school, was associated with increased reporting.

Non-Criminological Theories of Reporting Behavior

Outside of the criminological literature, there is evidence to suggest that the psychological process through which a "bystander" or "whistle-blower" decides to intervene is similar across emergency situations, regardless of the context in which those situations occur. Latane and Darley (1968) suggest that there are two types of intervention one might have in an emergency situation: direct (e.g., physically intervening to break up a fight, jumping in water and swimming out to save a drowning individual) and reportorial (reporting the emergency situation to one qualified to handle the situation, the type of intervention examined here). They suggest that the decision to engage in reportorial intervention in an emergency situation is based on a decision-making process where the bystander must know about the event, decide that the event is an emergency, and then decide that he or she is responsible for helping intervene to diffuse the situation. The bystander then must choose an appropriate method of intervention and successfully implement that intervention (Dozer & Micelli, 1985). Consequently, then, for weapon reporting in a school context, the student must first know another student has a weapon, decide that weapon poses a risk to others, make an individual decision to tell a responsible school authority about that weapon, and then actually report that weapon to an adult.

In the present study, we build on previous studies on students' willingness to report gun and other weapons possession at school to authorities by examining a range of predictors theoretically associated with weapon reporting. Our most significant contribution to the research in this area, however, comes in the exploration of the decision-making process of students who choose to report weapons possession at school. In an attempt to understand this process, we examine differences in willingness to report gun and other weapons possession to school authorities under three conditions: (1) if they heard another student had a gun or another weapon, (2) if they saw another student with a gun or other weapon, and (3) if they knew their best friend had a gun or other weapon. In addition, we examine the potential effects of involvement in school delinquency and youth alienation on students' willingness to report weapons possession.

Additionally, we also include two contextual predictors that have not been examined to date: school climate and youth victimization at school. Studies that have examined the impact of school climate on students' perceptions of school safety indicate that feelings of safety are promoted among students in schools where teachers challenge students, where students enjoy school, where teachers maintain discipline, and where there are clear school rules (Kitsantas, Ware, & Martinez-Arias, 2004; Welsh, 2000). As the studies by Brinkley and Saarino (2006) and Wylie et al. (2010) indicate, school climate does influence students' willingness to report students' weapons possession at school. In contrast, research on school victimization indicates that students who have been victimized are less likely to feel safe at school (Wallace & May, 2005). The influence of students' victimization experiences on their willingness to report weapons possession in school, however, has not been examined to date.

Method

The data for this study were taken from a larger study designed to assess students' perceptions of school safety and involvement in delinquency in and outside of school. The data were collected in one public middle school and one public high school in a predominately rural county in the Appalachian region of the U.S. (population approximately 73,000) during the first week of May 2006. The middle school was comprised of sixth, seventh, and eighth grades while the high school contained ninth through twelfth grades.

Table 3.1. Percent of Youths in the Sample and Youths Enrolled in the Schools at the Time of the Survey with Various Demographic Characteristics

Demographic Characteristic	Study Sample	Enrolled in Schools
Gender		
Females	58.3%	48.4%
Race		
White	85.0%	86.0%
African American	6.9%	10.3%
Hispanic	2.1%	1.8%
Other	5.9%	1.9%
Grade Level*		
Middle school	38.0%	28.1%
High school	61.4%	71.9%

*Note: 0.6% of the middle and high school respondents indicated that they were in a grade other than 6 through 12.

Subjects

A total of 1,521 surveys were completed by students at the two schools. A screening question, however, was used at the conclusion of the survey that asked students how often (never, some of the time, most of the time, all of the time) they had given honest responses on the survey. To ensure the most valid data for the variables under study, we conducted chi-square tests comparing the percentage of students who indicated that they would or would not tell a teacher or other adult about other students' possession of a weapon at school with whether or not they reported providing honest responses all of the time on the survey. Because the chi-square results revealed significant differences between youths who reported giving honest responses on all survey items and those who did not give honest responses on all survey items, only respondents who indicated that they had provided honest responses all of the time were used in the analysis.[2] We believe that restricting our analysis to only students who reported honest responses on each of the survey items improves the accuracy of the findings. Thus, the final sample used for this paper totals 895 respondents and consists of 334 middle school respondents, which comprised 54.2% of the middle school students enrolled in that school at the time of the survey administration, and 561 high school subjects, or 35.6% of the high school students enrolled in the high school.

In Table 3.1, we present the descriptive statistics for both the sample and the students enrolled in the school district at the time of the data collection. The descriptive statistics suggest that the majority (58.3%) of the students were female and most (85.0%) were white. Compared to students enrolled in the schools studied, the sample used in the following analysis contained proportionally more females, Hispanics, youths who identified themselves as of a race other than Black, White, or Hispanic, and fewer African American youths. In addition, our sample contained proportionally more middle school students and fewer high school youths than the school district.

Survey Administration

The survey instruments used to collect the data analyzed in this chapter were developed by university researchers at the request of school district administrators. After the survey instruments were finalized, packets containing instructions for administering the surveys and the survey instruments were delivered to the schools. The instruments were administered to each student in attendance on the day the survey was conducted, excluding those students in special education classes. Students completed a self-report survey under the supervision of their classroom teachers, who provided a brief introduction to the survey and its purpose. Survey administration took approximately 30 to 45 minutes and no major problems with the administration were reported.

Subjects participated on a volunteer basis. Prior to the survey, letters were mailed to students' homes by the schools. These letters explained the purpose of the survey and indicated that students would be omitted from the research at the request of the parent or guardian. Also, prior to survey administration, students were reminded that their participation was voluntary and that they could cease participation at any time. All subjects were assured of their anonymity and the confidentiality of the information they provided. After the subject completed the survey, s/he was instructed to place the forms in an envelope that accompanied the survey and to seal the envelope. Surveys were then placed in collection boxes and given to the researchers.

Study Measures

Six items on the survey served as the dependent variables in this research. These items asked respondents to indicate if they would tell a teacher, administrator, or another adult at school about other students' weapon possession under six conditions. Response options for each item were "Would not tell" (coded 0) and "would tell" (coded 1). The conditions presented were (1) "Saw another student with a gun," (2) "Knew my best friend had a gun," (3) "Heard another student had a gun," (4) "Saw another student with a weapon (other than a gun)," (5) "Knew my best friend had a weapon (other than a gun)," and (6) "Heard that another student had a weapon (other than a gun)."

Five items constituted demographic measures used in the analysis. These items included: "Do you qualify for free/reduced/full price lunch" (coded 0 = full price lunch, 1 = free or reduced lunch), "What is your gender?" (coded 0 = male, 1 = female), "Do you consider yourself: White, Black, Hispanic, Asian, American Indian, Other" (coded 0 = Nonwhite, 1 = White), and "Do you live with: both biological parents, one biological parent, one biological parent and a step-parent, your grandparents, some other relative, other:" (coded 0 = some other parental arrangement, 1 = both biological parents). In addition, one dichotomous variable was constructed to identify students' school level (coded 1 = high school and 2 = middle school).

The survey contained a variety of scales, 17 of which were chosen for use in the analysis because they were felt to reflect the theoretical focus of the study and were not highly correlated with one another. Because the original survey items employed various response formats such as "no" or "yes," Likert type options, and "none," "1," "2," "3," "4 or more," which were used on items asking about respondents' involvement in delinquency, we conducted contingency table analysis to screen for cells with expected frequencies less than five. Due to the size of our sample, several scales contained small expected frequencies. As a result, response categories were collapsed into dichotomous measures coded "0" or "1" for most measures. This eliminated large numbers of cells with expected frequencies less than five and made possible the use of the goodness-of-fit tests calculated by logistic regression (Tabachnick & Fidell, 2007). Reliability and factor analyses of the scales indicated that each had fair to very good reliability and each represented a unidimensional construct. Descriptive data for each of the measures used in the analysis can be seen in Table 3.2. The theoretical constructs and their associated predictors are discussed below.

Social Bonding/Social Capital

Four measures of social bonding/social capital were used in the analysis. These measures were: (1) family attachment, consisting of four items that measure youths' affinity for their family and parents; (2) adult social capital, a five-item measure that represented youths' belief that various adults could be counted on to help them with a problem; (3) school connectedness, comprised of four items that examined students' perceptions of whether they have a number of friends and acquaintances at school, whether or not they know a number of teachers, and whether or not they will be helped by peers if they are upset; and (4) alienation, consisting of six items that measured respondents' reports that they spend much of their time alone and are disconnected from others.

School Climate

Three measures of school climate were used in this analysis. These measures were: (1) positive school climate, a five-item scale that measured the respondents' belief that students understand school rules, are treated fairly when they break the rules, and respect teachers; (2) negative school climate, a three-item scale that measured students' belief that students are not treated fairly, and are singled out due to fashion preferences; and (3) school guardianship, a six-item scale that measured respondents' perception of whether or not teachers supervise hallways and restrooms.

School Misbehavior

One measure examined school misbehavior. This 11-item scale measured youths' self-reported involvement in various activities such as calling other students names;

Table 3.2. Descriptive Statistics for Variables Used in the Analyses

Scale	N	Mean	SD	Score Range	
Outcome variables					
Tell-saw another student with gun	876	.88	.322	0–1	
Tell-knew best friend had gun	877	.70	.458	0–1	
Tell-heard another student had gun	876	.72	.449	0–1	
Tell-saw another student with weapon (other than gun)	877	.70	.457	0–1	
Tell-knew best friend had weapon (other than gun)	873	.57	.495	0–1	
Tell-heard other student had weapon (other than gun)	869	.61	.488	0–1	
Demographic variables					
Gender (1 = female)	876	.59	.492	0–1	
Race (1 = White)	873	.85	.355	0–1	
Free lunch					
(1 = free or reduced)	870	.31	.462	0–1	
Living arrangement (1 = both biological parents)	874	.59	.492	0–1	
School (2 = middle school)	881	1.37	.484	1–2	
Theoretical Variables					**Alphas**
Family attachment	877	3.54	1.03	0–4	.83
Adult social capital	869	3.54	1.60	0–5	.77
School connectedness	871	3.33	1.05	0–4	.62
Alienation	859	2.25	2.237	0–6	.85
School Climate					
Positive school climate	854	3.50	1.489	0–5	.69
Teacher/staff bias toward outsider groups	857	1.04	1.112	0–3	.68
School guardianship	875	3.62	1.775	0–6	.62
School Misbehavior					
School misbehavior	877	3.24	3.155	0–11	.92
Strain					
Perceived risk of victimization at school	891	1.50	1.923	0–7	.82
School problems-delinquency	873	4.51	1.618	0–6	.75
School safety	774	5.76	1.756	0–7	.81
Self-efficacy	887	2.67	2.009	0–6	.68
Self-reported (SR) School Performance	885	2.51	.928	0–3	

bumping, pushing, kicking, or hitting another student; making fun of another student; getting into a serious argument with a student, teacher or another adult; being sent out of class; or being suspended.

Strain

Two measures of strain were used. They were (1) students' perceived risk of victimization at school, which was a seven-item scale that asks respondents to rate the chance that they could be the victim of actions such as having their locker broken into, being attacked by someone with a weapon, being bullied, being subjected to inappropriate sexual touching, or being threatened with harm; and (2) delinquency problems at school, a six-item scale measuring students' assessment of the seriousness of problems at school such as kids damaging property, fighting, gangs, bullying, and bringing weapons to school.

Self-Efficacy

One three-item measure of self-efficacy was used. This scale measured students' use of positive means to resolve anger, including talking things out with others, seeking the advice of an adult about how to handle problems, and seeking the advice of a friend.

School Safety

One seven-item measure of students' perceptions of school safety was used in the analysis. This scale measured students' perceptions of safety in various areas of the school such as school classrooms, hallways, restrooms, cafeteria, gym, parking lots, and locations outside school buildings such as recreation areas and entrances.

Self-Reported School Performance

Finally, the analysis included one measure of self-reported school performance. This item asked students "What grades do you usually get?" Response options were collapsed from nine categories into the following, "Mostly Fs" to "Mostly Ds" (coded 0), "Mostly Ds and Cs" to "Mostly Cs and Bs" (coded 1), and "Mostly Bs" to "Mostly As" (coded 2).

Analytic Plan

Because the outcomes of interest consist of dichotomous variables, binary logistic regression was used to assess relationships between each of the predictors and willingness of students to report weapons possession to school personnel.[3] Because none of the predictors used in this study contained more than 3% missing data and because various procedures for handling missing data are likely to produce similar results when less than 5% of cases are missing in large data sets (Tabachnick & Fidell, 2007), we employed listwise deletion of cases with missing data.

Table 3.3. Logistic Regression Results Regressing Whether Student Would Report if They Heard Another Student Had a Gun or a Weapon Other Than a Gun to an Adult

	Model 1		**Model 2**	
	Whether Student Would Report if They Heard Another Student Had a Gun (N=756)		Whether Student Would Report if They Heard Another Student Had a Weapon Other Than a Gun (N=751)	
Variable	**B/S.E.**	**Exp(B)**	**B/S.E.**	**Exp(B)**
School misbehavior	–.276/.091	.759**	–.375/.088	.687***
Perceived risk of victimization	.003/.052	1.003	–.034/.050	.967
School safety	–.089/.057	.915	–.069/.055	.934
Negative school climate	.017/.084	1.017	.205/.081	1.025
Positive school climate	.609/.213	.544**	.425/.207	.654*
School guardianship	.082/.054	1.085	.076/.053	1.079
School connectedness	.021/.090	1.021	.007/.088	1.007
Adult social capital	.259/.197	.772	.731/.191	.481***
Self-efficacy	.142/.047	1.153**	.118/.045	1.125**
Delinquency Problems at School	.054/.056	1.056	.022/.054	1.023
Alienation	.022/.042	1.022	.081/.041	1.085*
Family attachment	.673/.330	1.961*	.449/.328	1.567
Free lunch recipient	.102/.210	1.107	–.125/.206	.882
Males	–.260/.181	.771	–.427/.175	.652*
SR school performance	–.168/.164	.845	.098/.158	1.103
Parental arrangement	.054/.186	1.056	.071/.180	1.074
Nonwhite	–.145/.250	.865	.064/.248	1.066
School Level	–.286/.199	.752	–.875/.197	.417***
Constant	2.087/.902	8.057*	2.534/.881	12.601**
Chi-square (18 df)	72.490***		127.030***	
Nagelkerke R-Square	.131		.211	
–2 Log Likelihood	830.254		878.416	

* p<.05
** p<.01
*** p<.001

Results

The results presented in Table 3.3 demonstrate the impact of regressing whether a student would tell an adult if they heard that another student had a gun (Model 1) or a weapon other than a gun (Model 2) on the demographic, contextual, and theoretical variables described earlier. The logistic regression results presented in Table 3.3, Model 1 indicate that those students who felt their schools had lower levels of school misbehavior, more positive school climates, and had greater levels of self-efficacy and family attachment were significantly more likely than their counterparts to report that they would tell an adult at the school if they had heard another student had a gun. None of the other theoretical, demographic, or contextual variables had a significant association with the decision to report in this model. The variables included in the model explained slightly more than 10% (Nagelkerke R-square = .131) of the variance in the decision to report in this model.

In the second model in Table 3.3, we regressed students' decisions to report if they heard another student had a weapon other than a gun to an adult on the demographic, contextual, and theoretical variables described earlier. The logistic regression results presented in Table 3.3, Model 2 suggest that, once again, students who perceived lower levels of school misbehavior, felt their schools had more positive school climates, and who reported greater levels of self-efficacy were significantly more likely to report that they had heard a student had a weapon other than a gun to an adult. Additionally, females and middle school students, along with those students with higher levels of perceived social capital and alienation, were all significantly more likely than their counterparts to report that they would tell an adult if they had heard another student had a weapon other than a gun at school. The variables included in the model explained approximately 21% (Nagelkerke R-square = .211) of the variance in the decision to report in this model.

The results presented in Table 3.4 demonstrate the impact of regressing whether a student would tell an adult if they saw another student with a gun (Model 1) or saw another student with a weapon other than a gun (Model 2) on the demographic, contextual, and theoretical variables described earlier. The logistic regression results presented in Table 3.4, Model 1 suggest that those students who perceived lower levels of school misbehavior, felt their schools had more positive school climates, and who had greater levels of self-efficacy remained significantly more likely than their counterparts to report that they had seen another student with a gun to an adult. Additionally, those who experienced higher levels of school delinquency, females, and middle school students were also significantly more likely to tell an adult if they had seen another student with a gun at school. The variables included in the model explained slightly more than one quarter (Nagelkerke R-square = .262) of the variance in the decision to report in this model.

In the second model in Table 3.4, we regressed students' decisions to report if they saw another student with a weapon other than a gun to an adult on the demographic, contextual, and theoretical variables described earlier. The logistic regression results presented in the second model closely follow those in the first model in Table 3.4; females, middle school students, those students who perceived lower levels of school misbehavior and higher levels of positive school climate, and those students who had

Table 3.4. Logistic Regression Results Regressing Whether Student Would Report If They Saw Another Student With a Gun or a Weapon Other Than a Gun to an Adult

	Model 1		Model 2	
	Whether Student Would Report if They Saw Another Student With a Gun (N=756)		Whether Student Would Report if They Saw Another Student With a Weapon Other Than a Gun (N=757)	
Variable	B/S.E.	Exp(B)	B/S.E.	Exp(B)
School misbehavior	–.426/.142	.653**	–.378/.096	.686***
Perceived risk of victimization	–.095/.074	.909	.022/.055	.978
School safety	–.002/.080	.998	.025/.058	1.025
Negative school climate	–.077/.123	.926	.107/.088	1.113
Positive school climate	.941/.321	.390**	.573/.223	.564*
School guardianship	.074/.075	1.076	.002/.057	1.002
School connectedness	–.228/.138	.797	–.192/.096	.826*
Adult social capital	.267/.287	.766	.834/.206	.434***
Self-efficacy	.230/.076	1.258**	.149/.050	1.160**
Delinquency problems at school	.264/.082	1.302**	.138/.059	1.148*
Alienation	–.021/.060	.979	.002/.044	1.002
Family attachment	.468/.455	1.596	.651/.339	1.917
Free lunch recipient	.013/.309	1.013	.164/.223	1.179
Males	–.593/.272	.553*	–.703/.189	.495***
SR school performance	.266/.219	1.304	.001/.169	.999
Parental arrangement	–.470/.275	.625	.295/.196	1.343
Nonwhite	–.364/.338	.695	–.193/.262	.825
School level	–.922/.316	.398**	–1.173/.224	.309***
Constant	4.305/1.337	74.059**	3.392/.945	29.719***
Chi-square (18 df)	106.609***		151.145	
Nagelkerke R-Square	.262		.258	
–2 Log Likelihood	420.825		766.649	

* p<.05
** p<.01
*** p<.001

greater levels of self-efficacy and perceived delinquency at school were significantly more likely than their counterparts to report that they had seen another student with a weapon other than a gun to an adult. Additionally, those students with lower levels of school connectedness and higher levels of perceived social capital were also significantly more likely than their counterparts to report that they had seen another student with a weapon other than a gun at school. The variables included in the model also explained approximately one quarter of the variance (Nagelkerke R-square = .258) in the model.

The results presented in Table 3.5 demonstrate the impact of regressing whether a student would tell an adult if they knew their best friend had a gun (Model 1) or their best friend had a weapon other than a gun (Model 2) on the demographic, contextual, and theoretical variables described earlier. The logistic regression results presented in Table 3.5, Model 1 suggest that, once again, females, middle school students, those students who perceived lower levels of school misbehavior, higher levels of positive school climate, higher levels of perceived social capital, and higher levels of perceived self-efficacy were significantly more likely than their counterparts to report that their best friend had a gun. The variables included in the model explained slightly more than one fifth (Nagelkerke R-square = .222) of the variance in the decision to report in this model.

The logistic regression results presented in Table 3.5, Model 2 suggest that, similar to the previous models, females, middle school students, and those students who perceived lower levels of school misbehavior, higher levels of positive school climate, higher levels of perceived social capital, and higher levels of perceived self-efficacy were significantly more likely than their counterparts to report that their best friend had a weapon other than a gun. Additionally, students with lower levels of perceived school safety and higher levels of family attachment were significantly more likely to report that their best friend had a weapon other than a gun. The variables included in this model explained the most variation in reporting among the six models presented here (Nagelkerke R-square = .266).

Discussion

In this chapter, we used data from 895 middle and high school students in the Appalachian region of the U. S. to examine predictors of reporting weapons of various types to school authorities. The results presented here support many of the conclusions reached in previous studies with some notable exceptions. Our findings also reveal a number of interesting findings that are relevant for both policy and future research.

First, and most importantly, we determined that the vast majority of middle and high school students who had information that another student had a weapon on campus (whether the weapon was a gun or some other type of weapon) would report the student to school administrators. This finding mirrors previous research on students' willingness to report weapons possession at school (Brank et al., 2007; Brinkley & Saarino, 2006; Wylie et al., 2010). This suggests that students are willing to take an active part in protecting the safety of their own school. This finding is particularly encouraging and reaffirms the less publicized fact that many acts of violence are averted in schools each year because students tell school administrators or law enforcement about other

Table 3.5. Logistic Regression Results Regressing Whether Student Would Report if Their Best Friend Had a Gun or a Weapon Other Than a Gun to an Adult

	Model 1		Model 2	
	Whether Student Would Report if Their Best Friend Had a Gun (N=756)		Whether Student Would Report if Their Best Friend Had a Weapon Other Than a Gun (N=753)	
Variable	**B/S.E.**	**Exp(B)**	**B/S.E.**	**Exp(B)**
School misbehavior	–.440/.095	.644***	–.450/.089	.637***
Perceived risk of victimization	–.002/.053	.998	–.019/.052	.981
School safety	–.111/.058	.895	–.111/.056	.895*
Negative school climate	–.072/.085	.930	.030/.081	1.031
Positive school climate	.658/.218	.518**	.643/.209	.526**
School guardianship	.065/.055	1.067	.024/.054	1.024
School connectedness	–.020/.093	.981	–.072/.090	.931
Adult social capital	.426/.202	.653*	.737/.194	.479***
Self-efficacy	.178/.049	1.195***	.181/.045	1.199***
Delinquency problems at school	.082/.057	1.085	.083/.054	1.087
Alienation	.009/.042	1.009	.054/.041	1.055
Family attachment	.384/.338	1.468	.725/.339	2.065*
Free lunch recipient	.109/.214	1.115	–.147/.207	.863
Males	–.510/.186	.600**	–.726/.178	.484***
SR school performance	.053/.162	1.054	–.007/.161	.993
Parental arrangement	–.167/.190	.847	–.011/.181	.989
Nonwhite	–.403/.349	.668	–.344/.249	.709
School level	–.409/.206	.664*	–.637/.196	.529**
Constant	3.085/.931	21.861**	3.092/.895	22.023**
Chi-square (18 df)	128.227		166.551	
Nagelkerke R-Square	.222		.266	
–2 Log Likelihood	788.869		863.741	

* $p<.05$
** $p<.01$
*** $p<.001$

students who either threaten to or actually bring a weapon to school. Like previous studies, however, we found that willingness to report declines when those who possess weapons are close friends. Thus, this finding points to the need for school officials to develop strategies that help students understand that reporting weapons possession is extremely important, even when those weapons are possessed by one's friends.

Second, despite the finding that most students will report weapons possession, there were also a number of students who would not report the presence of a weapon at school. Additionally, the likelihood of reporting varied by a number of different factors, including the type of weapon brought to school and the relationship of the students who were aware of the weapon's presence at school, findings that mirror those of previous studies in this area (Brank et al., 2007; Brinkley & Saarino, 2006; Wylie et al., 2010). Several of these factors are discussed in detail below.

Students who perceived lower levels of school misbehavior were significantly more likely than their counterparts to report the presence of a weapon to an adult, regardless of how they became aware of the presence of the weapon, the type of weapon, or the relationship between the student and the student with the weapon. Thus, those students who felt their schools were orderly environments were significantly more likely to be willing to do their part in protecting that environment, including reporting the presence of weapons (regardless of type) when they became aware of the weapon presence. This finding is particularly encouraging for school administrators who seek to build a positive reporting climate by empowering students to take ownership of their own space. These findings suggest that these efforts will continue to be fruitful in maintaining a safe school environment.

Students who perceived the greatest levels of self-efficacy were also significantly more likely to report the presence of a weapon in every situation. Recall that these students report the use of more positive strategies for solving conflicts. Consequently, empowering students with the skills and knowledge to talk about their problems and resolve them in constructive ways will indirectly affect weapon reporting as well.

Students who perceived higher levels of positive school climate were also more likely to report the presence of a weapon in each of the situations presented to them. The direct relationship between positive school climate and willingness to report weapons possession is consistent with previous research by Wylie et al. (2010) and Brinkley and Saarnio (2006), who found a positive relationship between these measures, although Wylie et al. (2010) concluded that school climate is less important under conditions of anonymous reporting.

Only two demographic variables, gender and age/grade level, had a significant impact on weapon reporting in this sample. Similar findings have been uncovered in each of the earlier studies (Brank et al., 2007; Brinkley & Saarnio, 2006; Wylie et al., 2010). Female and middle school students were significantly more likely to report the presence of a weapon when they had direct knowledge of that weapon's presence at school (when they saw a student with a weapon or when they knew their best friend had a weapon) and when they heard that a student had a weapon other than a gun. Neither group was significantly more likely to report the presence of a weapon if they had heard a student had a gun. Consequently, it appears that the "culture of snitching" is much more prevalent among males than females, and it may be weapon specific. In other words, the stigma of being a "rat" appears to be much greater for males than females, and thus makes them less likely to report the presence of weapons in most cases. To address this situation, school administrators should develop programming and policies to encourage reporting among males and high school students, and they should stress the potential harm that can be caused by various types of weapons.

None of the other measures had a statistically significant association with the reporting of a weapon in all situations. Consequently, the impacts of the other theoretical variables depend on the weapon that was brought to school and/or the relationship the student has with the weapon carrier. Students who felt "strain" at school would report the presence of a weapon when they saw a student with a weapon or knew that their best friend had a weapon, regardless of the type of weapon, but were not significantly more likely to report second-hand knowledge of the presence of a weapon. These students, perhaps because of the negative relationships they perceive in the school environment, are not willing to assist the school by reporting unless they feel it will immediately impact them or one of their friends. Students with higher levels of family attachment, on the other hand, were significantly more likely to report when they heard a student had a gun and if they knew their best friend had a weapon other than a gun

Our findings regarding the relationships between students' willingness to report weapons possession at school and social capital are similar to the findings of Brank and associates (2007). For example, our results indicate that students with higher levels of perceived social capital were significantly more likely to report to an adult when they heard a student had a weapon other than a gun, when they saw another student with a weapon other than a gun, and when they knew their best friend had a weapon of any type. Thus, those students who trusted in adults to help them when they needed it were more likely to report the presence of a weapon other than a gun in every situation, and to report the presence of a gun when it was in the possession of their best friend. This bond of trust with adults, then, makes students more likely to report weapons other than guns, but not guns, except when guns are in the possession of their best friend. What is important here is that social capital appears to overcome some of the reluctance that many students have about reporting guns that are possessed by their friends. Quite possibly, the lack of association between increased social capital and reporting the presence of guns has more to do with higher levels of willingness to report guns across the sample than the lower levels of reporting of guns among students with a strong sense of social capital (remember, 72% of the students would report to an adult that they had heard a student had a gun on campus—this compares to only 61% who would report to an adult if they had heard a student had a weapon other than a gun). Given this finding, working to develop trusting relationships between students and adults is even more vital in operating safe schools.

Although the relationships discussed previously are important, there were a number of nonsignificant relationships uncovered in this study that are important as well. Among the demographic variables, students who received free lunch, performed poorly in school, were from single-parent homes, or were nonwhite were no more or less likely than their counterparts to report the presence of weapons at school to an adult. This calls into question a commonly held stereotype that only the "good" students (e.g., the middle class white students who perform well academically and live in homes where both biological parents live together) will report problems at school to teachers and administrators. These findings indicate that properly developed strategies to build trust and an "open reporting climate" will be successful or unsuccessful across all demographics and, when students do not report the presence of weapons, it is because of factors other than demographics.

Additionally, variables that intuitively would have a relationship with reporting the presence of weapons did not have an association with weapon reporting in this sample. Students with elevated levels of perceived risk of victimization, lower levels of perceived school safety, and lower levels of school guardianship were generally not more likely to report the presence of a weapon at school than their counterparts. This finding suggests that efforts to reduce fear and risk of victimization at school more generally may have little impact on encouraging weapon reporting among students. Consequently, school administrators need to target efforts to encourage weapon reporting among students to the aforementioned groups and let students know the specific purpose of those programs.

Finally, despite the extant literature indicating otherwise, student alienation, school connectedness, and perceptions of a negative school climate had little to do with weapon reporting among the youths in this sample. As a result, while all of those factors may be important in reducing delinquency and improving academic performance at school, they have little to do with weapon reporting among students in our sample.

Conclusions

The results presented here suggest a number of important implications for policy and future research. First, and perhaps most importantly, the results presented here suggest that efforts to encourage an "open reporting climate" where students feel empowered to report the presence of a weapon at school (and, intuitively, other actions that threaten the school environment) can be successful if properly designed and targeted. These efforts should begin with encouraging students to take ownership of their school, developing positive relationships between students and adults in the school, and building self-efficacy among students. Including students in the decision-making efforts of school administrators is a logical, yet often overlooked, step that can begin to accomplish this task. Inviting students to participate in assessments of school safety and crisis response planning is also essential; having these students report back to the larger student body and solicit feedback from their peers should create a larger sense of "buy-in" from the entire student body. Just as disgruntled voters often accuse their elected representatives of having a larger agenda that ignores the voters' needs, students who are not asked to provide feedback to administrators about their schools may feel ignored by those administrators. Because they feel the school administrators do not value their feedback, they may feel the administrators will not respond to their reports of weapons and other harmful behaviors and become apathetic about efforts of teachers and administrators to improve the school. Student empowerment will produce ownership; students who feel they own the space will not be apathetic. Although Wylie et al. (2010) argue that improving school climate may not be the most effective way to increase students' willingness to report weapons possession, and call for providing students with an anonymous avenue for reporting, we think it is too early to suggest that school climate improvement efforts will not produce significant results.

A second finding from this study needs future attention. Students who felt that the teachers and administrators were not helpful and created an environment of unfair and often nonexistent punishment for rule-breaking were less likely to report the presence of all weapons than those who felt school administrators and teachers treated students fairly and punished them when they broke the rules. Thus, schools exert considerable influence over the extent to which students are encouraged to report weapons possession. Importantly, with effort, schools can take steps to change students' perceptions of the school climate, which can increase levels of school safety. Our findings, in conjunction with earlier studies on this topic, indicate that students' willingness to report weapons possession is a highly nuanced phenomenon that is influenced by a variety of factors. These factors include the reporting climate of the school, students' perceptions of the potential consequences to themselves and others of reporting, the types of weapons involved, and the conditions under which reporting takes place. Moreover, previous research in this area (Brank et al., 2007; Wylie et al., 2010) indicates that allowing students an anonymous way to report weapons possession may be an important factor in encouraging student reporting. Unfortunately, we were not able to test this measure. Future studies, however, should examine how the ability to report misbehavior anonymously interacts with a variety of factors including those explored in this paper.

The developing body of research in this area provides a starting point for understanding students' willingness to report weapons possession at school and can serve as a basis for policies designed to enhance school safety. Moreover, our findings support and compliment previous studies in this area that highlight the relevance of school climate, social bonding, and the development of social capital and self-efficacy in the development of safe schools. Additional research is needed, however, to more fully understand the circumstances and factors that will be the most effective in encouraging students to report weapons possession in schools. This research is important because it can play a major role in developing strategies for reducing some of the most serious forms of violence that occur in our schools.

Notes

1. We introduce social learning theory because the hypotheses explored by Brank et al. (2007) and Wylie et al. (2010) are compatible with the social learning perspective, although this is not noted in either study.

2. Because the school system collected the data for this project, we were concerned that some students might not take the questionnaire as seriously as they might if outside researchers were collecting the data. In addition to including a protocol providing teachers step-by-step instructions regarding how the questionnaires should be administered, we also included an item asking students how honest they were during the completion of the questionnaire. The chi-square tests to examine the relationship between respondent honesty and reporting the presence of a weapon suggested that, compared to those students who indicated they provided honest responses all the time, larger percentages of respondents who indicated that they never gave honest responses, were honest some of the time, or were honest most of the time indicated that they

would not tell about the presence of a weapon. These percentage differences ranged from 9.9% to 13% and each was statistically significant ($p = .000$).

3. Although logistic regression is a robust technique that does not require assumptions about the distributions of predictors for purposes of analysis, it does assume a linear relationship between continuous predictors and the logit transformation of the outcome variables. Moreover, the power of the test is likely to be improved when there is multivariate normality and linearity among the predictors (Tabachnick & Fidell, 2007). Consequently, a number of steps were taken to screen the data prior to running the final models. We computed tolerance statistics for each of the continuous predictors, all of which exceeded .68, thus indicating that multicollinearity was not present. To test for linearity between continuous predictors and the logit transformation of the outcome variables, we computed interaction terms consisting of each continuous predictor and its natural log and conducted a logistic regression with the continuous predictors and the interaction terms. This test revealed that the assumption of linearity in the logit was violated in the case of four of the predictors. As a result, a square root transformation of school misbehavior, a reflect and square root transformation of positive school climate and adult social capital, and a reflect and inverse transformation of family attachment was computed. A subsequent test of linearity of the logit revealed that the assumption was no longer violated. In addition, we screened the data for univariate outliers through plots of standardized residuals and for multivariate outliers by calculating Mahalanobis distances and evaluating extreme cases using the chi-square distribution ($\chi^2(17) = 40.790$, $p. = .001$). As a final step prior to conducting the analysis, we computed DFBETAS to check for cases that might exert extreme influence on the regression coefficients. Together, these efforts led to the identification of 15 cases that were considered for removal from the database. Models were then estimated both with and without these cases. Minor changes in three of the models were found. Consequently, the following analysis is the result of the models run without the 15 outliers.

In three of the six models, the final model with outliers removed resulted in one predictor either being added to or being removed from the initial model. In the final model regressing "Heard Another Student Had a Weapon" on the predictors, alienation did not reach significance when it was found to be significant in the initial model. When "Knew Best Friend Had a Weapon (Other than a Gun)" was regressed on the predictors, family attachment reached significance; it was not significant in the initial model. Finally, with outliers removed, when "Saw Another Student with a Weapon" was regressed on the predictors, family attachment did not reach statistical significance when it was significant in the initial model.

References

Akers, R. L., & Sellers, C. S. (2004). *Criminological theories*. Los Angeles: Roxbury.

Bailey, S. L., Flewelling, R. L., & Rosenbaum, D. P. (1997). Characteristics of students who bring weapons to school. *Journal of Adolescent Health, 20*, 261–270.

Beger, R. (2003). The "worst of both worlds": School security and the disappearing fourth amendment rights of students. *Criminal Justice Review, 28*, 336–354.

Brank, E. M., Woolard, J. L., Brown, V. E., Fondacaro, M., Luescher, J. L., Chinn, R. G., & Miller, S. A. (2007). Will they tell? Weapons reporting by middle-school youth. *Youth Violence and Juvenile Justice, 5*(2), 125–146.

Brinkley, C.J., & Saarino, D.A. (2006). Involving students in school violence prevention: Are they willing to help? *Journal of School Violence, 5*(1), 93–106.

Cao, L., Zhang, Y., & He, N. (2008). Carrying weapons to school for protection: Analysis of the 2001 school crime supplement data. *Journal of Criminal Justice, 36*, 154–164.

Darley, J. M., & Latane, B. (1968). Bystander intervention in emergencies: Diffusion of responsibility. *Journal of Personality and Social Psychology, 8*(4), 377–383.

Dinkes, R., Kemp, J., Baum, K., & Snyder, T. D. (2009). *Indicators of school crime and safety: 2008.* Washington, DC: U. S. Department of Education and U. S. Department of Justice.

Dozier, J. B., & Miceli, M. P. (1985). Potential predictors of whistle-blowing: A prosocial behavior perspective. *The Academy of Management Review, 10*(4), 823–836.

DuRant, R. H., Getts, A. G., Candenhead, C., & Woods, E. R. (1995). The association between weapon carrying and the use of violence among adolescents living in and around public housing. *Journal of Adolescent Health, 17*, 376–380.

Eaton, D. K., Kann, L., Kinchen, S., Shanklin, S., Ross, J., Hawkins, J. et al. (2008). Youth risk behavior surveillance—United States, 2007. *Surveillance Summaries* [June 6]. Atlanta, GA: Centers for Disease Control and Prevention.

Erikson, K. G., Crosnoe, R., & Dornbusch, S. M. (2000). A social process model of adolescent deviance: Combining social control and differential association perspectives. *Journal of Youth and Adolescence, 29*, 395–425.

Estell, D. B., Farmer, T. W., Cairns, B. D., & Clemmer, J. T. (2003). Self-report weapon possession in school and patterns of early adolescent adjustment in rural African American youth. *Journal of Clinical Child and Adolescent Psychology, 32*(3), 442–452.

Farmer, G.L. (1999). Disciplinary practices and perceptions of school safety. *Journal of Social Work, 26*(1), 1–37.

Fitzgerald, D. L. & Ferrara, P. S. (2008). *Border gate: The story the government doesn't want you to read.* New York: Universe, Inc.

Forrest, K. Y. Z., Zychowski, A. K., Stuhldreher, W. L., & Ryan, W. J. (2000). Weapon-carrying in school: Prevalence and association with other violent behaviors. *American Journal of Health Studies, 16*, 133–140.

Friman, P. C., Woods, D. W., Freeman, K. A., Gilman, R., Short, M., McGrath, A. M., & Handwerk, M. L. (2004). Relationships between tattling, likeability, and social classification: A preliminary investigation of adolescents in residential care. *Behavior Modification, 28*(3), 331–348.

Glazer, M. P., & Glazer, P. M. (1989). *The whistleblowers: Exposing corruption in government and industry.* New York: Basic Books.

Grieger, T., Kauffman, J. M., & Grieger, R. M. (1976). Effects of peer reporting on cooperative play and aggression of kindergarten children. *Journal of School Psychology, 14*, 307–313.

Hindelang, M. (1973). Causes of delinquency: A partial replication and extension. *Social Problems, 21*, 471–487.

Hirschi, T. (1969). *Causes of delinquency*. Berkeley, CA: University of California Press.

Ingram, G. D., & Bering, J. M. (2010). Children's tattling: The reporting of everyday norm violations in preschool settings. *Child Development, 81*(3), 945–957.

Kalafat, J., & Elias, M. (1992). Adolescents' experience with and response to suicidal peers. *Suicide and Life-Threatening Behavior, 22*, 315–321.

Kitsantas, A. Ware, H. W., & Martinez-Arias, R. (2004). Students' perceptions of school safety: Effects by community, school environment, and substance use. *The Journal of Early Adolesence, 24,* 412–430.

Kulig, J., Valentine, J., Griffith, J., & Ruthazer, R. (1998). Predictive model of weapon carrying among urban high school students: Results and validation. *Journal of Adolescent Health, 22,* 313–319.

Lancelotta, G., & Vaughn, S. (1989). Relation between types of aggression and sociometric status: Peer and teacher perceptions. *Journal of Educational Psychology, 81,* 86–90.

Lockwood, D. (1997). Violence among middle school and high school students: Analysis and implications for prevention. *NIJ Research in Brief.* Washington, DC: National Institute of Justice.

MacNamara, D. E. J. (1991). The victimization of whistle-blowers in the public and private sectors. In R. J. Kelly & D. E. J. MacNamara (Eds.), *Perspectives on deviance: Dominance, degradation, and denigration* (pp. 121–134). Cincinnati, OH: Anderson.

Martin, S. L., Sadowski, L. S., Cotton, N. U., & McCarraher, D. R. (1996). Response of African-American adolescents in North Carolina to gun carrying by school mates. *Journal of School Health, 66,* 23–26.

Marvell, T. B. (2001). The impact of banning juvenile gun possession. *Journal of Law and Economics, 44,* 691–714.

May, D. C. (1999). Scared kids, unattached kids, or peer pressure: Why do students carry firearms to school? *Youth & Society, 13,* 100–127.

Mayer, M. J. & Leone, P. E. (1999). A structural analysis of school violence and disruption: Implications for creating safer schools. *Education and Treatment of Children, 22*(3), 333–356.

National Center for Chronic Disease Prevention and Health Promotion (n.d.). *Trends in the prevalence of behaviors that contribute to violence on school property: National YRBS: 1993–2007.* Retrieved October 26, 2009, from http://www.cdc.gov/HealthyYouth/yrbs/pdf/yrbs07_us_violence_school_trend.pdf.

Pershing, J. L. (2002). Whom to betray? Self-regulation of occupational misconduct at the United States Naval Academy. *Deviant Behavior, 23,* 149–175.

Robers, S., Zhang, J., & Truman, J. (2010). *Indicators of School Crime and Safety: 2010* (NCES 2011-002/NCJ 230812). National Center for Education Statistics, U.S. Department of Education, and Bureau of Justice Statistics, Office of Justice Programs, U.S. Department of Justice. Washington, DC.

Rosenfeld, R., Jacobs, B. A., & Wright, R. (2003). Snitching and the code of the street. *British Journal of Criminology, 43,* 291–309.

Rountree, P. W. (2000). Weapons at school: Are the predictors generalizable across context? *Sociological Spectrum, 20,* 291–324.

Samuelson, L., Hartnagel, T. & Krahn, H. (1990). Crime and social control among high school dropouts. *Journal of Crime and Justice, 18,* 129–161.

Scheckner, S., Rollins, S.A., Kaiser-Ulrey, C., & Wagner, R. (2002). School violence in children and adolescents: A meta-analysis of effectiveness. *Journal of School Violence, 1,* 5–34.

Simon, T. R., Crosby, A. E., & Dahlberg, L. L. (1999). Students who carry weapons to high school: Comparison with other weapon carriers. *Journal of Adolescent Health, 24,* 340–348.

Stein, K. B., Sarbin, T. R., Chu, C.-L., & Kulik, J. A. (1967). Adolescent morality: Its differentiated structure and relation to delinquent conduct. *Multivariate Behavioral Research, 2,* 199–210.

Tabachnick, B. G. & Fidell, L. S. (2007). *Using multivariate statistics.* Boston: Pearson.

Toomey, K. A. (2004). Practice pointer: The snitch rule. *Utah State Bar, 17*, 24–36.

Verdugo, R.R., & Schneider, J.M. (1999). Quality schools, safe schools: A theoretical and empirical discussion. *Education and Urban Society, 31*, 286–308.

Vossekuil, B., Fein, R. A., Reddy, M., Borum, R., & Modzeleski, W. (2002). *The final report and findings of the safe school initiative: Implications for the prevention of school attacks in the United States.* Washington, DC: United States Secret Service and United States Department of Education.

Wallace, L., & May, D. C. (2005). The Impact of relationship with parents and commitment to school on adolescent fear of crime at school. *Adolescence, 40*(159), 458–474.

Welsh, W.N. (2000). The effects of school climate on school disorder. *Annals*, 567, 88–107.

Westmarland, L. (2005). Police ethics and integrity: Breaking the blue code of silence. *Policing and Society, 15*, 145–165.

Wilcox, P., & Clayton, R. R. (2001). A multilevel analysis of school-based weapon possession. *Justice Quarterly, 18*, 509–539.

Wylie, L. E., Gibson, C. L., Brank, E. M., Fondacaro, M. R., Smith, S. W., Brown, V. E., & Miller, S. A. (2010). Assessing school and student predictors of weapons reporting. *Youth Violence and Juvenile Justice, 8*(4), 351–372.

Chapter 4

Parental Aggression against Teachers: A New Threat or an Old Myth?

*David C. May, Jerry Johnson, Yanfen Chen, Lisa Hutchinson, and Melissa Ricketts**

In the previous chapters, we have considered the dangers posed by students who carry and use weapons at school. Of all the dangers faced by students at school, weapons have the potential to inflict some of the greatest harm and, consequently, are important to consider in any book about school safety. Nevertheless, to this point, we have concentrated primarily on student safety in schools. Along with the students, another important group has concerns about school safety as well: the teachers.

While the research reviewed so far in this book has identified a number of characteristics and causal influences related to aggressive behaviors among students in school settings, similar research focusing on aggression against teachers is limited and typically is concerned only with incidents that involve students as perpetrators. Given the fact that there is a large body of literature that describes an inherent conflict in parent-teacher relationships, the emerging recognition of the "pushy parent" (Beard, 1991; Estes, 2002; Frean, 2002), and anecdotal evidence that has brought about an increased recognition of the existence of incidents of parental aggression against school personnel, a more thorough examination of the issue of parental aggression is warranted. The research reported here is an attempt to fill that void by (1) examining public school teachers' perceptions of (and experiences with) parental behaviors they perceive as aggressive or otherwise problematic and (2) investigating the extent to which perceptions and experiences vary according to selected teacher, school, and community characteristics.

We begin with a review of the literature on teacher experiences with (and perceptions of) instances of parental aggression and violence, followed by a description of the methods that we used to analyze the data we used for the research in this chapter. Using self-reports from a cross-section of elementary, middle, and high school teachers from the state of Kentucky, we then provide a descriptive analysis of teacher perceptions of (and experiences with) problematic behaviors on the part of parents. We follow that

---

* The information presented in this chapter is largely drawn from an article I coauthored with four colleagues that appeared in print elsewhere. The citation for that article is included below:

May, David C., Jerry Johnson, Yanfen Chen, Lisa Hutchison, and Melissa Ricketts
2010 Exploring Parental Aggression toward Teachers in a Public School Setting. *Current Issues in Education*, 13(1), 1–34.

with results from analyses investigating variations in perceptions and experiences according to individual teacher characteristics, school characteristics, and community characteristics. Finally, we conclude with policy recommendations and suggestions for future research.

Literature Review

The majority of information presented both in this book and in the area of school safety in general has focused primarily on student-on-student behaviors (Bauer et al., 2008; Dinkes et al., 2009) and includes only a small amount of information regarding aggression towards teachers (Callahan & Rivara, 1992; Johnston, O'Malley, & Bachman, 1993). Moreover, a growing literature has also sought to identify the causal influences of aggressive behaviors among students. Out of this research has emerged a wealth of information regarding the influential nature of parents as predictors of student aggression within schools (Batsche & Knoff, 1994; Farrington, 1989; Hotaling, Strauss, & Lincoln, 1989; Loeber & Stouthamer-Loeber, 1986; Olweus, 1980; Paperny & Deisher, 1983; Patterson, Dishion, & Bank, 1984; Trickett & Kuczynski, 1986). A related literature has also examined the adversarial nature of the parent-teacher relationship (Anderson-Levitt, 1989; Attanucci, 2004; Fine, 1993; Katz, 1996; Lasky, 2000; Lightfoot, 2003; Lodish, 1994; Trumbull, Rothstein-Risch, & Greenfield, 2000). In response to this body of knowledge regarding the importance of parents' role in the school environment and culture, researchers have also attempted to develop appropriate methodologies for dealing with the inherent conflict between parents and teachers (Ames, 1995; Epstein, 2001; Fenwick, 1993; Krumm, 1989; Rucci, 1991; St. John-Brooks, 2001).

Much of the aforementioned literature focuses on how to resolve the inherent teacher-parent conflict or improve the nature of parental involvement in the school, yet little attention has been paid to the specific issue of parental aggression in education. This lack of attention is surprising given that studies have identified parental attitudes as a significant source of stress for teachers (Brown, 1984; Heads fear, 2000; Moses, Slough, & Croll, 1987; Phillips, 2005). In fact, the strain of dealing with parents has been cited as one of the primary factors in new teachers leaving the profession (Phillips, 2005). Further, documented incidents of parental aggression towards school administrators and teachers are numerous. Nearly one in four Philadelphia public school teachers and staff said they were assaulted in the 2008–2009 school year (Sullivan, Snyder, Graham, & Purcell, 2011). In a 2001 study of school administrators in one Florida county, Trump and Moore (2001) found that 70% of respondents had been threatened by a parent. They identified three primary types of threats that occurred: verbal threats accompanied by intimidation, non-contact threats accompanied by intimidation, and intimidation with physical contact. While the study results confirmed the anecdotal belief that parental aggression towards teachers existed in their district, the authors cautioned against generalizing beyond their district and suggested replicating their study in other places (Trump & Moore, 2001). From an international perspective, 140 members of the National Association of Head Teachers reported being assaulted in the United Kingdom in the year 2001 (Figures confirm, 2001; Rights culture, 2001). In Edinburgh alone, over 70 parental assaults of teachers occurred during 2004 (Meglynn, 2005).

Recent incidents of parental aggression in a variety of other contexts further demonstrate the need for this line of research. Parental involvement in extracurricular activities has been linked to a wide range of behaviors, including relatively harmless acts of overextending their child's involvement in youth sports to more serious acts of physical aggression and even murder (Freivogal, 1991; Kanter, 2002; Sports Illustrated, 2000). Indeed, increasingly close parental involvement in extracurricular activities and debates between parents and teachers regarding academic grades has resulted in the emergence of a "pushy parents" typology (Beard, 1991; Estes, 2002; Frean, 2002).

Although society has recognized the existence of "pushy parents" and educators have sought to develop strategies to address conflict in parent teacher relationships, limited empirical research examines parental aggression towards teachers. Specifically, while some research is available, it is limited in scope and geography.

Here we fill a void by conducting a descriptive and exploratory analysis focusing on parental aggression toward teachers. This work provides empirical evidence about both (1) the prevalence and incidence of behaviors perceived as aggressive or problematic by teachers, and (2) the teacher, school, and community characteristics associated with the presence and prevalence of such behaviors.

Methods

Survey Construction

To begin this research, the limited availability of literature on parental aggression towards teachers required developing original constructs to include in the survey instrument for the data collection around this topic. To facilitate that development, we convened a focus group following a structured group format (Morgan, 1997) with a representative group of administrators and teachers (n = 10). The purpose of the focus group was to solicit information regarding the following issues: (1) conceptual definition of parental aggression, (2) forms of parental aggression, (3) frequency and extent of parental aggression, (4) issues around which parental aggression arises, (5) current responses to parental aggression, and (6) possible recommendations for dealing with aggressive parents.

Several themes emerged from analysis of the focus group data. The question concerning the conceptualization of parental aggression resulted in the identification of two primary sources of conflict, communication and issues of control, as well as a suggestion for a more appropriate conceptualization of the problem. Participants stressed the need to frame the survey instrument to conceptualize the issue from the standpoint of a *problem* rather than a *conflict* (to extend the range of behaviors to be considered beyond just overtly aggressive behaviors to other problematic interactions as well). The question concerning the types of parental aggression also yielded several themes, with verbal, property, and physical aggression identified as the most common. The question concerning the frequency and extent of parental aggression produced results suggesting that while few parents were problematic, dealing with those problematic parents consumed an inordinate amount of the teacher's time. A total of seven themes emerged for the question concerning the issues around which parental aggression arises: grades, discipline, special education, curriculum, absences, extracurricular activities, and negative media portrayal. The aforementioned themes served as the basis for developing the survey instrument.

Data Collection

Data were collected via electronic questionnaire. While electronic questionnaires may not yield representative results for surveys of the general public, valid, reliable electronic surveys involving members of organizations that have both access to the Internet and valid email addresses can be conducted with minimal issues of coverage (Dillman, 2000).

To begin the data collection process, a letter was mailed to all Kentucky superintendents (n = 176) describing the purpose and methodology of the study and asking for the email addresses of all school principals in the district and permission to send an email to each principal asking for their help in administering the questionnaire. The initial letter was followed up with three follow-up mailings and a phone call. In the end, 161 (91.5%) superintendents agreed to allow the principals in their district to participate.

Using an email distribution list of principals created from addresses provided by the superintendents, an informational letter was emailed to the principals. Approximately one month later, principals were sent an email containing the link to the web-based survey and were asked to forward the email to all the teachers in their school. Two follow-up emails were sent over the next month reminding principals to remind all the teachers in their school about the survey opportunity. The website was deactivated after approximately six weeks. After cleaning the data, the sample consisted of responses from 5,971 public school teachers.

Estimating an accurate response rate for this project is problematic. If each of the principals forwarded the email to all teachers in their school, then 33,106 teachers, the number of teachers in the 161 districts who agreed to participate in the research, had the opportunity to complete the questionnaire. Because the sample under study here consists of 5,971 respondents, our response rate using that calculation strategy is 18.0 percent. This estimate is conservative, at best, because it assumes that (1) all principals in all districts whose superintendent cooperated were able and willing to forward the email containing the link to the web-based survey to all the teachers in their school and (2) all teachers in those schools received and read that email. Nevertheless, the low response rate is indicative of the literature suggesting that lower response rates generally result from online versus pen and paper survey administrations (Handwerk, Carson, & Blackwell, 2000; Matz, 1999; Sax, Gilmartin, & Bryant, 2003; Tomsic, Hendel, & Matross, 2000; Underwood, Kim, & Matier, 2000). Given the exploratory nature of this analysis, the results presented below make an important contribution to this discussion, despite the limitations of the data collection process.

Demographic characteristics of teachers in the sample were remarkably similar to the overall population of Kentucky teachers in terms of race and gender, suggesting that non-response bias is not a serious issue (Dillman, 1991; Krosnick, 1999). While the findings presented here need to be taken in the context of this sample and are not immediately generalizable to the state as a whole, it is reasonable to expect that future research efforts with more representative samples would produce similar results.

Moreover, if we construe the 5,971 respondents as a sample for the population of 33,106 teachers, sample size calculations using a confidence level of 95% result in a confidence interval of 1.15 when based on the most stringent range of responses (two-item, or 50%).

Data Analysis

The following research questions guided the investigation:

1. To what extent have public school teachers in Kentucky experienced aggressive or otherwise problematic parental behaviors?
2. What do public school teachers in Kentucky perceive to be the primary causes of problematic interactions with parents?
3. How do teachers' experiences and perceptions with regard to problematic interactions with parents vary according to key characteristics of the teacher (e.g., gender, age, years of education experience, education level)?
4. How do teachers' experiences and perceptions with regard to problematic interactions with parents vary according to key characteristics of the school and community (e.g., grade level, school enrollment, community population size)?

The research questions were addressed through the use of descriptive statistics, one-way analysis of variance (ANOVA), and multiple linear regression analysis. Specifically, descriptive statistics were used to present a general overview of characteristics of the teachers, schools, and communities represented in the sample, and were also used to describe experiences with aggressive or problematic interactions for the sample as a whole. A one-way ANOVA test was then used to investigate the extent that incidences of problematic behaviors vary according to the level of the school (i.e., elementary, middle, or high). Finally, multiple linear regression analysis was used to investigate the impact of relevant teacher and school characteristics on the number of instances of aggressive or problematic interactions with parents reported by respondents.

This study is responsive to key gaps in the literature regarding parental aggression toward teachers. In general, researchers, policymakers, and practitioners have little information about: (1) the prevalence or incidence of parental aggression toward teachers; and (2) situational and contextual factors associated with parental aggression toward teachers. Thus, despite the caveats indicated by the sampling limitations, we feel this chapter lays an important foundation for future work in this area.

Results

Descriptive Analyses

In Tables 4.1 to 4.4, we provide descriptive and frequency statistics for demographic and professional characteristics of respondents in the sample. The descriptive statistics for respondents' age and years of teaching experience are presented in Table 4.1. The results presented in these tables suggest that the average teacher responding to the ques-

Table 4.1 Summary of Descriptive Statistics for Respondents' Age and Tenure in Education

	N	Min.	Max.	Mean	SD
Teacher's Age	5,743	21	75	41.636	10.493
Years of Experience	5,933	0	43	12.670	8.976

Table 4.2 Summary of Frequency Statistics for Teacher Gender, Race, and Education Level

Variable	Frequency	Percent	Valid Percent	Cumulative Percent
Gender				
Female	4,856	81.3	81.6	81.6
Male	1,097	18.4	18.4	100.0
Total	5,953	99.7	100.0	
Missing	18	.3		
Race				
Black	109	1.8	1.8	1.8
White	5,757	96.4	96.9	98.7
American Indian	24	.4	.4	99.1
Hispanic	17	.3	.3	99.4
Asian	11	.2	.2	99.6
Other	17	.3	.3	99.9
Multiracial	7	.1	.1	100.0
Missing	29	.5		
Education				
Some College	9	.2	.2	.2
Bachelor's	1,428	23.9	24.0	24.2
Master's	2,957	49.5	49.7	73.9
Master's +30 hours	1,502	25.2	25.3	99.2
Ed.D./Ph.D.	48	.8	.8	100.0
Total	5,945	99.6	100.0	
Missing	26	.4		

Table 4.3 Summary of Frequency Statistics for School Level, Enrollment, and Community Size

Variable	Frequency	Percent	Valid Percent	Cumulative Percent
School Level				
Elementary	2,598	43.5	43.6	43.6
Middle	1,501	25.1	25.2	68.7
High	1,865	31.2	31.3	100.0
Missing	7	.1		
Total	5,971	100.0		
Enrollment				
Less than 250	471	7.9	8.0	8.0
251 to 500	1,922	32.2	32.5	40.5
501 to 750	1,874	31.4	31.7	72.2
751 to 1,000	754	12.6	12.8	84.9
1,001 to 1,250	335	5.6	5.7	90.6
1,251 to 1,500	272	4.6	4.6	95.2
1,501 to 1,750	151	2.5	2.6	97.8
1,751 to 2,000	73	1.2	1.2	99.0
2,001 to 2,500	59	1.0	1.0	100.0
Missing	60	1.0		
Total	5,971	100.0		
Community Size				
Less than 2,500	974	16.3	16.6	16.6
2,501 to 5,000	1,047	17.5	17.8	34.4
5,001 to 10,000	861	14.4	14.7	49.0
10,001 to 25,000	1,169	19.6	19.9	68.9
25,001 to 50,000	784	13.1	13.3	82.3
50,001 to 150,000	388	6.5	6.6	88.9
Over 150,000	653	10.9	11.1	100.0
Missing	95	1.6		
Total	5,971	100.0		

tionnaire was approximately 42 years of age with 13 years of experience in education (Table 4.1).

In Table 4.2, we provide frequency statistics describing gender, race, and education level distributions among the sample. Four in five respondents (81.3%) were female, while the vast majority (96.4%) were white. Approximately half (49.5%) of the respondents had obtained a master's degree, while approximately equal percentages had a Bachelor's degree and a Rank I designation (Master's degree plus 30 hours graduate education) (23.9% and 25.1%, respectively).

Table 4.4 Incidence of Respondents Reporting Various Problematic Interactions with Parents

Interaction	Frequency	Valid Percent
A parent has shouted at me in anger	1,930	36.0
A parent has used profanity directed toward me	1,506	27.9
A parent has verbally threatened me	820	15.2
A parent has sent numerous emails to harass me	443	8.3
A parent has detained or attempted to detain me against my will	300	5.6
A parent has damaged my property at home or school	122	2.3
A parent has hit, pushed, or attempted to hit or push me	91	1.7

In Table 4.3, we provide frequency statistics for school level, school size, and community size in discrete categories. Almost half of the respondents (43.5%) taught in elementary schools while one in three respondents (31.2%) taught in high school. Approximately three in four respondents (72.2%) taught in schools with enrollments of less than 750 students and respondents were widely distributed across a variety of community sizes.

In Table 4.4, we provide frequency and descriptive statistics related to respondents' experiences with aggressive or problematic interactions with parents. The most prevalent form of aggressive/problematic behavior was verbal aggression. More than one in three respondents reported that a parent of a child at the school had shouted at them in anger; more than one in four teachers reported that a parent had used profanity directed toward the respondent, and more than one in seven reported having been threatened verbally. Considerably less common, about 1 in 12 respondents reported having been harassed as a result of receiving numerous emails. Far fewer respondents had experienced any of the more serious situations. About 1 in 20 (5.6%) responded that a parent had detained or attempted to detain them in a location in which they did not want to be. Less than 1 in 40 teachers responded that a parent had damaged their property at school or at home (2.3%) and that a parent had pushed, hit, or attempted to push or hit them (1.7%). In results not presented in tabular form here, respondents reported experiencing an average of three of the seven problematic interactions (3.22), although approximately 60% reported no interactions in any of these categories. Thus, the majority of respondents in the sample have never experienced aggressive or otherwise problematic behavior from a parent *at any point in their career.* A sizable minority did report having been involved in some type of problematic parental behavior; an additional 30% reported between one and eight total instances of aggressive parent behavior or problematic interactions with parents. Less than 3% of respondents reported 20 or more incidents of such interactions over the course of their career.

In Table 4.5, we report frequency statistics for the variable measuring respondents' perceptions of the most important causes of problems between teachers and parents. More than half of the respondents reported that discipline was the most important

Table 4.5 Summary of Frequency Statistics for Respondents' Perception of Most Important Causes of Problems with Parents

	Variable	Frequency	Percent	Valid Percent	Cumulative Percent
Valid	Discipline	3,016	50.5	51.4	51.4
	Grades	1,637	27.4	27.9	79.3
	Special Education	417	7.0	7.1	86.4
	Other Issues	285	4.8	4.9	91.3
	Attendance	228	3.8	3.9	95.2
	Curriculum	117	2.0	2.0	97.2
	Sports	120	2.0	2.0	99.2
	Other Extracurricular	44	.7	.8	100
	Total	5,864	98.2	100.0	
Missing		107	1.8		
Total		5,971	100.0		

cause of problems with parents, while another 28% cited grades as the leading cause. Other notable causes included special education, cited as most important by 1 in 14 respondents, and attendance issues, cited as most important by 1 in 25 respondents.

Table 4.6
Summary of ANOVA for Number of Incidents Reported by School Level

	Sum of Squares	df	Mean Square	F
Between Groups	1467.307	2	733.654	6.581**
Within Groups	603802.379	5416	111.485	
Total	605269.686	5418		

**p=0.001

Post-hoc Bonferroni Comparison for Number of Incidents Reported by School Level

Comparisons	Mean Difference (in reported incidents)	Std. Error	95% CI Lower Bound	95% CI Upper Bound
Elementary vs. Middle	–1.130*	0.358	–1.989	–0.271
Elementary vs. High	–0.972*	0.336	–1.777	–0.166
Middle vs. High	0.158	0.384	–0.762	1.079

* p<0.05

Investigative Analyses

The results reported in the previous section depict the respondents' collective experiences with aggressive or otherwise problematic parent behavior directed toward teachers. As a follow-up to those analyses, below we investigate the extent to which reported experiences vary according to characteristics of the respondent, the school, and the community. In Table 4.6, we begin with the results from a one-way analysis of variance (ANOVA) that was performed to investigate whether experiences with aggressive or otherwise problematic parent interactions vary according to the level of the school in which respondents taught. In these analyses, the dependent variable operationalizes respondents' experiences as the total number of incidents reported from among the categories in Table 4.4 while the independent variable is the grade level of the school (i.e., elementary, middle, or high school).

The ANOVA results presented in Table 4.6 indicate that the grade level of the teacher's school has a significant impact on the number of aggressive/problematic parent incidents experienced by the teacher ($F=6.581$, $df=2$, $p<.01$). Results of post hoc comparisons indicate that experiences for teachers at the elementary level differ significantly from those of middle and high school teachers; elementary teachers experienced significantly fewer incidents than either group. Elementary teachers, on average, experienced 1.1 fewer incidents than middle school teachers, and .9 fewer incidents than high school teachers. The difference in the number of incidents experienced by middle school teachers when compared to high school teachers was not statistically significant.

Table 4.7 Summary of Regression Analysis for Variables Predicting Number of Incidents Reported by Teacher (n = 5, 691)

Variable	B	SE B	β
Sex of Respondent	.129	.062	.048
Age of Respondent	–.010	.004	–.100**
Years Experience in Education	.004	.005	.031
Level of Educational Attainment	.080	.038	.054*
School Enrollment	.020	.018	.030
Community Size	.057	.012	.108***

Notes: Adjusted $R^2=.162$; *p≤.05; **p≤.01;***p≤.001

We next performed a multiple linear regression analysis to investigate whether the respondents' experiences with problematic parental behaviors (i.e., the variable measuring the total number of instances of aggressive or problematic interactions with parents reported by the respondent) varied by gender, age, total years of experience in education, educational attainment, school enrollment size, or community population size. Prior to performing the analysis, relevant statistical tests and transformations were performed to ensure that variables met assumptions for regression analysis.

The results presented in Table 4.7 suggest that respondent's age, respondent's level of educational attainment, and community size where the respondent was located all had statistically significant associations with problematic parental behavior. Specifically, the regression results suggest that, on average: (1) the higher the age of the teacher, the less likely it is that the teacher will experience aggressive and/or problematic interactions with parents; (2) the higher the education level of the teacher, the more likely it is that the teacher will experience aggressive and/or problematic interactions with parents; and (3) the larger the community, the more likely it is that a teacher will experience aggressive and/or problematic interactions with parents. None of the other variables had a statistically significant influence on the number of problematic parental behaviors the respondent had experienced in their career. The R^2 statistic in Table 4.6 indicates that 16.2 percent of the variation in experiences with problematic parent behaviors is explained by the variables included in the regression equation.

Discussion

Interpretation of Results

As noted earlier, data limitations in this study prevent us from making generalizations to the larger population with statistical certainty. In other words, we cannot draw *statistical conclusions*. Given the close similarities between teachers, schools, and communities in the sample and in the larger population, we can, however, draw *logical conclusions* based upon the results reported here.

First, the results presented here suggest that although a substantial minority of teachers had experienced verbal abuse and threats from parents, only a small percentage of teachers had actually experienced any physical aggression from parents. In other words, while the problem of parental aggression was present for many of the teachers in the study, the issue was more verbal than physical.

This finding, coupled with the fact that much of the literature on parental aggression against teachers is found in popular or trade magazines (e.g., *Time*, *Good Housekeeping*, *Times Educational Supplement*), further suggests the need for scholarly research in this area. Based on the results of this study, some teachers are likely to experience somewhat regular, if primarily verbal, conflict with parents. Contradicting anecdotal evidence and media accounts of numerous threats and assaults on parents, however, the results presented here suggest that teachers in this sample experienced only a small amount of physical confrontations with parents. The explanation for this perception that teachers are at great risk of physical assault by parents may be attributed to the rarity of these types of events, rather than their frequency. Whenever a teacher is assaulted by a parent, it becomes a newsworthy event, not just at the local level, but often at the state, regional, and sometimes national levels as well. Thus, these rare events often dominate the news, saturating those areas with news accounts about these events. This saturation increases public perceptions that these events are regular occurrences in the school setting when, in actuality, verbal threats from parents far outnumber any sort of physical threat against teachers in the school setting.

Secondly, respondents indicated that the primary cause of conflict between parents and teachers is discipline. This finding suggests that teachers who regularly discipline students may increase the likelihood of parental conflict by doing so. Consequently, it is important that school administrators be aware of this relationship and take steps to reduce potential for conflict between parents and teachers over disciplinary actions in their schools. One method through which administrators can do so is by supporting teachers when they discipline students and, if needed, by serving as the disciplinarian for teachers for particularly problematic children so teachers can focus on the academic tasks at hand, and not worry about increasing their risk for victimization by firmly and fairly enforcing classroom rules.

Our results also suggested that elementary teachers experienced significantly less parental aggression or problematic interactions than either middle school or high school teachers. Specifically, both middle and high school teachers are, on average, likely to experience about one more incident of problematic parental behavior than an elementary teacher. To characterize the practical significance of this one incident difference, it is worth recalling that approximately 60% of respondents reported no such incidents, and that 90% of respondents reported eight or fewer incidents. The one incident difference represents a 33% increase over the mean of 3.2, and a 100% increase over the median of 0. Thus, differences in the experiences of elementary school teachers, when compared to those of middle school and high school teachers, are not only statistically significant, but substantively significant as well. The grade-level differences suggest that efforts in this area should be targeted at the middle and high school levels.

Younger teachers were more likely to experience incidents of parental aggression or other problematic interactions than their older counterparts, as were teachers working in larger communities. The relationship between age and exposure to increased incidents of parental aggression is intuitive, as younger teachers often do not have the life experience and maturity of their older counterparts, who have often developed strategies through the "school of hard knocks" that are effective in avoiding parental conflict. Additionally, given that teachers working in smaller communities are generally more likely to have long-standing roots in that community (and often have attended the same school in which they are currently working) and are also more likely to interact with the parents of their children in settings outside of the school, this finding makes sense as well. It is also possible that differences in the number and/or severity of disciplinary incidents is a contributing factor—rural and small town schools, on average, experience fewer incidents and fewer serious incidents (NCES, 2006). This difference is thus impacted by differences in community dynamics in urban, suburban, and rural settings.

The regression results also suggest that teachers with more advanced degrees were more likely to experience incidents of parental aggression or other problematic interactions than their counterparts without those advanced degrees. Although this relationship was somewhat unexpected, it is not completely surprising. It may be that teachers who return for additional graduate courses are more willing to experiment with innovative educational practices and theories than their counterparts who do not. These practices may make parents that are unfamiliar with these strategies uncomfortable and thus more likely to confront these teachers than they would be to confront their less innovative counterparts. It could also be that teachers with higher levels of education are less willing to tolerate questions or suggestions about their educational strategies and methods from parents. This resistance may make conflict with parents more likely. Further analysis is needed to unravel these relationships.

Recommendations for Future Research

The results of this descriptive and exploratory project warrant further inquiry into this line of research. Specifically, we suggest that this project should be replicated using a more representative data sample and additional potentially important variables not measured in this research. Additional variables that could be added to enhance the work include (1) data about discipline strategies and frequencies of teachers and schools, which would allow for examination of the influence of the frequency and type of teachers' disciplinary actions on problematic parental behavior and also provide some additional context for exploring school level influences; and (2) locale codes from NCES, which would enable better examinations of the influence of community characteristics on problematic parental behaviors. The use of national datasets such as the Schools and Staffing Survey and the National Household Education Survey, both products of the National Center for Education Statistics, should also be explored.

Secondly, future work should attempt to understand parental perceptions at different grade levels about school discipline, attendance, and other issues that were identified here as causes of parent aggression and other problematic interactions. Results of these efforts could confirm teacher perceptions that certain types of issues and interactions lead to aggression and problematic interactions. Moreover, and more exploratory in nature, this inquiry would further allow researchers to explore the hypothesis that differences in parent behaviors at different school grade levels are in part the result of changes in the perceptions of those parents as their children move through the different schooling levels, with a particular focus on the middle school transition years.

Recommendations for Policy and Practice

The results presented here reveal that incidents involving problematic interactions with parents are far more likely to be verbal than physical, that middle school and high school teachers are more likely to experience such incidents, and that discipline is a primary cause of such incidents. With that in mind, the following recommendations for policy and practice are offered: (1) pre-service training and in-service professional development should incorporate strategies for dealing effectively with verbal conflict; and (2) schools should involve parents in developing, implementing, and monitoring discipline policies and procedures.

Because teachers are most likely to experience *verbal* conflict with parents, providing training for teachers on how to avoid, prevent, and resolve verbal confrontations with parents (e.g., de-escalation strategies for preventing verbal confrontations from turning into physical conflict) is recommended for both pre-service and in-service teachers. Additionally, training and support for teachers in developing non-confrontational approaches to student discipline are recommended. While providing training and support in these areas for all teachers is clearly warranted by results reported here, findings also suggest, if more tentatively, that inexperienced teachers likely need the most support and assistance if they are to build capacity in these areas.

Because discipline incidents are a primary cause of teacher-parent conflict (from the teachers' perspectives), disciplinary policy and practice should be procedurally clean, should involve parents, and should provide for transparency in its development, implementation, and monitoring. Schools can be proactive in preventing problems here by: (1) developing clear discipline codes, including consequences for specific infractions; (2) enforcing rules consistently and without favoritism; (3) communicating the rules to parents, students, and the community at large; and (4) creating and maintaining a process through which parents can address their concerns regarding discipline issues with the principal and, if needed, the superintendent and school board. Involving parents in the process of developing discipline codes can be a very effective approach (Sheldon & Epstein, 2002). A clear disciplinary code and a process for addressing appeals and other issues should also be thoroughly explained in the student handbook. Recent research (NCES, 2006) suggests that only 60% of schools have a formal process to obtain parent input on policies related to school crime and discipline, and only 19% of schools have a program that involves parents at school in helping to maintain school discipline.

Moreover, data on disciplinary incidents should be assembled and published in a manner that is accessible to parents and other interested parties in the community. Schools should also be proactive in disseminating this information to parents at every opportunity and through a variety of media (e.g., print, electronic). Clearly and proactively communicating this information may reduce the number of potentially problematic situations that arise. While these strategies will certainly not completely eradicate parent-teacher conflicts, any strategy that reduces this conflict is a worthwhile strategy to explore.

References

Ames, C. (1995). *Teachers' school-to-home communications and parent involvement: The role of parent perceptions and beliefs.* Washington, D.C.: Center on Families, Communities, Schools and Children's Learning.

Anderson-Levitt, K. (1989). Degrees of distance between teachers and parents in urban France. *Anthropology and Education Quarterly, 20*(2), 97–117.

Attanucci, J. S. (2004). Questioning honor: A parent-teacher conflict over excellence and diversity in a USA urban high school. *Journal of Moral Education, 33*(1), 57–69.

Batsche, G. M., & Knoff, H. M. (1994). Bullies and their victims: Understanding a pervasive problem in the schools. *School Psychology Review, 23*(1), 165–174.

Bauer, L., Guerino, P., Nolle, K.L., & Tang, S. (2008). *Student victimization in U.S. schools: Results from the 2005 school crime supplement to the national crime victimization survey.* Washington D.C.: National Center for Education Statistics, NCES 2009-306.

Beard, L. (1991, Sept.). Pushy parents, problem children. *Good Housekeeping, 21*(3), 172–175.

Brown, J. (1984). *Missouri teachers experience stress.* Urbana, IL. ERIC Clearinghouse on Elementary and Early Childhood Education, (ERIC Document Reproduction Service No. ED 253313).

Callahan, C. M., & Rivara, F. P. (1992). Urban high school youth and handguns. *Journal of the American Medical Association, 267*, 3038–3042.

Dillman, D.A. (2000). *Mail and Internet surveys: The tailored design method (2nd ed.).* New York: John Wiley & Sons.

Dillman, D. A. (1991). The design and administration of mail surveys. *Annual Review of Sociology, 17*(2), 225–249.

Dinkes, R., Kemp, J., & Baum, K. (2009). *Indicators of school crime and safety: 2008* (NCES 2009-022/ NCJ 226343). Washington, DC: National Center for Education Statistics, Institute of Education Sciences, U.S. Department of Education, and Bureau of Justice Statistics, Office of Justice Programs, U.S. Department of Justice.

Eaton, D.K., Kann, L., Kinchen, S., Shanklin, S., Ross, J., Hawkins, J., Harris, W.A., Lowry, R., McManus, T., Chyen, D., Lim, C., Brener, N.D., & Weschsler, H. (2007). *Youth risk behavior surveillance survey—United States, 2007.* Atlanta: Centers for Disease Control.

Epstein, J. (2001). *Schools, family and community partnerships.* Boulder, CO: Westview Press.

Estes, C. A. (2002). Parents and youth sports, *Parks & Recreation, 37*(12), 20.

Farrington, D. P. (1989). Early predictors of adolescent aggression and adult violence. *Violence and Victims, 4*, 79–100.

Fenwick, K. (1993). Diffusing conflict with parents: A model for communication. *Child Care Information Exchange, 93*, 59–60.

Figures confirm surge in violence. (2001, June 1). *Times Educational Supplement, 4431*, 1–6.

Fine, M. (1993). Apparent involvement: reflections on parents, power and urban schools. *Teachers College Record, 94*(4) 682–729.

Frean, A. (2002, June 6). Pushy parents 'cause school phobia'. *Times*, p. 4.

Freivogal, M. W. (1991, September 2). Cheerleader case in Texas makes pushy parents feel a bit less pushy. *St. Louis Post-Dispatch.*

Handwerk, P.G., Carson, C., & Blackwell, K. M. (2000). Online versus paper-and-pencil surveying of students: A case study. Paper presented at the Annual Forum of the Association for Institutional Research, Cincinnati, OH, May 21–24, 2000.

Harris, K.M., & Udry, J.R. (2010). *National longitudinal study of adolescent health (Add Health), 1994–2002: Wave III supplemental files [restricted use].* Ann Arbor, MI: Interuniversity Consortium for Political and Social Research

Heads fear violent parents. (2000, April 6). *BBC News Online.* Retrieved June 10th, 2005 from http://news.bbc.co.uk/1/low/education/704042.stm

Hotaling, G. T., Strauss, M. A., & Lincoln, A. J. (1989). Intrafamily violence and crime and violence outside the family. In L. Ohlin & M. Tonry (Eds.), *Family violence* (pp. 315–375). Chicago: University of Chicago Press.

Johnston, L.D., O'Malley, P. M., & Bachman, J. G. (1993). *Monitoring the future study for goal 6 of the national education goals: A special report for the National Education Goals Panel.* Ann Arbor, MI: University of Michigan, Institute for Social Research.

Kanter, M. (2002). Parents and youth sports. *Park and Recreation, 37*(12), 20–28.

Katz, L. G. (1996). *Preventing and resolving parent-teacher differences.* Urbana, IL. ERIC Clearinghouse on Elementary and Early Childhood Education, (ERIC Document Reproduction Service No. 401048).

Krosnick, J. A. (1999). Survey research. *Annual Review of Sociology, 50*(4), 537–567.

Krumm, V. (1989). *How open is the public school? On cooperation between teachers and parents.* Austria: Educational Management.

Lasky, S. (2000). The cultural and emotional politics of teacher-parent interactions. *Teaching and Teacher Education, 16*(8), 843–860.

Lightfoot, S. (2003). *The essential conversation: What parents and teachers can learn from each other.* New York: Random House Publishing.

Lodish, R. (1994). Parents and teachers. *Independent School, 55*(1), 96–97.

Loeber, R., & Stouthamer-Loeber, M. (1986). Family factors as correlates and predictors of juvenile conduct problems and delinquency. In M. Tonry & N. Morris (Eds.), *Crime and justice: An annual review of research* (Vol. 7) (pp. 29–150). Chicago: University of Chicago Press.

Matz, C. M. (1999). Administration of web versus paper surveys: Mode effective and response rates. Master's Research Paper, University of North Carolina, Chapel Hill.

Meglynn, F. (2005, March 4). Violence against teachers drops after crackdown. *Education Reporter*, p. 11.

Morgan, D. L. (1997). *Focus groups as qualitative research.* Thousand Oaks, CA: Sage Publications.

Moses, D., Slough, E., & Croll, P. (1987). Parents as partners or problems? *Disability, Handicap & Society,* 2(1), 75–84.

National Center for Education Statistics. (2006). *Crime, violence, discipline, and safety in U.S. public schools: Findings from the school survey on crime and safety: 2003–04.* Washington, DC: Author.

National Center for Education Statistics. (2007). *School Survey on Crime and Safety (SSOCS), 2004.* Washington, DC: Author.

Olweus, D. (1980). Familial and temperamental determinants of aggressive behavior in adolescent boys: A causal analysis. *Developmental Psychology, 1*(4), 644–660.

Paperny, D., & Deisher, R. (1983). Maltreated adolescents: The relationship to a predisposition toward violent behavior and delinquency. *Adolescence, 18,* 499–506.

Patterson, G. R., Dishion, T. J., & Bank, L. (1984). Family interaction: A process model of deviancy training. *Aggressive Behavior, 10,* 253–268.

Phillips, S. (2005, April 08) Strain of dealing with violent or meddling parents. *Times Educational Supplement.*

Rights culture fuels school violence. (2001, May 29). *BBC New Online.* Retrieved June 4th, 2005 from http://news.bbc.co.uk/1/low/education/1357670.stm

Rucci, R. (1991). *Dealing with difficult people: A guide for educators.* Washington, D.C.: Office of Educational Research. (ERIC Document Reproduction Service No. 336810).

Sax, L. J., Gilmartin, S. K., & Bryant, A. N. (2003). Assessing response rates and non-response bias in web and paper surveys. *Research in Higher Education, 44*(4), 409–431.

Sheldon, S., & Epstein, J. (2002). Improving student behavior and school discipline with family and community involvement. *Education and Urban Society, 35*(1), 4–26.

Sports Illustrated. (2000, July). Out of control. *Sports Illustrated,* 87–95.

St. John-Brooks, C. (2001). Mutual respect will tame pit-bull parents. *Times Educational Supplement, 4437,* 23.

Sullivan, J., Snyder, S., Graham, K.A., & Purcell, D. (2011, March 27). Climate of violence stifles city's schools. *Philadelphia Inquirer.* Retrieved June 30, 2014 from http://www.philly.com/philly/news/special_packages/inquirer/school-violence/118574199.html?c=r

Tomsic, M. L., Hendel, D. D., & Matross, R. P. (2000). A World Wide Web response to student satisfaction surveys: Comparisons using paper and Internet formats. Paper presented at the 40th Annual Meeting of the Association for Institutional Research, Cincinnati, OH, May 21–24, 2004.

Trickett, P., & Kuczynski, L. (1986). Children's misbehaviors and parental discipline strategies in abusive and nonabusive families. *Developmental Psychology, 22,* 115–123.

Trumbull, E., Rothstein-Fisch, F., & Greenfield, P. M. (2000). *Bridging cultures in our schools: New approaches that work.* Washington, D.C.: Office of Educational Research. (ERIC Document Reproduction Service No. ED404954).

Trump, K. S., & Moore A. (Eds.). (2001). Deal effectively with hostile visitors to the front office. *Inside School Safety*, 6(2), 1–10.

Underwood, D., Kim, H., & Matier, M. (2000). *To mail or to web: Comparisons of survey response rates and respondent characteristics.* Paper presented at the Annual Forum of the Association for Institutional Research. Cincinnati, OH. (ERIC Document Reproduction Service No. ED 446513).

Chapter 5

Fear of Crime in Schools

*David C. May**

Before you start reading this chapter, I want you to conduct an experiment. Find the nearest computer, smart phone, iPad or E-pad, or anything that will allow you to "google." "Google" the word "lockdown" and the word "school" as a two-word combination. The chances are really good that, if you are reading this chapter between August and early June, your search took you to an article about a school lockdown that occurred today, yesterday, or, at the very most, last week. When I conducted this experiment on my own (June 30, 2014), I read about a primary school in Australia that "locked down" that morning because of an armed robbery that occurred near the school.

If you have never been involved in a "lockdown," you probably are not acutely aware of the emotions experienced by children taking part in that event. In a school setting, a lockdown is "a security measure taken during an emergency to prevent people from leaving or entering a building" (www.dictionary.com). Students attending K–12 public schools in the United States typically participate in at least one lockdown drill each year so they are familiar with the procedure. Nevertheless, when a "real" lockdown occurs, students can often tell that the action is not a drill and thus take it much more seriously. However, when the lockdown occurs, many students experience fear.

Fear can be defined as an " ... usually unpleasant feeling that arises as a normal response to danger" (Scruton, 1986, p. 30). Fear has been the subject of more scientific investigation than any other emotion and affects every human being in some fashion (Izard, 1977). Fear is a typical, rational response to a current or perceived threat and can serve as a coping function to allow humans to increase their chances of survival in the face of a fear-inducing threat (Lazarus, Kanner, & Folkman, 1980; Marks, 1978). When individuals face dangerous situations (like a lockdown for elementary students), small levels of fear induce caution, while more fear allows individuals to flee in the face of danger, thus increasing their chances of survival. Just as humans fear snakes, spiders, and public speaking, they often fear that which they cannot control or do not understand. Crime fits both of those criteria.

Fear of crime has a variety of negative consequences. In fact, some scholars have argued that fear of crime may be a more severe problem than crime itself (Doerner & Lab, 2012) and the fear of crime is often incongruent with actual crime levels. Even

---

* The second half of this chapter presents results from an article I wrote that appeared in *Sociological Spectrum* in 2001.

May, David C. (2001). The Effect of Fear of Sexual Victimization on Adolescent Fear of Crime. *Sociological Spectrum* 21(2):141–174.

though the crime rate has declined dramatically since 1992 (Federal Bureau of Investigation, 2012), crimes such as the recent Sandy Hook elementary school mass murder (CNN, 2013) continue to make Americans fearful of crime, particularly violent crime.

Each year, the Bureau of Justice Statistics surveys public school youths regarding their fear of crime at school. The most recent report in that series indicates that the percentage of students aged 12–18 that report being afraid at school has dropped from 12 percent in 1995 to 4 percent in 2011 (Robers, Kemp, Rathbun, & Morgan, 2014). Nevertheless, although less than 1 in 20 students agreed that they "had been afraid of an attack at school or on the way to and from school," the percentage agreeing with that statement (4 percent) is twice as high as the percentage of students who agreed that they were afraid of an attack "away from school" (2 percent) (Robers et al., 2014).

Thus, it is important to have a good understanding of what drives those fears. As Doerner and Lab (2012) argue, fear of crime is sometimes more important than actual crime—in other words, perceptions of crime often are more important for feelings of safety among students, parents, and administrators than the actual incidence of crime at school. To provide a better understanding of the causes of fear among children at school, in this chapter I begin by reviewing the literature around how fear of crime became a topic of research. I will then discuss how the measurement of fear of crime has progressed over the past four decades and identify the correlates and causes of fear of crime among both adults and adolescents. I will then examine research that specifically examines fear of criminal victimization at school and close by discussing strategies whereby schools can reduce fear of crime among students in their buildings.

History of Fear of Crime Research

Although the scientific study of the fear of crime began earlier, in 1995, Kenneth Ferraro published what remains a seminal work in the field of fear of crime. In that book, Ferraro used data from telephone interviews of 1,101 adult respondents regarding their levels of fear of crime and perceptions of risk to conduct one of the first in-depth fear of crime surveys of people across the United States. Ferraro (1995) thus set the stage for much of the subsequent fear of crime research that has grown dramatically over the past two decades.

One of the most important contributions Ferraro made was the distinction he highlighted between fear of crime and perceptions of risk. Ferraro defined fear of crime as "... an emotional response of dread or anxiety to crime or symbols that a person associates with crime" (Ferraro, 1995, p. 4). Ferraro's definition highlighted two important components of fear: (1) fear is an emotional response and (2) fear results from both personal crime victimization and symbols of crime. Thus, Ferraro's definition was one of the first to suggest that the emotional response of fear of crime can be evoked by symbols of crime. This is particularly important for settings where relatively few crimes, particularly violent crimes, occur. Consequently, elements commonly found in schools such as graffiti, litter, students loitering in the restrooms or in front of the lockers, may cause an emotional response of fear from other students, even though the student is not victimized by crime directly.

Ferraro was also among the first to articulate the differences between fear of crime and perceptions of risk which, up until that point, had often been confused in both measurement and understanding. Ferraro defined perceived risk as a more cognitive element than fear by stating that it was "... recognition of a situation as possessing at least potential danger, real or imagined..." (Ferraro, 1995, p. 4). Fear of crime research prior to Ferraro's book had largely used measures of fear of crime that blurred distinctions between risk and fear or ignored perceptions of risk altogether. Ferraro (1995) conceptualized fear of crime as a distinct phenomenon from perceived risk and estimated the impact of perceived risk on fear of crime in the United States. Ferraro determined that while a number of factors affected perceptions of victimization risk, perceived risk was the strongest predictor of fear of crime, regardless of the other variables included in the model. This finding profoundly influenced the fear of criminal victimization research by stressing the importance of treating fear of crime as a conceptually distinct phenomenon from perceived risk of crime and continues to impact the study of fear of crime even until today.

Although it has been over two decades since Ferraro published his seminal work, many fear of crime researchers today appear to either be unaware of his work or have chosen to consciously ignore it altogether. Lane, Rader, Henson, Fisher, and May (2014) provide a thorough discussion of the measurement of fear of crime, how it has evolved over time, and the controversies surrounding its measurement. In general, they determine that the best measures of fear of crime (1) use the words "fear" or "afraid" in their measures; (2) examine fear of specific types of crime (e.g., burglary, terrorism) instead of more abstract notions of crime (e.g., walking alone in the neighborhood at night); (3) differentiate between intensity (how fearful) and prevalence (how often); and (4) include measures of relationships between respondents and potential offenders (e.g., friend, family member, stranger). Unfortunately, even most measures of fear of crime among adults fall far short of meeting these criteria; measurement in adolescent fear of crime still has even further to go.

Measuring Fear of Crime among Adolescents

The measurement problems around fear of crime are even more nuanced when considering fear of criminal victimization among juveniles. These problems are amplified by the fact that relatively few published studies examine fear of crime among juveniles; among those that do, the vast majority are either largely descriptive (like the previously reviewed *Indicators of School Crime and Safety*) or use self-report data collected from small, local or regional samples of juveniles with specific measures of fear that meet some of the criteria specified by Lane et al. (2014). In fact, Hale (1996), in his extensive review of the fear of crime literature published at that time, noted that adolescents have generally been ignored by fear of crime researchers, and recommend that fear of criminal victimization among this group be "... an important research priority" (Hale, 1996, p. 100). Because juveniles often have higher rates of victimization than adults (May, 2014), it is quite possible that adolescents may have higher levels of fear than either young, middle-aged, or elderly adults. Youths may accurately sense that they are differentially exposed to criminal victimization which might cause them to have higher levels of perceived risk. Because higher levels of perceived risk are often associated with increased levels of fear, this would thus lead to higher levels of fear of crime among adolescents.

Correlates of Fear of Crime among Adults

In the four decades that have passed since fear of crime research became popular in the 1970s, several variables have emerged as predictors of fear of crime. These variables include gender, race, place of residence, and neighborhood incivilities. Although the vast majority of studies examining demographic differences in fear of crime use adult samples, with limited exceptions discussed below, these demographic predictors of fear of crime apply to both adults and adolescents.

Gender and Fear of Crime

The vast majority of studies investigating fear of crime among both adults and adolescents have determined that females are more fearful of crime than males (see Lane et al., 2014, for review). A number of explanations have been offered for women's higher levels of fear of crime. The oldest explanation for this relationship can best be described as the physical vulnerability hypothesis (Rader, Cossman, & Porter, 2012), which suggests that females feel more vulnerable than males because they believe they are physically weaker than men and thus would be less able to physically fend off a would-be attacker. Another commonly used explanation is the "shadow of sexual assault" explanation (Ferraro, 1995, p. 86). This argument posits that females have an inordinate fear of sexual assault, especially rape, and this fear of rape pervades all aspects of their lives, causing them to express greater overall fear levels (May, 2001). The shadow hypothesis argues that females associate rape with numerous forms of crime (burglary, robbery, etc.) because they realize that, if victimized by any of these offenses, there is the possibility that they will be raped. A third common explanation for higher fear among females is the socialization hypothesis. This position argues that females are socialized to believe that males are necessary for their protection and that they are taught to be especially wary of strangers in public places (Rader, Cossman, & Porter, 2012). Regardless of the explanation that one accepts, the finding that females are more fearful of crime than males is the strongest empirical relationship in this research area.

Race and Fear of Crime

Almost without exception, in those studies where race is found to have a significant association with fear, Blacks are more fearful of crime than Whites (Hale, 1996). The most common explanation for the association between race and fear of criminal victimization is the "social vulnerability" explanation, which argues that certain groups, primarily the poor and minorities, realize that they are both frequently exposed to the threat of criminal victimization and that, if victimized, they have fewer resources, both economic and emotional, to help them recover from the victimization. This realization thus makes them more fearful of crime (May, 2001).

Social Class and Fear of Crime

Most research suggests that individuals of lower socioeconomic status are more fearful of crime than their counterparts of higher socioeconomic status (May, 2001). This relationship between socioeconomic status and fear of crime may be explained by (1) the limited exposure of higher socioeconomic groups to criminal conditions; (2) the additional security provided to members of higher socioeconomic status because of their additional financial, social and political resources; and (3) their greater confidence in societal agencies of justice and security (May, 2001).

Victimization and Fear of Crime

Intuitively, victims of crime should be more fearful of crime than their counterparts who have not been victimized. Unlike the variables discussed above, however, there is no consensus regarding the association between victimization and fear of crime. Some authors have suggested that victims of crime are more fearful than individuals who have not been victimized, while others have found the relationship between victimization and fear of crime to be weak or nonexistent (see Hale, 1996, for review). Hale (1996) suggests that the disparate findings around victimization and fear of crime are at least partially explained by measurement differences in those studies that examine this relationship. Hale suggests that additional research is needed to settle this debate (Hale, 1996).

Incivilities and Fear of Crime

In recent years, the focus has moved from individual level predictors of fear to more structural level predictors. One structural explanation for fear of crime was first known as the broken windows theory (Wilson & Kelling, 1982) but is commonly known today as the neighborhood incivility hypothesis (Ferraro, 1995). The neighborhood incivility hypothesis argues that various features of the physical environment are related to criminal realities, including increased levels of fear of crime. In other words, residents from areas with features such as trash, litter, graffiti, broken windows in buildings, and abandoned houses and cars will have higher levels of fear of crime than their counterparts in more "civil" areas. Nearly all the studies that examine the relationship between neighborhood incivility and fear of crime report a significant positive relationship between the two (Lane et al., 2014).

Fear of Crime among Adolescents

As reviewed earlier, the most comprehensive examination of fear of crime among students is *Indicators of School Crime and Safety*. Nevertheless, that study is largely descriptive and provides little insight into why certain groups of adolescents are more fearful of crime than their counterparts. A limited number of studies explored why certain adolescents are more fearful of crime, however. In addition to studies that I have coauthored that are reviewed below (May, 2001; May & Dunaway, 2000; May, Vartanian, & Virgo, 2002; Wallace & May, 2005), a small number of others (Alvarez & Bachman, 1997; Baker & Mednick, 1990; Hepburn & Monti, 1979; Melde, 2009; Parker & Onyekwuluje, 1992; Wayne & Rubel, 1982) have explored fear of crime among adolescents as well. Each will be discussed in detail below.

Alvarez and Bachman (1997) used a nationally representative sample of over 10,000 respondents to examine fear of crime among adolescents. Students were asked "How often are you afraid that someone will attack or harm you at school?" and "How often are you afraid that someone will attack or harm you on the way to and from school?" Alvarez and Bachman determined that younger students, poor students, those who had been assaulted at school, and those who said gangs were noticeably present at their school were more fearful of crime at school. Race, ethnicity, gender, and location of school had nonsignificant effects on fear of crime at school. Blacks, Latinos, females, younger students, and poorer students were all more fearful than their counterparts outside of the school context. In general, these associations remain in schools even until today (Robers et al., 2014).

Parker and Onyekwuluje (1992) examined data collected from a subsample of 112 teenage respondents from Washington D.C. and Atlanta in 1981. Parker and Onyekwuluje (1992) unearthed two important findings. First, the direction of the association between fear of criminal victimization and the demographic variables associated with fear of crime among adolescents was the same for young adult, adult, and elderly subsamples. Secondly, none of the demographic variables examined in the analysis (residence, gender, income status, education, marital status, and neighborhood crime rate) had a statistically significant association with fear of crime among adolescents, although this may have been due in part to the small size of the subsample and the measurement of the variables, as there was little variation in marital status, education level, and residence (Parker & Onyekwuluje, 1992).

Hepburn and Monti (1979) used data collected from 1799 public high school students in St. Louis, Missouri to examine the relationship between school-related victimization, fear of victimization, and subsequent behaviors among the students. They operationalized fear by asking whether the student "has been afraid that someone will hurt or bother you at school" (p. 123) and scoring responses as a dichotomous variable representing fear. Using bivariate analyses, Hepburn and Monti determined that white youth, those youth who had been victimized by crime, and younger students were more likely to admit fear of crime. Gender did not have a statistically significant association with fear of crime.

Wayne and Rubel (1982) used a national sample of 30,000 students to examine fear of crime. Although they do not include the measure they used to assess fear of criminal victimization in their research, it appears that the measure would better be described as a measure of "apprehensiveness" rather than fear, as respondents were coded as not apprehensive, slightly apprehensive, moderately apprehensive, and very apprehensive. Those coded as moderately apprehensive or very apprehensive were considered to be fearful. Despite the methodological limitations of their analysis, the sheer volume of their sample makes their work an important descriptive work. They determined that younger students, minority students, those with poor grades, those with less educated parents, those who had been robbed/assaulted, those from urban schools, and those students that reported incidents of violent crime in their neighborhood were all more likely to be fearful of crime.

May and Dunaway (2000a) examined fear of criminal victimization in the school setting using data collected from a sample of 742 public high school students in Mississippi. This study improved on the studies reviewed earlier by incorporating the suggestions of Ferraro (1995) and others and utilizing a four-item index that asked students to indicate their agreement with statements regarding how "afraid" they were of specific school situations (e.g., I am afraid to stay late after school because I might become a victim of crime). May and Dunaway (2000a) confirmed that students in lower grades, those who perceived their neighborhood as criminogenic, and those who "felt unsafe" at school were all more likely to agree that they were fearful of crime at school. Additionally, they also discovered a race/gender interaction in adolescent fear, and determined that while females were generally more fearful than males, black males were also more fearful than white males. May, Keith, Rader, & Dunaway (2013) extended this research in a follow-up study and determined that adolescents who perceived their opportunities as blocked had significantly higher levels of fear of crime than their counterparts. Additionally, those youth whose peers have attitudes favorable to delinquency are less fearful of crime than their counterparts. None of these findings have been uncovered by fear of crime research among adults, and indicate that, at least with the sample that they examined, the determinants of fear of crime among adolescents are somewhat different than those of adults.

One of the most recent examinations of adolescent fear of crime was done by Melde and his colleagues (Melde, 2009; Melde & Esbensen, 2009; Melde, Taylor, & Esbensen, 2009). With the exception of the impact of a deviant lifestyle on fear of crime discussed below, these studies largely support those reviewed above.

Although the research remains somewhat limited in the area of adolescent fear of crime, it appears that the predictors of fear for adolescents are somewhat different than those of adults. Blacks, those who perceive themselves at risk of victimization, and those from criminogenic neighborhoods are most fearful among both adolescents and adults. Younger adolescents are more fearful than their older counterparts. Further, while gender and socioeconomic status are two of the stronger determinants of fear among adults, the effect of both gender and socioeconomic status on fear of crime among adolescents is less well established, as a number of studies find no relationship between the two. The impact of victimization on fear of crime also is inconclusive for adolescents. While each of these findings may be an artifact of measurement, they point to the fact that predictors of adolescent fear of crime are somewhat different than that of adults, and thus need further exploration.

Explanations for Fear of Crime among Adolescents

A variety of explanations have been offered for fear of crime among adolescents. These explanations can be broadly grouped into three categories: socialization, lifestyle, and vulnerability explanations. Lane et al. (2014) provide a thorough discussion of each of those areas. We include parts of that discussion below then expand the discussion of the vulnerability explanation based on previous work I have published in other outlets.

Socialization

Lane et al. (2014) argue that an adolescent's socialization experience is an important determinant of their fear of crime. Because adolescents are heavily influenced by both their parents and peers, it makes sense that fear of crime would be transmitted through socialization from these groups. In previous work that I have published with Lisa Wallace (Wallace & May, 2004) and Lesa Vartanian and Keri Virgo (May, Vartanian, & Virgo, 2002), we determined that parental supervision had an important association with an adolescent's fear of crime because of a potential "sheltering effect" on adolescent fear of crime. Because of this shelter, youth with close supervision are not as likely to be around dangerous youth who may victimize them. De Groof (2008) extended our work by arguing that fear of crime may be transmitted intergenerationally. De Groof (2008) found that children with smothering parents or unattached parents had children with higher fear of crime levels. Consequently, then, the socialization experiences a youth have are important predictors of their levels of fear of crime.

Lifestyles

Recently, work with incarcerated juveniles by Jodi Lane and I has made important contributions in the area of fear of crime among juveniles. Melde (2009) built on that work, as he examined delinquent lifestyle risk factors and how these factors impact fear of victimization among youth. He found that the impact of crime victimization on adolescents' levels of fear of crime varied by age; when controlling for other factors such as victimization frequency, younger children feared crime more than older children. He also found that, unlike the research with adults, the impact of perceptions of risk only had a small association with adolescent fear of crime.

In her explanations of fear among juvenile offenders Lane (2009) found that, with the exception of being shot and/or murdered, juveniles who were engaged in criminal activity were not more fearful of crime than their less criminal counterparts. In fact, both May (2001) and Lane determined that only small proportions of juvenile offenders indicated they were fearful of crime at all. Lane (2009) argued that the diminished levels of fear among juvenile offenders may be due to the fact that these offenders were raised in environments where they were socialized not to be fearful (or admit fear) or they may really be "tougher" and not as afraid as their noncriminal counterparts.

Consequently, it appears the impact of both perceived and actual risk on fear of crime may be different for adolescents than for adults. Intuitively, those youths most engaged in deviant lifestyles should be more fearful because they realize they have an increased likelihood of victimization. Whether it is because of underdeveloped reasoning processes, the perceived invincibility of adolescence, or some other reason, this is clearly not the case. Risky lifestyles do not appear to increase fear of crime among adolescents; if anything, they decrease it.

Vulnerability

Perhaps the most important determinant of fear of crime among adolescents is vulnerability. Lane et al. (2014) suggest that physical vulnerability is the primary explanation for fear of crime among the young. They suggest that younger individuals are smaller than older individuals and thus may believe they are less likely to be able to successfully protect themselves from victimization; this perceived vulnerability thus produces fear of crime. For example, Goodey's (1994) study found that physically smaller children were more afraid of crime than their larger counterparts. She explained this finding through the notion that children who are smaller in size were more likely to view themselves as potential victims. Most recently, Melde (2009) found that younger teenagers feel more vulnerable to potential victimization.

Nevertheless, perhaps the best vulnerability explanation for increased fear of crime among adolescents is the "shadow of powerlessness" explanation I introduced in 2001. Below, I have included the results of a study I conducted that was published in *Sociological Spectrum* (May, 2001). Although the data used in that article are 15 years old, the findings are still as relevant for examining fear of crime at school in 2014 as they were when the article first appeared in print. After presenting evidence around the fear of crime at school among public school students, I use the shadow of powerlessness as a partial explanation for that finding.

Methodology

The data for this analysis were obtained from the 1997 Mississippi High School Youth Survey, conducted in the spring of that year by the Mississippi Crime and Justice Research Unit (MCJRU) at the Social Science Research Center at Mississippi State University. Public high schools were randomly selected and the State was divided into four regions, and an attempt was made to sample schools from each region. Although none of the superintendents from the Northeast region agreed to participate in the study, four schools allowed the researchers to administer the questionnaire at their schools, one each from the southeast (Southeast) and northwest regions (Northwest) and two from the southwest region (Southwest 1 and Southwest 2).

In those schools where permission was granted to administer the self-report instrument used for data collection, researchers distributed parental consent forms to the school principal at least one week prior to the scheduled survey administration with instructions to distribute the consent forms to each student in grades ten through twelve. On the day of the questionnaire administration, researchers distributed the instrument to all students who could produce a signed parental consent form or identification verifying that they were 18 years of age or above.

A number of superintendents, particularly in the northeast region of the state, refused to allow students from their school system to participate in this data collection effort. Additionally, even in those schools that agreed to participate, the response rate was considerably influenced by a large number of students who failed to present a signed parental consent form and thus were not allowed to participate. There are a wide variety of reasons why this might have been the case. Further, some of the schools did a much better job circulating the consent forms and encouraging and reminding students about the study and the need to return the parental consent forms than others. Consequently, it appears that the school's level of enthusiasm and preparedness probably affected the response rate more than the student's willingness to participate.

Using the total number of students enrolled in grades ten through twelve on the day of the survey administration as the population at each school, response rates were as follows: 21.4 percent at Southwest 2, 25.6 percent at Southeast, 38.3 percent at Southwest 1, and 47.1 percent at Northwest. Although all of the aforementioned factors are important limitations in their own right, the final sample of students is representative of adolescents in the state, with the exception of white females (who are slightly over represented) and black males (who are slightly under represented) (U.S. Census Bureau, 1999).[1]

Prior to the distribution of the survey, students were read detailed instructions that assured them of confidentiality and anonymity and informed them that their participation was completely voluntary and they were free to answer any, all, or none of the questions. In each class where the survey was administered, research assistants distributed and collected the questionnaires in an effort to reduce any influence the teacher might have had on the student responses.

The instrument used to collect the data for this study was a 17-page questionnaire that consisted of 234 questions and statements. The statements used a Likert-type format designed to assess adolescent's attitudes and perceptions of crime. Several questions were also included to assess demographic characteristics (e.g., race, gender, income, parent's occupation), along with a number of questions that examined the adolescent's participation in deviant activities. Students required approximately 45 minutes to complete the surveys.

As the respondent's gender is critical in the "shadow of sexual assault" argument by Ferraro (1995), any respondent not indicating their gender was omitted from the analysis. Additionally, inasmuch as over 97 percent of the sample consisted of either black or white respondents, only Whites and African-Americans were included in the study. Further, as this study focuses on adolescents, any respondent born prior to 1977 was also excluded from the study (as they would have been 20 years of age at the time of the survey). Thus, the sample for this study consisted of a total of 725 students, 310 (42.6 percent) of whom were black and 417 (57.4 percent) of whom were white. Over half (415, 57.1 percent) of the respondents were female, while 312 (42.9 percent) of the respondents were male. Finally, the age distribution of the respondents was as follows: 17.6 percent (128) were 15 years of age; 34.3 percent (249) were 16; 232 (31.9 percent) were 17; 106 (14.6 percent) were 18; and the remaining 1.7 percent (12) were 19 years of age. Measures of the independent variables are included in the Appendix.

Dependent Variables

Two cumulative indexes assessed adolescent fear of criminal victimization. One included a variable representing fear of sexual victimization, while the other omitted the fear of sexual victimization variable (hereinafter referred to as the fear of nonsexual victimization index).

The dependent variable representing adolescent fear of criminal victimization was operationalized by asking students to indicate their level of agreement with a number of statements concerning their fear of various occurrences. Responses were scored using a six-point Likert type format ("strongly agree," "agree," "somewhat agree," "somewhat disagree," "disagree," and "strongly disagree"). The answers were coded with the number 6 representing strongly agree and 1 representing strongly disagree. The statements were as follows:

I am afraid of being attacked by someone with a weapon.
I am afraid of being shot.
I am afraid of having my money/possessions taken from me.
I am afraid to go to school because I might become a victim of crime.
I am afraid to stay late after school because I might become a victim of crime.
I am afraid to go out at night because I might become a victim of crime.
I am afraid of being beaten up.
I am afraid to attend school events (i.e., football games, dances, etc.) because of fights.
I am afraid of being sexually assaulted.

The nine-item index including the fear of sexual assault variable (hereinafter referred to as the fear of sexual victimization index) had an internal reliability of .821 while the eight-item fear of nonsexual victimization index that excluded the fear of sexual assault variable had an internal reliability of .800.

Independent Variables

A number of variables were included as independent variables in the linear regression models used in this study. Each of these variables has previously demonstrated an association with fear of criminal victimization in earlier studies. These variables include age, race, gender, economic status, violent crime victimization experience, property crime victimization experience, perceived risk of victimization, and perceived neighborhood incivility. The contextual variables are discussed in detail below.

Economic Status

The measurement of social class or economic status among adolescents is a controversial issue. May and Dunaway (2000) contend that economic status, particularly among adolescents, should be ascertained by distinguishing between those who fall below the absolute poverty line and those who are above it. While father's education is often used as a measure of class among adolescents, it is plausible to suggest that asking adolescents whether their family receives forms of public assistance is a more valid measure of economic status than asking them to estimate their father's level of education. It can be argued that the adolescent is much more likely to know that her family receives public assistance than she would be to know the level of her father's education. Consequently, economic status was determined by the question "In the past year, has your family received some form of public assistance (such as WIC, AFDC/welfare, or food stamps)?" Those reporting yes were coded (1) while those not receiving public assistance were coded(0).[2]

Victimization Experience

Given the importance of measurement in predicting the relationship between crime victimization and fear of crime highlighted by Hale (1996), two questions asked the respondent whether they had been victimized by a violent or property crime. While some may argue that neither question is a good measure of victimization experience (particularly the violent victimization question, which asks whether the adolescent has been threatened with violence on their way to and from school), these questions were the only questions included in the survey that examined this phenomenon. At best, these are weak measures of victimization and the generalizability of their relationship with fear of crime is therefore limited. Those who had been victimized by crime were coded (1). Because both perceived risk of criminal victimization and perceived neighborhood incivility have been demonstrated to affect fear of crime, both were included as control variables in this study. The measures used to create those variables are included in the Appendix.

Missing Data

Although initial analysis of the data indicated no severe missing data problems, several of the indicators used to comprise the incivility and the fear indices contained missing information. It appeared that most of the missing data was due to respondent attrition, in that most of the indicators that contained missing information were found on the latter three pages of the survey. For most of these respondents, the entire pages containing these indicators were left blank. Even with this attrition, none of the variables included in the analysis had more than 10 percent of the questions unanswered. Thus, listwise deletion was used in the models below.

Results

The percentage distributions for the indicators used to comprise the independent and dependent variables not discussed previously are presented in Table 5.1. The table contains both the proportion of the total sample and the proportion of males and females that agreed with the measures used to construct the independent and dependent variables.

There were 120 students (16.7 percent) in the sample who responded affirmatively that their family received some form of public assistance. Further, over half the sample (55 percent, 399 respondents) answered that someone had threatened to hurt them while 611 (84 percent) of the respondents admitted that someone had stolen something from them. In both cases, a larger proportion of males responded that they had been victimized by crime. The vast majority of the respondents (88.4 percent) felt safe when they were out with their friends. Further, most students (82.9 percent) agreed that their neighbors are good, upstanding citizens, while less than half of the respondents agreed with each statement included as a measure of perceived neighborhood incivility. For each of the latter indicators, males were more likely to agree with the statement than their female counterparts.

Table 5.1. Frequency and Percentage Distributions for Responses to Dependent and Independent Variables for Adolescent Sample

Independent Variables	Total Sample	N and % Yes Males	N and % Yes Females
Economic Status	120 (16.5)	37 (11.9)	83 (20.0)
Property Crime Victim	611 (84.0)	272 (87.2)	339 (81.7)
Violent Crime Victim	399 (54.9)	174 (55.8)	225 (54.2)
I feel safe when I'm with my friends	639 (88.4)	280 (90.6)	359 (86.7)
There are drug dealers in neighborhood	296 (42.6)	124 (41.8)	172 (43.7)
There are gangs in neighborhood	253 (36.3)	114 (38.1)	139 (34.9)
Neighborhood is noisy and has litter	133 (19.0)	64 (21.3)	69 (17.3)
Neighborhood is getting worse	167 (25.0)	77 (27.2)	90 (23.4)
Neighbors are good, upstanding citizens	549 (82.9)	226 (81.6)	323 (83.9)
Dependent Variable Indicators			
Of being sexually assaulted	337 (47.0)	63 (20.6)	274 (66.7)
Of being attacked by someone with a weapon	424 (59.0)	145 (47.2)	279 (67.7)
Of being shot	423 (58.9)	152 (49.5)	271 (65.9)
Of having my money/possessions taken from me.	429 (59.7)	146 (47.6)	283 (68.7)
To go to school because I might become a victim of crime	85 (12.6)	28 (10.0)	57 (14.5)
To stay late after school because I might become a victim of crime	76 (11.3)	28 (9.9)	48 (12.4)
To go out at night because I might become a victim of crime	123 (18.4)	38 (13.5)	85 (21.9)
Of being beaten up	109 (16.5)	41 (14.9)	68 (17.7)
To attend school events because of fights	106 (16.1)	42 (15.2)	64 (16.7)

The percentage distributions for the statements used to create the fear of victimization indices reveal much greater gender differences than are found with the aforementioned statements used for the independent variables. Approximately half of the respondents agreed that they were afraid of being sexually assaulted, being attacked by someone with a weapon, being shot, and having their money/possessions taken from them; conversely, less than one in five of the respondents agreed that they were fearful in the remaining situations. In each case, a larger proportion of females agreed that they were fearful of the scenario described; however, the gender differences were much greater

Table 5.2. Results of Regressing Adolescent Fear Index with Sexual Victimization Variable Included on Known Predictors of Fear

	B	Std. Error	Beta	t	Sig.
Age	–.780	.332	–.085	–2.346	.019
Female	5.392	.672	.290	8.025	.000
Black	2.793	.803	.148	3.476	.001
Economic Status	1.030	.963	.041	1.070	.285
Property Crime Victim	.832	.926	.034	.899	.369
Violent Crime Victim	.059	.689	.003	.086	.931
Perceived Neighborhood Incivility	.256	.060	.175	4.283	.000
Perceived Risk	.815	.302	.103	2.704	.007
(Constant)	27.513	5.727		4.804	.000

R Square	.210
F	20.690; $p < .001$
Listwise N	631

for sexual assault than any of the other variables, lending credence to the "shadow of sexual assault" phenomenon described earlier.

The results obtained from regressing adolescent fear of criminal victimization on the demographic variables are presented in the Table 5.2. The results indicate that, as expected, gender, age, race, perceived neighborhood incivility, and perceived risk all had statistically significant associations with adolescent fear of criminal victimization. The regression coefficients indicate that, as with adults and adolescents in previous studies, gender emerged as the strongest predictor of adolescent fear of criminal victimization; females were significantly more likely to be fearful of crime than males. Additionally, those who perceived their neighborhood as criminogenic, Blacks, younger adolescents, and those who perceived themselves most at risk of criminal victimization were significantly more likely than their counterparts to indicate higher levels of fear of crime. These findings also concur with those of previous studies among adolescents.

None of the other variables included in the model had a statistically significant association with adolescent fear of criminal victimization. The variables included in this model explain 21 percent of the variation in adolescent fear of criminal victimization.

The results obtained from regressing adolescent fear of nonsexual criminal victimization on the demographic and contextual variables are presented in Table 5.3. The removal of fear of sexual assault from the index did not cause a substantive change on the effects of the independent variables, although the strength of the relationships changed somewhat. Gender remained the strongest predictor of fear of nonsexual victimization. The results further indicate that, as in Table 5.2, those who perceived their neighborhood as criminogenic, those with higher levels of perceived risk, Blacks, and

Table 5.3. Results of Regressing Adolescent Fear Index without Sexual Victimization Variable on Known Predictors of Fear

	B	Std. Error	Beta	t	Sig.
Age	−.721	.290	−.091	−2.489	.013
Female	3.442	.586	.216	5.877	.000
Black	2.294	.699	.143	3.281	.001
Economic Status	.798	.837	.037	.953	.341
Property Crime Victim	.669	.808	.031	.827	.408
Violent Crime Victim	.309	.601	.020	.515	.607
Perceived Neighborhood Incivility	.235	.052	.187	4.505	.000
Perceived Risk	.730	.262	.108	2.786	.005
(Constant)	32.817	4.991		5.017	.000

R Square .178
F 16.901; $p < .001$
Listwise N 633

younger respondents were all significantly more likely to be fearful of nonsexual criminal victimization. None of the other variables included in the model had a statistically significant effect on fear of criminal victimization. Thus, the removal of fear of sexual assault from the fear index did not, upon initial review, appear to affect which groups were most fearful of either sexual or nonsexual victimization. However, with the removal of fear of sexual assault from the fear index, the variables included in the model explained only 17.8 percent of the variation in adolescent fear of nonsexual criminal victimization.

The results obtained from regressing adolescent fear of nonsexual criminal victimization on the demographic and contextual variables and fear of sexual assault are presented in Table 5.4. With the addition of the fear of sexual assault variable as an independent variable, the associations between the demographic variables and the fear of nonsexual victimization index changed dramatically. First, as Ferraro (1995) determined with adults, fear of sexual victimization became the strongest predictor of fear of nonsexual victimization in the model. With the inclusion of fear of sexual assault as a control variable, however, the association between gender and fear of nonsexual victimization became nonsignificant. Thus, as with adults (Ferraro, 1995) and previous studies of adolescents (May & Dunaway, 2000), when fear of sexual assault was controlled for or excluded, females were no more fearful of criminal victimization than males. Thus, it appears that the "shadow of sexual assault" thesis applies to adolescents as well as adults.

With the inclusion of fear of sexual assault, Blacks, younger respondents, those who perceived their neighborhoods as most criminogenic, and those who perceived themselves to be most at risk of criminal victimization remained more fearful of nonsexual criminal

Table 5.4. Results of Regressing Adolescent Fear Index of Nonsexual Victimization Variable on Known Predictors of Fear and Fear of Sexual Victimization Variable

	B	Std. Error	Beta	t	Sig.
Age	–.581	.251	–.074	–2.317	.021
Female	–.649	.578	–.041	–1.124	.262
Black	1.218	.610	.075	1.997	.046
Economic Status	.369	.726	.017	.508	.612
Property Crime Victim	.324	.698	.015	.465	.642
Violent Crime Victim	.821	.520	.052	1.577	.115
Perceived Neighborhood Incivility	.193	.045	.153	4.259	.000
Perceived Risk	.562	.228	.083	2.469	.014
Fear of Sexual Assault	2.082	.142	.540	14.699	.000
(Constant)	19.598	4.333		4.523	.000

R Square	.390
F	44.089; $p<.001$
Listwise N	631

victimization than their counterparts. None of the other variables included in the model were significant at the .05 level. With the inclusion of fear of sexual assault in the model, the amount of variation in fear of nonsexual victimization more than doubled to 39.0 percent, adding further credence to the argument that fear of nonsexual victimization is differentially driven by fear of sexual assault.

As May and Dunaway (2000) determined that the effect of gender on fear of crime was conditioned by race (black males are more fearful than white males), I tested for the interaction between race, gender, and fear of nonsexual victimization in this study as well. Thus, the sample was separated into subsamples of males and females, and the fear of nonsexual victimization index was regressed on the independent variables used in previous models for each group. The results of that model are presented in Table 5.5.

The results presented in Table 5.5 indicate that even with the inclusion of fear of sexual assault, the association between gender and fear of nonsexual victimization is conditional on race; in other words, black males are more fearful of nonsexual victimization than their white counterparts, while there was no significant difference in the level of fear between white females and their black counterparts. The effects of the other variables included in the model were similar for both genders, as fear of sexual assault was the strongest predictor of fear of nonsexual victimization for both males and females. For females, however, those who had higher levels of perceived neighborhood incivility and those who had higher levels of perceived risk were more fearful of nonsexual

Table 5.5. Results of Regressing Adolescent Fear on Nonsexual Victimization on Known Predictors of Fear by Gender (Male)

	B	Std. Error	Beta	t	Sig.
Age	– .729	.398	–.097	–1.829	.069
Black	3.522	1.030	.223	3.418	.001
Economic Status	1.801	1.320	.074	1.365	.174
Property Crime Victim	– .329	1.202	–.015	– .273	.785
Violent Crime Victim	.769	.843	.050	.912	.362
Perceived Neighborhood Incivility	.132	.076	.060	1.743	.083
Perceived Risk	.455	.409	.109	1.113	.267
Fear of Sexual Assault	1.648	.248	.366	6.654	.000
(Constant)	23.577	6.830		3.452	.001

R Square .308
F 14.127; p<.001
Listwise N 263

Table 5.5 (cont.). Results of Regressing Adolescent Fear on Nonsexual Victimization on Known Predictors of Fear by Gender (Female)

	B	Std. Error	Beta	t	Sig.
Age	– .431	.320	–.055	–1.345	.180
Black	– .202	.759	–.013	– .266	.791
Economic Status	– .482	.866	–.025	– .557	.578
Property Crime Victim	.774	.841	.039	.921	.358
Violent Crime Victim	.882	.652	.057	1.353	.177
Perceived Neighborhood Incivility	.217	.056	.174	3.858	.000
Perceived Risk	.803	.273	.131	2.937	.004
Fear of Sexual Assault	2.301	.171	.556	13.456	.000
(Constant)	15.018	5.541		2.710	.007

R Square .423
F 32.886; p<.001
Listwise N 368

victimization than their counterparts. This effect did not occur for males. None of the other variables had a statistically significant relationship on fear of nonsexual victimization for either males or females. Finally, the independent variables included in the model explained a much higher percentage of variation in the score on the fear of nonsexual victimization index for females (42.3 percent) than for males (30.8 percent), lending further support to the argument that the "shadow of sexual assault" impacts fear of nonsexual victimization among adolescent females more than among males.

The results presented above confirm the findings of May and Dunaway (2000) that gender and race interact to impact fear of nonsexual victimization among adolescents. It is plausible to suggest, however, that adolescent fear of nonsexual victimization may impacted by the interaction between race, gender, and some other variable. To test this interaction, a regression model was calculated for each race/gender subgroup. As the sample size is reduced to 225 or less for each subgroup, a relationship is said to be statistically significant when $p < .10$.

In the model presented in Table 5.6, the sample is separated into subsamples of black males, white males, black females, and white females, and regression models are estimated using each sample. This additional step reveals an interaction between race, gender, and perceived risk for females, and race, gender, age, and economic status for males. While fear of sexual assault remains the strongest predictor of fear of nonsexual victimization among all groups, perceived risk of victimization significantly impacts adolescent fear of crime among black females only; the effect is not statistically significant for either white females or males of either race. Additionally, perceived neighborhood incivility continued to be a significant predictor of fear of crime among females of both races, but not among males.

The effects of the other variables included in the model were similar for both genders, with the exception of age and economic status. For white males, age and economic status both had a statistically significant effect on fear of nonsexual victimization; this effect was not statistically significant for any of the other groups. Thus, white males who were younger and received public assistance were more fearful of nonsexual victimization than their counterparts who were older and did not receive public assistance.

Finally, the independent variables included in the model explained a much higher percentage of variation in the score on the fear of nonsexual victimization index for females, both white (43.5 percent) and black (37.4 percent), than for males (19.9 percent for white males and 16.9 percent for black males), lending further support for the "shadow of sexual assault" hypothesis.

Discussion

The purpose of this chapter was to provide the reader insight into what drives fear of crime among students at school by examining factors that have been linked to fear of crime in previous studies. Guided by research on the determinants of adult and adolescent fear of crime garnered from previous studies, I included a study I had published previously to demonstrate the effect of background and contextual factors on both fear of sexual victimization and fear of nonsexual victimization. While the measures included in the study were not all school-specific measures, the administration

Table 5.6. Adolescent Fear of Nonsexual Victimization Index Regressed on Known Predictors of Fear for Race-Gender Subgroups

	Black Females		White Females		Black Males		White Males	
Variable	*B/SE*	*Beta*	*B/SE*	*Beta*	*B/SE*	*Beta*	*B/SE*	*Beta*
Age	– .661/.509	–.090	– .261/.416	–.033	– .461/.725	–.063	– .982/.473	–.150**
Economic Status	.360/1.088	.023	–1.786/1.463	–.065	.575/1.961	.029	3.679/2.003	.133*
Property Crime Victim	– .578/1.545	–.027	1.351/1.007	.072	.006/2.480	.000	– .697/1.332	–.040
Violent Crime Victim	.474/1.067	.032	1.105/.828	.072	.735/1.596	.046	.978/.988	.077
Perceived Neighbor-hood Incivility	.158/.085	.132*	.283/.076	.197**	.206/.143	.144	.092/.089	.077
Perceived Risk	.803/.349	.160**	.733/.451	.084	.131/.682	.019	.816/.528	.112
Fear of Sexual Assault	1.964/.267	.517***	2.536/.225	.586***	1.658/.412	.403***	1.666/.327	.368***
(Constant)	22.157/8.996**		10.284/7.202		22.049/12.706*		27.500/8.073***	
Listwise N	143		225		100		163	
F	11.515***		23.827***		2.669*		5.500***	
R Square	.374		.435		.169		.199	

* p<.10
** p<.05
*** p<.01

of the survey in the school setting, coupled with the fact that the study was conducted during the school year when the majority of the students' time awake was spent at school, suggest that the findings presented here would apply to school-specific fear as well (and subsequent studies in this area confirm that evidence).

The findings presented in this chapter suggest that there is a great deal of similarity in the determinants that impact both adult and adolescent fear of crime, particularly the relationship between fear of sexual assault and fear of nonsexual victimization. Specifically, both male and female adolescents most fearful of sexual assault are also most fearful of nonsexual victimization. This confirms the findings of previous research among adults, and indicates that this relationship exists, regardless of the age of the respondent. Additionally, adolescents, particularly female adolescents, who perceive their immediate community environment as exhibiting signs of incivility and perceive themselves most at risk of criminal victimization are likely to have higher levels of fear of both sexual and nonsexual victimization. These findings again mirror those of adults.

On the other hand, actual criminal victimization, a significant predictor of adult fear of crime in many studies, did not demonstrate a statistically significant association with adolescent fear of crime for any of the race-gender subgroups. Thus, it appears that the perception that one is more likely to be a victim of crime in a school setting is a more important determinant of fear among adolescents than the actual victimization experience in that setting. This relationship may not be conclusive, however, as the limitations of the victimization measures discussed earlier limit the generalizability of this finding. Future studies should follow Lane et al. (2014) and use better measures of victimization to understand the relationship between victimization and fear for adolescents.

The findings reviewed here suggest that, among adolescents, race and gender interact with a number of other variables. Specifically, after controlling for fear of sexual assault, I found that black male youths were more likely to experience fear of nonsexual victimization than white youths, a finding confirmed by previous work I had conducted (May & Dunaway, 2000). On the other hand, after controlling for fear of sexual assault, black females were no more likely to be fearful of nonsexual crime victimization than their white counterparts. As May and Dunaway (2000) suggest, this finding is congruent with actual victimization data which show that black males are the subgroup most likely to be victimized by crime. Thus, it may be that black males accurately perceive that they are at greatest risk of victimization by crime and are thus more fearful of crime.

The findings from this study further add to the adolescent fear of crime literature because, unlike previous research on adolescent fear of crime, I compared the results of regressing fear of nonsexual victimization on fear of sexual victimization and other background variables across race/sex subgroups among adolescents. The results revealed that race and gender combine to have a differential impact on fear of nonsexual victimization among adolescents above and beyond the interaction discussed earlier. While fear of sexual victimization is the strongest predictor of fear of nonsexual victimization for all four groups, the impact of a number of the background variables is contingent upon the combination of race and gender of the respondent, particularly for white males. Younger white males and white males whose family received public assistance were more fearful than their white male counterparts who were older and did not receive public assistance.

The differential impact of age and economic status among white males may be explained by the previously discussed social vulnerability hypothesis. The social vulnerability hypothesis states that certain groups in the larger society, primarily the poor and minorities, realize that they are frequently exposed to the threat of victimization and actual victimization will impact them economically and socially (Rohe & Burby, 1988). Historically, white males have been the least socially vulnerable subset in the population. When restricting the population to white males, then, the groups most socially vulnerable would be the young and the poor; in both cases, these groups are more fearful of nonsexual crime victimization than their counterparts.

The findings from this study are of particular importance in the area of adolescent fear of crime. Among both adolescent males and females, fear of sexual assault is the most powerful predictor of fear of nonsexual victimization. Interestingly, however, when controlling for fear of sexual assault, none of the other statistically significant predictors of fear of nonsexual victimization among adolescents are the same. For females, it appears that fear of sexual assault, combined with a heightened perception of their risk for victimization and a perception that their neighborhood is criminogenic, increases female fear of nonsexual victimization. Thus, it appears that fear of nonsexual victimization among adolescent females is a combination of two factors: the social vulnerability explanation (Rohe & Burby, 1988) and the "shadow of sexual assault" explanation (Ferraro, 1995).

The impact of fear of sexual assault on fear of nonsexual victimization for males, however, should not be overlooked. Fear of sexual assault is the strongest predictor of fear of nonsexual victimization for males in this study as well. Three other factors (race, age, and economic status) also have statistically significant effects upon fear of nonsexual victimization among at least some adolescent males. Again, the social vulnerability explanation may partially explain this relationship as well. Black males are more likely to be fearful of crime than white males; this finding is consistent with actual victimization patterns which indicate that young black males have the highest rate of criminal victimization. Further, white males who were younger and of lower economic status are more fearful of nonsexual crime than their older counterparts. It may be that these adolescents (many in their first or second year of high school) realize that their older counterparts are more mature, both physically and mentally, and thus may have heightened levels of fear of nonsexual victimization because they realize their susceptibility to victimization from these older, larger youth.

This realization by adolescent males that their bodies are not as physically mature as many of their older counterparts may also contribute to the effect of fear of sexual assault on their fear of nonsexual victimization. Ferraro (1995) has suggested that fear of sexual assault drives fear of nonsexual victimization for females. The results of this study indicate that, while the fear of sexual assault has a stronger impact on fear of nonsexual victimization for females than males, the effect of the "shadow of sexual assault" may be an important contributor to fear of nonsexual victimization for males, particularly white males, as well.

Thus, it may be that the "shadow of sexual assault" for females works in a similar manner for adolescent males. Some males may realize that they are physically weaker than their older and stronger counterparts, and may perceive that they are less powerful and less able to resist both sexual and nonsexual crime. This realization of their differential vulnerability to crime may make them more fearful of both sexual and nonsexual crime victimization than their less vulnerable counterparts. Thus, it may be that a "shadow of powerlessness" for adolescent males may work in a similar manner as the "shadow of sexual assault" works for females.

For this reason, it becomes increasingly important to alleviate adolescent fear of sexual assault and their perceptions of risk of criminal victimization. Thus, an increase in rape awareness programs may be a needed step in reducing fear of criminal victimization (both sexual and nonsexual) among both males and females. Additionally, these programs need to be targeted toward younger audiences, perhaps beginning in elementary and middle school.

Conclusions and Policy Implications

There are a number of additional steps that could be implemented to reduce fear of criminal victimization among students at school that are already in place with adult populations. First, as May and Dunaway (2000) suggest, students should be empowered to make use of available resources at their school to reduce fear and disorder. Problem-solving methods widely used by police and neighborhood watch programs throughout the country could be used in schools to allow students to identify sources of fear of crime in their environment and take steps to alleviate those conditions. This empowerment may reduce the feelings of powerlessness for both males and females and may lead (either directly or indirectly) to a decreased fear of criminal victimization; even if it does not reduce fear, it will give students a sense of ownership of their own school environment which should lead to increased school safety.

Another important step to begin to alleviate this fear of crime among students is to lessen the stigma of the feelings of powerlessness commonly found among adolescents. Adolescents, particularly adolescent males, are often hesitant to discuss their sense of powerlessness with adults; by internalizing these feelings of powerlessness, they may heighten their fears and perceptions of risk. Programs should be implemented in schools to encourage open discussion of the effects of rape, sexual assault, and feelings of powerlessness and should highlight steps that students can take to lessen their chances of being sexually assaulted and increase their sense of power over their surroundings.

When published over a decade ago, the findings presented here uncovered a challenging new area within adolescent fear of crime research. Nevertheless, not much has changed in that time. The concept of the "shadow of powerlessness" needs to be further refined and tested to determine if those feelings of powerlessness among adolescent males persist in larger, more urban samples than the one I used in 2001. A better understanding of the causes of the shadow of powerlessness will lead to better ways to prevent it.

Appendix

Race
How do you describe yourself?

1. African American/Black
2. White
3. American Indian
4. Mexican American/Latino
5. Asian or Asian American
6. Other (______________)

Coded: African-American (1); White (0); All other responses (missing)

Gender
What is your sex? 1. Male 2. Female
Coded: Female (1); Male (0)

Economic Status
In the past year, has your family received some form of public assistance (such as WIC, AFDC/ welfare, or food stamps)?
1. Yes 2. No
Coded: Yes (1); No (0)

Violent Crime Victimization Experience
Please indicate whether any of the following things have ever happened to you:
Had someone threaten to hurt me 1. Yes 2. No
Coded: Yes (1); No (0)

Property Crime Victimization Experience
Please indicate whether any of the following things have ever happened to you:
Had something stolen from me 1. Yes 2. No
Coded: Yes (1); No (0)

Perceived Risk of Criminal Victimization
Responses to the following statement were scored using a six-point Likert-type format, with responses including "strongly agree," "agree," "somewhat agree," "somewhat disagree," "disagree," and "strongly disagree." The answers were coded with the number 1 representing "strongly agree" and the number 6 representing "strongly disagree."
Please indicate the extent to which you agree or disagree with the following statements:
I feel safe when I am out with my friends.

Perceived Neighborhood Incivility Index
Responses to the following statements were scored using a six-point Likert-type format, with responses including "strongly agree," "agree," "somewhat agree," "somewhat disagree," "disagree," and "strongly disagree." The answers to the first four statements were coded with the number 6 representing "strongly agree" and 1 representing "strongly disagree," while responses to the last statement were reverse coded, with the number 1 representing "strongly agree" and the number 6 representing "strongly disagree."

My neighborhood is noisy and the streets always seem to have litter on them.
There are drug dealers in my neighborhood.
There are gangs in my neighborhood.
My neighborhood is getting worse and worse all the time.
Most of the people living in my neighborhood are good, upstanding citizens.

Cronbach's alpha: .809.

Notes

1. In the 1997 Census projections for the state of Mississippi for ages 16 to 19, 27.6 percent of Mississippians were white males, 26.0 percent were white females, 23.1 percent were black males, and 23.4 percent were black females (U.S. Census Bureau, 1999). The sample used in this paper consists of 24.7 percent white males, 32.3 percent white females, 17.5 percent black males, and 25.5 percent black females. In models not included in this study, data were weighted to be representative of the adolescent population of Mississippi. While the strength of the effects were somewhat different than the models using unweighted data, there were no substantive or statistical differences in the associations examined in this study. Thus, I included the models with unweighted data in the paper. The models using weighted data are available upon request.

2. Father's education was also used as a measure of class in other models not included in this study. The effect of father's education was not statistically significant in any of the models.

References

Alvarez, A., & Bachman, R. (1997). Predicting the fear of assault at school and while going to and from school in an adolescent population. *Violence and Victims 12*(1), 69–85.

Baker, R.L., & Mednick, B.R. (1990). Protecting the high school environment as an island of safety: Correlates of student sear of in-school victimization. *Children's Environments Quarterly, 7*(3), 37–49.

Craske, M.G. (1999). *Anxiety disorders: Psychological approaches to theory and treatment.* Boulder, CO: Westview Press.

Doerner, W.G., & Lab, S.P. (2012). *Victimology (6th ed).* Burlington, MA: Elsevier.

Federal Bureau of Investigation. (2012). *Crime in the United States—2011.* http://www.fbi.gov/about-us/cjis/ucr/crime-in-the-u.s/2011/crime-in-the-u.s.-2011 (accessed August 1, 2013).

Ferraro, K.F. (1995). *Fear of crime: Interpreting victimization risk.* Albany, NY: State University of New York Press.

Hale, C. (1996). Fear of crime: A review of the literature. *International Review of Victimology, 4*, 79–150.

Hepburn, J.R., & Monti, D.J. (1979). Victimization, fear of crime, and adaptive responses among high school students, pp. 121–132 in W.H. Parsons (ed.) *Perspectives on Victimology.* Beverly Hills, CA: Sage.

Izard, C.E. (1977). *Human emotions.* New York: Plenum Press.

Lane, J. (2006). Explaining fear of general and gang crimes among juveniles on probation: The impacts of delinquent behaviors. *Youth Violence and Juvenile Justice, 4*(1), 34–54.

Lane, J., Rader, N.E., Henson, B., Fisher, B.S., & May, D.C. (2014). *Fear of crime in the United States: Causes, consequences, and contradictions.* Durham, NC: Carolina Academic Press.

Lazarus, R.S., Allen, D.K., & Folkman, S. (1980). Emotions: A cognitive-phenomenological analysis, pp. 189–217 in *Theories of Emotion (vol. 1)*, R. Plutchik & H. Kellerman (eds). New York: Academic Press.

Marks, I.M. (1978). *Living with fear.* New York: McGraw Hill Book Company.

May, D.C. (2001). *Adolescent fear of crime, perceptions of risk, and defensive behaviors: An alternate explanation of violent delinquency.* Lewiston, NY: Edwin Mellen Press.

May, D.C. (2014). Victimization, crime, and fear of Crime. Forthcoming chapter in M. Krohn & J. Lane's *Handbook on Juvenile Delinquency and Juvenile Justice.* Hoboken, NJ: Wiley Blackwell.

May, D.C., & Dunaway, R.G. (2000). Predictors of adolescent fear of crime. *Sociological Spectrum, 20*(2), 149–168.

May, D.C., Rader, N.E., & Dunaway, R.G. (2009). Predicting adolescent fear of crime through the lens of general strain theory. Paper presented at the annual meetings of the Southern Criminal Justice Association, Charleston, SC.

May, D.C., Vartanian, L.R., & Virgo, K. (2002). The impact of parental attachment and supervision on fear of crime among adolescent males. *Adolescence, 37*(146), 267–288.

Melde, C. (2009). Lifestyle, rational choice, and adolescent fear: A test of a risk-assessment framework. *Criminology, 47*(3), 781–811.

Melde, C., & Esbensen, F.A. (2009). The victim–offender overlap and fear of in-school victimization: A longitudinal examination of risk assessment models. *Crime and Delinquency, 55*(4), 499–525.

Melde, C., Taylor, T. J., & Esbensen, F.A. (2009). 'I got your back:' An examination of the protective function of gang membership in adolescence. *Criminology, 47*(2), 565–594.

Parker, K.D., & Onyekwuluje, A.B. (1992). The influence of demographic and economic factors on fear of crime among African-Americans. *The Western Journal of Black Studies*, 16(3), 132–140.

Rader, N.E., Cossman, J.S., & Porter, J.R. (2012). Fear of crime and vulnerability: Using a national sample of Americans to examine two competing paradigms. *Journal of Criminal Justice, 40*, 134–141.

Robers, S., Kemp, J., Rathbun, A., and Morgan, R.E. (2014). *Indicators of school crime and safety: 2013* (NCES 2014-042/NCJ 243299). National Center for Education Statistics, U.S. Department of Education, and Bureau of Justice Statistics, Office of Justice Programs, U.S. Department of Justice. Washington, DC.

Rohe, W. M., & Burby, R. J. (1988). Fear of crime in public housing. *Environment and Behavior, 20*(6), 700–720.

Scruton, D.L. (1986). The anthropology of an emotion, pp. 7–49 in D.L. Scruton (ed.) *Sociophobics: The Anthropology of Fear.* Boulder, CO: Westview Press.

Wallace, L., & May, D.C. (2005). The impact of relationship with parents and commitment to school on adolescent fear of crime at school. *Adolescence, 40*(159), 458–474.

Wayne, I., & Rubel, R.J. (1982). Student fear in secondary schools. *Urban Review, 14*(3), 197–237.

Chapter 6

Corporal Punishment in the United States

*Timothy McClure and David C. May**

In recent years, most school districts have moved away from corporal punishment as a disciplinary action, relying more on alternative forms of punishment such as in-school suspension, after-school detention, and a wide range of other punishments. Nevertheless, not all school districts have made that change. The most recent estimates available indicate that 18 states still allow corporal punishment to be used as a discipline strategy in their schools. Use of corporal punishment in schools is most prevalent in the southeastern United States. In fact, in the 2009–2010 school year (the most recent for which nationwide data are available), an estimated 216,346 students received corporal punishment (Office of Civil Rights, 2014). This continues a steady decline that began in the early 1980s (The Center for Effective Discipline, 2010).

In Table 6.1, we present a comparison of states using corporal punishment and states banning corporal punishment. The results presented there suggest that although corporal punishment was used in 18 states in 2009–2010, corporal punishment in schools is largely a southern phenomenon. In fact, with the exception of Virginia and West Virginia, corporal punishment was used in all of the states typically classified as southern states in 2009–2010. Additionally, Mississippi (7.5% of enrolled students received corporal punishment), Alabama (4.7%), and Arkansas (4.5%) use corporal punishment as discipline more than any other state (The Center for Effective Discipline, 2010).

Corporal punishment is defined as "... the use of physical force with the intention of causing a child to experience pain, but not injury, for the purpose of correction or control of the child's behavior" (Straus & Donnelly, 2001, p. 4). This practice has been allowed in public schools by the U.S. Supreme Court case *Ingraham v. Wright* (1977), but, as previously demonstrated, its use and support for its use varies significantly across different geographic, cultural, and economic characteristics. In fact, despite the evidence of a recent decline in its use throughout the United States, it remains a hotly debated topic.

Because the majority of states ban its use in schools, we begin with a discussion of the arguments against corporal punishment then review those arguments that support it. Benatar (1998) provides a thorough discussion of the arguments for and against

* The information presented in this chapter is largely based on an article I coauthored with Timothy McClure that appeared elsewhere. The citation for this article is included below:
McClure, Timothy D. and David C. May. (2008). Dealing with Misbehavior at School in Kentucky: Theoretical and Contextual Predictors of Use of Corporal Punishment. *Youth and Society, 39*(3), 406–429.

Table 6.1. States Authorizing and Banning the Use of Corporal Punishment in Schools

States Using Corporal Punishment in Public Schools in 2009–2010	States Not Using Corporal Punishment in Public Schools in 2009–2010
Alabama	Alaska
Arkansas	California
Arizona	Colorado
Florida	Connecticut
Georgia	Delaware
Idaho	District of Columbia
Indiana	Hawaii
Kansas	Illinois
Kentucky	Iowa
Louisiana	Maine
Mississippi	Maryland
Missouri	Massachusetts
North Carolina	Michigan
Oklahoma	Minnesota
South Carolina	Montana
Tennessee	Nebraska
Texas	Nevada
Wyoming	New Hampshire
	New Jersey
	New Mexico
	New York
	North Dakota
	Ohio
	Oregon
	Pennsylvania
	Rhode Island
	South Dakota
	Utah
	Vermont
	Virginia
	Washington
	West Virginia
	Wisconsin

Table 6.2. Philosophical Arguments Surrounding Corporal Punishment

Arguments Against Corporal Punishment	Arguments in Support of Corporal Punishment
Corporal punishment leads to abuse. People that administer corporal punishment may lose control and turn what was intended as a minor punishment into physical abuse.	Corporal punishment punishes only the guilty student while other forms of punishment (suspension, in-school detention, expulsion) punish the teachers and/or the parents responsible for supervising the punished child.
Corporal punishment is degrading to the victim because it lowers their sense of self-worth.	Corporal punishment offers educators a punishment alternative less punitive than suspension or expulsion but more punitive than in-school detention
Corporal punishment is psychologically damaging to victim by causing depression, anxiety, and lowered self-esteem.	Corporal punishment is unpleasant and thus sends a clear message of punishment; other forms of punishment (e.g., additional schoolwork) may make a student avoid a "good" thing in the future because of their punishment experience with it.
Corporal punishment stems from and causes sexual deviance by causing sexual excitement for either the person delivering or the person receiving the punishment.	Some parents support corporal punishment at school for their children because they use corporal punishment in their homes.
Corporal punishment teaches the wrong lesson that violence is an appropriate way to settle differences between people or solve arguments.	
Corporal punishment does not deter those that are being punished from further wrongdoing.	
When corporal punishment is used, it suggests all other behavioral management efforts have failed.	

corporal punishment. Benatar (1998) presents seven arguments against the use of corporal punishment in school then reviews four arguments in support of corporal punishment. These arguments are presented in Table 6.2. Benatar (1998) suggests that empirical evidence for both sides is limited and, in many cases, criticisms that are levied against corporal punishment are just as relevant for other forms of school punishment as well. Following Benatar, then, it would make sense that the states and school districts that use (or do not use) corporal punishment make that choice based on reasons other than its effectiveness or ineffectiveness in controlling misbehavior at school.

In this chapter, we highlight one of those explanations by expanding the work of Owen (2005) regarding the relationship between social capital and use of corporal punishment in the school. Owen used data from 48 states to reveal that states with higher levels of social capital (measured in terms of state rates of social trust and participation in civic, political, and social activities) were less likely to use corporal punishment in the school. While his work is an important contribution to the literature, he suggests a number of areas of future research. In this chapter, we attempt to fill some of those voids by using sociological and criminological theory (as well as the relevant literature in this area) to guide the analysis of several social and demographic factors' associations with the use of corporal punishment in schools.

Literature Review

Few researchers have examined characteristics surrounding corporal punishment in the schools (see Owen, 2005, for a notable exception). However, several studies have demonstrated an association between the support and use of parent-to-child corporal punishment and various parental characteristics (i.e., religion, age, marital status, temperament, and parenting style) (see Xu, Tung, & Dunaway, 2000, for review). This body of literature has uncovered a number of variables associated with corporal punishment at both the societal and individual level, but these relationships must be viewed in the context of their methodological and theoretical challenges.

First and foremost, most of the findings in this research are merely correlational results. It is rather easy to demonstrate which parents use corporal punishment and corporal punishment's correlation with other behaviors. Due to the limited use of longitudinal data, however, it is much more difficult to determine why parents use it and what effect it has on children. Because most current research only provides a snapshot of corporal punishment, students of corporal punishment are left to theoretically determine which came first: corporal punishment or the variable(s) with which it is correlated. Nevertheless, the effort to determine *who* uses corporal punishment is the first step in answering *why* and *should* they use it.

It is also difficult to point to any variable as a sole determinant of corporal punishment. Because so many variables that have been found to be linked to corporal punishment are also linked to one another (both across and within different studies) (e.g. Xu et al., 2000), it is often difficult to determine the effect of any single variable, even with the help of regression models. Thus, the findings throughout this research support the idea of an integrated theory of corporal punishment, encompassing many different aspects of psychology, sociology, and criminology, and should be read in that context.

Parent-to-Child Corporal Punishment

A significant portion of the literature surrounding corporal punishment has related a wide array of parent and child characteristics with the support and use of corporal punishment. These studies largely focus on the demographic characteristics, psychological traits, and family dynamics associated with parent-to-child corporal punishment. General support for corporal punishment (along with self-reported prevalence, incidence, and severity of corporal punishment) is considered throughout this body of literature. Overall, these studies indicate that most parents support corporal punishment in the home and use (or have used) some form of corporal punishment at some point in their child(ren)'s lifetime (e.g., Crandall, 2002; Straus & Donnelly, 1993; 2001).

Nevertheless, specific subgroups of parents support and use corporal punishment more often. Parents are more likely to support and/or use corporal punishment if they are African-American (Regaldo, Sareen, Inkelas, Wissow, & Halfon, 2004; Xu et al., 2000), male (Xu et al., 2000), poor (Straus & Donnelly, 1993; 2001; Straus & Stewart, 1999; Xu et al., 2000), employed in blue-collar occupations (Wauchope & Straus, 1990), less educated (Ellison & Sherkat, 1993; Xu et al., 2000), single (Crouch & Behl, 2001; Ellison, Bartowski, & Segal, 1996; Regaldo et al., 2004; Straus & Stewart, 1999), older (Xu et al., 2000), Conservative Protestants, and/or "Biblical-literalists" (those who have a literal interpretation of the Bible) (Ellison et al., 1996; Ellison & Sherkat, 1993; Xu et al., 2000).

School Corporal Punishment

Despite the wealth of research on corporal punishment at the individual level, there is only a small body of literature regarding predictors of corporal punishment in schools. While the literature surrounding corporal punishment in school is scarce, the actual practice of corporal punishment is not all that rare. Using a nationally representative sample of public schools, the U.S. Department of Education Office for Civil Rights projected that around 216,000 public school students received corporal punishment in 2009–2010 (less than one percent of all public school students). This number is significantly lower than the yearly average of a million or so in the 1980s, but corporal punishment is still a common practice in a number of school districts in the United States (U.S. Department of Education, Office of Civil Rights, 2014). Estimates suggest that corporal punishment is used in about 15% of all public schools in the United States (National Center for Education Statistics, 2000).

Parental Factors

Although a nationally representative poll conducted by ABCNEWS indicated that most parents (72%) disapprove of school corporal punishment (Crandall, 2002), the author of the report and Grasmick, Morgan, and Kennedy (1992) were able to point to specific subgroups for which school corporal punishment is more acceptable. Southerners and Midwesterners were more likely to support school corporal punishment in the ABCNEWS poll (35% and 31%, respectively) than respondents from the West and the East (19% and 13%, respectively) (Crandall, 2002). Additionally, Grasmick et al. (1992) found that, in an Oklahoma school district, parents who were members of Protestant denominations, male, had lower levels of education, and were younger were significantly more likely to support corporal punishment in schools. However, the homogeneity of the sample in this study made it difficult to apply these findings to any population outside of this school district.

Socioeconomic Status

While Arcus (2002) found a significant positive relationship between state poverty rates and the use of corporal punishment, few studies have investigated the relationship between socioeconomic status and corporal punishment at the district level. However, in 2005, the Kentucky Center for School Safety compared receipt of corporal punishment among free-lunch students, reduced-lunch students, and paid-lunch students. This comparison showed the percentage of punishments that involved paddling for free-lunch students was 2.5 times higher than the percentage of paid-lunch students and 1.5 times higher than the percentage of reduced-lunch students, overall. However, these differences were much less dramatic when examining only those districts that use corporal punishment (Kentucky Center for School Safety, 2005).

Geographic Setting

Corporal punishment appears to be most prevalent in "town" and "rural" settings, as 41% and 36% of principals in those settings, respectively, reported the availability of corporal punishment as compared to 20% and 15% for the "urban" and "urban fringe" principals, respectively (National Center for Education Statistics, 2000). Southeastern and southwestern states also use corporal punishment more often than other regions of the United States (Arcus, 2002; Owen, 2005; The Center for Effective Discipline, 2010; United States Department of Education Office of Civil Rights, 2014).

Crime Statistics

Researchers have also compared school corporal punishment rates to other statewide data on different sociological factors including criminal justice statistics. Using data from all 50 states, Arcus (2002) found that higher corporal punishment rates are associated with higher school shooting fatality rates. Hyman and Wise (1979) found that permissiveness toward school corporal punishment is positively correlated with both statewide homicide rates and statewide student violence rates.

Theoretical Explanations of Corporal Punishment

Social Capital

Durkheim argues in his *Moral Education* (1973) that the level of involvement in a culture by its members is indicative of the *level* of morality in that culture. In other words, the more citizens are devoted to the altruistic practice of shaping and improving their community, the more moral their community is. Owen (2005) calls such devotion "social capital" and extends Durkheim's arguments to school corporal punishment. He does so by first showing that school corporal punishment is a negative practice (because of its negative effects on those who receive it) and then demonstrating a significant association between the use of corporal punishment in schools and social capital—or the interconnectedness of communities as defined by the members' social trust and civic, political, and social involvement. Using state-level data, he examined the relationships between social capital and three indicators of school corporal punishment: prevalence of corporal punishment in schools, incidence of corporal punishment in schools (among those states that allow it), and support for corporal punishment in general. He found a significant inverse relationship between social capital and all three indicators of school corporal punishment. There were also lower levels of social capital and higher levels of corporal punishment support and use in the Southeastern and Southwestern regions of the United States. Interestingly, Xu et al. (2000) made and tested a similar argument regarding parents' use of corporal punishment. They also found a significant negative correlation between corporal punishment use and social capital, when it was operationalized as the amount of help parents received from others.

While Owen (2005) reveals a link between social capital and the use of corporal punishment in schools, he also suggests a number of areas for future research. First, he recognizes that the pronounced regional difference in the use of corporal punishment may be partially explained by social capital, but may also be influenced by other factors as well. Secondly, he also recognizes the importance of culture in explaining corporal punishment and calls for further research in this area. As such, other theoretical perspectives may also be helpful in understanding corporal punishment in schools.

Culture

The use of corporal punishment is in large part a function of culture. Changes in the organization and collective morals of society have led to the decreased use of corporal punishment in schools in much the same way they led to the abolition of corporal punishment in the criminal justice system. According to Durkheim (1933), as societies grow in economic interdependence and heterogeneity of values, their division of labor grows and their systems of punishment focus more on individual rights and practical outcomes rather than religious values and emotion. Thus, these societies are less likely to use corporal punishment because it has the potential of violating individuals' cultural mentalities and sensibilities. A logical extension of Durkheim's theory would purport that societies with a greater division of labor and low rates of religious fundamentalism and conservatism (characteristics of mechanical societies) would be less likely to use corporal punishment. This same reasoning can be applied to corporal punishment in the school. If Durkheim is correct, those societies with less sophisticated labor forces, conservative religious and political philosophies, and less religious and political heterogeneity would be more likely to use corporal punishment in the school.

To test if the theoretical assumptions made by Durkheim, Owen, and Xu et al. (2000) extend to the use of school corporal punishment at the county level in Kentucky, we analyzed the relationship between school corporal punishment and indicators of both social capital and culture. To measure social capital at the county level, we used total church adherence rates from the Glenmary Research Center and total voter registration and turnout percentages from the Kentucky State Board of Elections. Unfortunately more powerful measures of social capital used by Owen (2005) were not available at the county level. The indicators for the *type* of culture included: type of religious adherence, type of political affiliation, urbanicity, population density, type of labor force, income, racial composition, and region. These variables served as proxies for the county's dominant religious, political, geographic, and social characteristics.

The type of religious adherence was derived from data collected by the Glenmary Research Center regarding the adherence rates for five major religious groups in the year 2000. Political affiliation was determined by registration and turnout statistics from the Kentucky State Board of Elections (2004) for Republican, Democratic, and "Other" political parties in the 2004 general election. Data from the 2000 U.S. Census provided measures of urbanicity (the percentage of housing units considered urban), population density (population per square mile), type of labor force (percentage of workers considered white collar or "white-collar rate"), and racial composition (percentages for White, African-American, Latino and Other). Finally, a variable representing regional culture was introduced using the U.S. Congressional districts provided by the Kentucky Legislative Research Commission (2002).

The link between culture and corporal punishment can also be explained by how corporal punishment is learned from society. Murray Straus, one of the foremost modern researchers and theorists on parent-to-child corporal punishment, asserts that corporal punishment is, in part, learned from a culture of aggression. For Straus, corporal punishment is one part of a cycle of aggression. Like other forms of violence, corporal punishment can be caused by an underlying culture of aggression, but can also add to the culture of aggression. This occurs through a process that Straus calls "cultural spillover" (Straus & Donnelly, 2001). The correlation between corporal punishment and aggressive behavior is strongly supported by empirical research, but again, a causal relationship is difficult to identify (Crouch & Behl, 2001; Ellison, et al., 1996; Regaldo et al., 2000; Sears, Maccoby, & Levin, 1957; Straus & Donnelly, 2001).

A logical extension of Straus' work would purport that schools in areas where other forms of physical aggression are present and endorsed would have higher levels of corporal punishment and vice versa. However, the evidence to support this claim is either outdated (Hyman & Wise, 1979) or is based only on state-level data (Arcus, 2000). In this chapter, we sought to determine if violent crime rates and aggression in schools are, in fact, associated with school corporal punishment rates on the county level. To do so, we examined county level child physical and sexual abuse rates, child sexual abuse rates, adult abuse rates, and spouse abuse rates provided by the Kentucky Cabinet for Health and Family Services. Using data from the Kentucky State Police's *Crime in Kentucky: 2000 Crime Report*, we also calculated crime rates to determine their association with corporal punishment in school. These included rates for: (1) Part I violent offenses, (2) Part I property offenses, (3) total Part I offenses, (4) total Part II arrests, (5) offense against family arrests, and (6) total arrests.

Strain

There is ample evidence that parent-to-child corporal punishment is associated with economic and psychological strain among parents (Bronfenbrenner, 1958; Bryan & Freed, 1982; Crouch & Behl, 2000; Ellison et al., 1996; Ellison & Sherkat, 1993; Regaldo et al., 2004; Straus & Donnelly, 1993; 2001; Straus & Stewart, 1999; Xu et al., 2000). Studies that correlate lower socio-economic status with high rates of corporal punishment can be explained by Merton (1938) and Agnew's (2005) arguments that deviance from more socially acceptable patterns of behavior is often the result of a disjunction between cultural goals and an individual's means to achieve them. The use of corporal punishment among parents may indeed be the result of not having the means (e.g., time or education) to use other forms of punishment.

Like individuals, institutions can also experience strain as a result of not having the means to achieve all of society's goals. For example, while all schools have the same goal of creating a safe school environment, not all schools have the same economic or political support to use the most desirable prevention and discipline programs. Their desire to use such programs may take a back seat to their economic resources and goals set by society. Messner and Rosenfeld (2001) explain this phenomenon in their theory of institutional anomie by examining the interrelation of the four major groups of social institutions—economy, polity, family, and education. They argue that all four of these groups influence (and interact with) one another. For example, an educational policy (in this case, corporal punishment) can be influenced by the economic system through the political bodies of the school board and state legislature, with support from the family system. Educational policy may also affect the economy by how well it develops human capital, which is needed for a strong economy.

Messner and Rosenfeld also argue that while the other groups of social institutions are important, American culture is primarily determined by its capitalistic and materialistic nature. This, in turn, causes economic goals to take precedence over all others. Not only does American society devalue noneconomic goals, it also pushes economic goals into noneconomic institutions with little resistance from those institutions (Messner & Rosenfeld, 2001). This precedence of economic goals is evident in the dominance of the budget in the educational system today. Schools often determine their educational policies based on the policies' affordability and economic efficiency. Messner and Rosenfeld also assert that American society fosters an environment where both individuals and institutions will strive to achieve goals by any means necessary. As such, in order to achieve their economic goals, districts with fewer financial resources may continue the use of corporal punishment, even if it is not the most effective or beneficial punishment because it is financially efficient and keeps the student (and his or her assigned tax dollars) in the school.

Messner and Rosenfeld's hypotheses are supported by the link between poverty rates and school corporal punishment at the state level (Arcus, 2000). To determine whether or not institutional economic strain is associated with corporal punishment use at the county level, we examined several socioeconomic variables that may cause institutional strain in a county. County level median household incomes, poverty rates, percentages of households that have a single householder (single parent rate), and percentages of residents with a high school education or above (educational attainment) that were derived from the 2000 U.S. Census data, as well as the county's unemployment rate (reported by the Kentucky Cabinet for Health and Family Services) served as indicators of institutional strain in this study.

Purpose of This Study

Guided by the extant literature and theoretical perspectives, in this study, we attempt to determine the macro-level predictors of the prevalence and incidence of corporal punishment in Kentucky public schools. We explore three theoretical explanations of corporal punishment by examining a wide range of factors theoretically and empirically linked to the use of corporal punishment in the home and/or in the school. Such an effort adds to the understanding of a largely under-researched practice in American public education by (1) providing a profile of those counties in Kentucky that use corporal punishment and those that do not and (2) identifying factors that influence the frequency with which they use it. While the data analyzed allow only for correlational inferences, this effort is the first step in determining what actually causes policy makers and parents to support and implement corporal punishment in the school.

Method

Sample

The 120 counties in Kentucky comprised the sample in this study. While this is a small sample size, it is rather high compared to other states. Kentucky has the fourth most counties in the U.S. and one of the highest county-to-population ratios. There is a school district for every county in Kentucky plus an additional 56 independent school districts. Data from these 56 districts were combined with the data from the other district(s) in the county in which they sit to create a county-wide index of corporal punishment. Most of these independent school districts are relatively small and matched the county district in corporal punishment policy (Kentucky Center for School Safety, 2005).

Dependent Variables

As part of the Kentucky Center for School Safety (KCSS) annual data reporting process, each of the over 1,200 public schools in Kentucky submitted data in July, 2005 that enumerated the number of expulsions, out-of-school suspensions, and corporal punishments they had within that school in the 2004–2005 academic year. Approximately one-third of the 176 districts reported at least one use of corporal punishment in 2004–2005 (McCoy-Simandle, May, & Chen, 2005).

From these data, two dependent variables were created. The first dependent variable, prevalence, was a dichotomous variable measuring whether or not the county had any instances of corporal punishment in the 2004–2005 school year. Those 44 counties that had at least one instance of corporal punishment were coded (1). The second dependent variable, incidence, measured the rate at which counties used corporal punishment—the number of corporal punishment incidents divided by the public school enrollment in that county (obtained from the Kentucky Department of Education). This variable was an interval/ratio level variable whose scores ranged from 0 (no instances of corporal punishment) to 15.83 (rate of corporal punishment per 100 students).

Independent Variables

While the literature reviewed above suggests that there are no studies that have examined the use of corporal punishment within a state using the county as the unit of analysis, a number of studies suggest that there are social and demographic factors that are associated with the use and support of the use of corporal punishment by individuals. As such, data were collected from numerous state and federal sources on a wide variety of social and demographic variables that might be associated with the use of corporal punishment. These variables and their sources are discussed below.

U.S. Census Bureau Data (2000)

The Census Bureau provides county-level data on several variables that will be used in this analysis. The data that comprise the variables representing median household income, urbanicity, population density, poverty rate, and educational attainment were obtained from the 2000 U.S. Bureau of the Census' data set. The total population of each county was also used to create rates in other categories (e.g., crime rates) (U.S. Census Bureau, 2000).

Kentucky Cabinet for Health and Family Services

The Kentucky Cabinet for Health and Family Services' Epidemiology and Health Planning Data Branch provides county health profiles for each county in Kentucky. These profiles provide information across a wide spectrum of demographic variables. The variables used in this analysis were: unemployment rates, spouse abuse rates, adult abuse rates, child sex abuse rates, and child neglect rates (Kentucky Cabinet for Health and Family Services Division of Epidemiology and Health Planning, 2000).

Kentucky State Police

Data regarding crime incidents were collected from the Kentucky State Police's *Crime in Kentucky: 2000 Crime Report*. These data were combined with county population data from the U.S. Census to create rates for: (1) Part I violent offenses, (2) Part I property offenses, (3) total Part I offenses, (4) total Part II arrests, (5) offense against family arrests, and (6) total arrests.

Glenmary Research Center

In 2000, the Glenmary Research Center conducted a comprehensive study of church adherence in America. This project collected adherence rates for denominations in 149 religious bodies across the U.S. A total county-level adherence rates was obtained from this data set, as well as adherence rates for the following groups of denominations: Evangelical Christian, Mainline Protestant, Catholic, Jewish, Muslim, and Other (American Religion Data Archive, 2005).

Kentucky State Board of Elections (KSBE)

The KSBE publishes party registration and voter turnout data after each national election. The data from the 2004 General Election were used in this analysis. Overall voter turnout and voter registration percentages were calculated, along with percentages for Democrat, Republican, and Other categories provided in the data (Kentucky State Board of Elections, 2004).

Kentucky Legislative Research Commission

Counties were divided into five regions using U.S. Congressional Districts provided by Kentucky's Legislative Research Commission Geographic Information Systems Office. While there are six Congressional Districts in Kentucky, only five were used in this analysis, as Jefferson County comprises the entirety of Congressional District 3 and was combined with District 2 to allow for regional comparisons. These districts were renamed Western Kentucky (District 1), Mid-western Kentucky (Districts 2 & 3), Northern Kentucky (District 4), Eastern Kentucky (District 5), and Central Kentucky (District 6). Those counties that do not lie entirely in one Congressional District were placed in the district that included the majority of its land mass (Kentucky Legislative Research Commission, 2002)

Results

Table 6.3. Bivariate Pearson Correlations between All Independent Variables and the Prevalence and Incidence of Corporal Punishment

	Corporal Punishment	
	Prevalence	Incidence
Culture variables		
Evangelical adherence rate	–.009(.922)	–.115(.458)
Mainline Protestant adherence rate	–.212(.020)*	.074(.632)
Catholic adherence rate	–.288(.001)**	–.221(.150)
Jewish adherence rate	–.124(.179)	———#
Muslim adherence rate	–.094(.307)	.005(.975)
2004 Democrat registration rate	–.022(.816)	–.047(.764)
2004 Republican registration rate	.061(.508)	.064(.681)
2004 Other registration rate	–.367(.000)***	–.275(.071)*
2004 Democrat turnout rate	–.349(.000)***	–.462(.002)**
2004 Republican turnout rate	–.345(.000)***	–.477(.001)**
2004 Other turnout rate	–.403(.000)***	–.456(.002)**
White collar rate	–.242(.008)**	–.173(.262)
Urbanicity	–.207(.023)*	–.228(.137)
Population density	–.195(.033)*	–.211(.168)
White	151(.100)*	.087(.575)
African-American	–.120(.190)	–.064(.681)
Latino	–.194(.034)*	–.232(.130)
Other	–.241(.008)**	–.197(.199)
Child-physical abuse rate	.085(.356)	–.056(.718)
Child-sexual abuse rate	–.019(.838)	–.084(.588)
Child-neglect rate	.271(.003)**	.180(.588)
Spouse abuse rate	.141(.126)	.135(.382)
Adult abuse rate	–.090(.327)	.030(.848)
Total arrest rate	.043(.638)	.212(.167)
Violent offense rate	–.214(.019)*	–.060(.701)
Property offense rate	–.129(.159)	.082(.598)
Part I offense rate	–.141(.124)	.106(.495)
Part II arrest rate	.041(.657)	.204(.183)
Offense against family offense rate	–.183(.046)*	–.230(.133)

Social Capital		
Total church adherence rate	–.209(.022)*	–.112(.468)
2004 Total registration rate	–.012(.896)	.043(.781)
2004 Total turnout rate	–.356(.000)***	–.454(.002)**
Strain Variables		
Median household income	–.454(.000)***	–.482(.001)**
Poverty rate	.455(.000)***	.450(.002)**
Unemployment rate	.393(.000)***	.084(.588)
High school education rate	–.417(.000)***	–.427(.004)**
Single parent rate	.041(.657)	.385(.010)**

*p<.10, **p<.01, ***p<.001, # No Jewish adherence in counties that use corporal punishment.

After the data were collected and coded, bivariate correlation models were estimated in order to determine if the independent variables were correlated with the prevalence and/or incidence of corporal punishment in each county's schools. These results are presented in Table 6.3. Those variables that demonstrated a statistically significant relationship with prevalence and/or incidence were then included in multivariate logistic regression models to examine predictors of prevalence of corporal punishment and linear multivariate regression models to examine predictors of the incidence of corporal punishment in those districts that used it. Due to the small sample size under study (N = 120), those correlations with a probability level of .10 or less were included in the multivariate models. To avoid redundancy and issues of multicollinearity, in cases where sets of variables demonstrated a high correlation with one another (r = .70 or above), only one variable from the set was entered into the multivariate models.

In order to test for regional differences in the prevalence of corporal punishment, we conducted cross-tabulations and tests for association. These results are presented in Table 6.4. To test for regional differences in the incidence of corporal punishment, we conducted a one-way analysis of variance (ANOVA) test and post-hoc tests using the regions described above. While there were no significant regional differences in the incidence of corporal punishment (results not presented here), there were moderate regional differences in the prevalence of corporal punishment. The proportion of counties that used corporal punishment was highest in the Western Region (40.6%) and the Eastern Region (64.3%).

Table 6.4. Cross-tabulations Between Region and Prevalence of Corporal Punishment

Region	Counties using CP	Counties not using CP	Total Counties
Western	13 (40.6%)	19 (59.4%)	32
Mid-western	4 (19.0%)	17 (81.0%)	21
Northern	6 (26.1%)	17 (73.9%)	23
Central	3 (18.7%)	13 (81.3%)	16
Eastern	18 (64.3%)	10 (35.7%)	28
Total	**44**	**76**	**120**

$\chi^2 = 15.541$ (p = .004), Lambda (λ) = .098 (p = .179), Goodman & Kruskal $tau_{yx} = .130$ (p = .004)

Table 6.5. Results from Multivariate Logistic Regression Model Regressing Prevalence of Corporal Punishment on Variables Demonstrating a Significant Bivariate Correlation in Table 6.3

Enter Method

Variable	B	S.E.	Wald	Exp(B)
Median Household Income	.000	.000	3.092	1.000*
Unemployment rate	.176	.127	1.918	1.192
Population density	–.009	.010	.899	.991
Rurality	.043	.020	4.808	1.044*
White collar rate	–.036	.067	.296	.992
Violent offense rate	–.514	.491	1.093	.598
Total church adherence rate	.000	.002	.015	1.000
Catholic church adherence	–.008	.006	1.567	.992
2004 Total turnout rate	.077	.078	.983	1.081
2004 Other registration rate	–.121	.238	.259	.886
Western region	–.441	.927	.227	.643
Mid-western region	–.606	1.053	.331	.546
Northern region	–.449	.942	.227	.639
Central region	–.479	1.087	.194	.620
Constant	1.145	3.745	.094	3.144
Chi-Square	42.981***			
–2 Log Likelihood	114.737			
Nagelkerke R-Square	.412			

*p<.10, ***p<.001

Results from Multivariate Stepwise Forward Conditional Logistic Regression Model

Variable	B	S.E.	Wald	Exp(B)
Median household income	.000***	.000	21.243	1.000
Constant	4.429***	1.064	17.319	83.846
Chi-Square	30.532***			
–2 Log Likelihood	127.186			
Nagelkerke R-Square	.307			

***p<.001

The second stage of analysis involved the estimation of the two multivariate regression models alluded to above. Those variables that demonstrated a significant correlation with the prevalence of corporal punishment were included in two multivariate logistic regression models. In the first model, the independent variables that demonstrated a significant correlation with the prevalence of corporal punishment were entered in one stage. Given the findings presented in Table 6.4, to control for cultural and geographic regional differences, the regions in which the county was located were used to create four dummy variables (West, Mid-west, Central, and North) with the Eastern region used as the reference category.

In an effort to estimate the most efficient model, we then ran a logistic regression model using the forward stepwise method in which only the variables with the strongest effects were retained in the model (Knoke, Bohrnstedt, & Mee, 2002). Those results are presented in Table 6.3. Although several variables were correlated with the prevalence of corporal punishment in the county in the original model, median household income was the only variable to survive the stepwise logistic regression model. While there were significant differences across the different regions of Kentucky in the prevalence of corporal punishment in Table 6.4, the lack of a significant effect in the regression analyses shows that factors other than regional culture, namely median household income, better predict the use of corporal punishment.

Table 6.6. Results from Multivariate Linear Regression Model Regressing Prevalence of Corporal Punishment on Variables Demonstrating a Significant Bivariate Correlation in Table 6.3

Enter Method

Variable	B/SE	Beta	t	Significance
Median household income	.000/.000	–.388	–4.593	.000***
Single parent rate	.083/.048	.144	–1.7.2	.091*
Constant	1.659/1.227		1.353	.179
Listwise N	44			
F	13.953			
R Square	.193			

*p<. 10, ***p<.001

Results from Multivariate Stepwise Linear Regression Model

Variable	B/SE	Beta	t	Significance
Median household income	.000/.000	–.415	–4.961	.000***
Constant	3.513/.569		6.179	.000***
Listwise N	44			
F	24.615			
R Square	.173			

***p<.001

The incidence of corporal punishment was then regressed on those independent variables that had demonstrated a statistically significant bivariate correlation (p<.10) with incidence of corporal punishment in Table 6.3 in a linear regression model. Because we analyzed variance in the predictor variables independent of whether or not the county allows corporal punishment, we included only those counties with at least one incident of corporal punishment in this analysis.

In those counties that use corporal punishment, every variable other than the rate of single-parent households in a county that was significantly correlated with the incidence of corporal punishment demonstrated multicollinearity with median household income. Thus, these variables (poverty rate, educational attainment, and 2004 voter turnout) were excluded from the linear regression model. After removing those variables, median household income and the rate of single-parent households in a county were the only variables that demonstrated a significant bivariate correlation with incidence of corporal punishment. These variables were then entered into in the linear regression model using the enter method. To determine the strength of the effects of these variables on the incidence of corporal punishment, we then ran a forward stepwise regression model. After the first step in this model, only median household income remained with a significant effect. The results of these models are presented in second model in Table 6.6.

The first linear regression model revealed that median household income and the county single-parent household rate both had a significant effect on the incidence of corporal punishment. However, median household income was the only variable to survive the forward stepwise regression model. The county single-parent household rate did not meet the criteria to be entered into the model. Thus, the regression models under study here demonstrate that median household income is the strongest predictor of both the prevalence and incidence of corporal punishment in the state of Kentucky.

Discussion

While most school districts in Kentucky have abandoned the use of corporal punishment, many continue to use it to deal with problem behavior. Although several variables had significant bivariate correlations with the prevalence of corporal punishment, the factor that best predicted the prevalence of corporal punishment in a multivariate context was median household income. Those counties that had higher median household incomes were significantly less likely to use corporal punishment than those counties with lower median household incomes. Even when controlling for regional culture, median household income still predicted the prevalence of school corporal punishment. Also, after removing those districts that prohibit the use of corporal punishment, median household income predicted the incidence of corporal punishment. Those districts that had higher median household incomes were less likely to use it, even though their school board policy allowed its use.

It is important to consider the multi-collinearity between median household income, poverty rate, educational attainment, and total voter turnout (which was also multi-collinear with Republican and Democrat turnout). Such multi-collinearity and the strength of median household income's effect on corporal punishment in the regression models supports the idea that overall socioeconomic status and social capital are both associated with the use of corporal punishment.

At least two alternative explanations for the relationship between median household income and corporal punishment use in a school district exist: Messner and Rosenfeld's institutional strain theory and reproduction theory. According to Messner and Rosenfeld (2001), the strong relationship between median household income and corporal punishment use extends the theory of institutional anomie to the school setting. Those counties with the most economic strain were most likely to use corporal punishment and use it often. These districts may indeed be attempting to attain societal goals of budget efficiency and school discipline through a cost-efficient punishment. They may also be more apt to reject evidence that corporal punishment can have negative psychological effects on children and does not reduce behavior problems any better than other forms of punishment. Thus, Messner and Rosenfeld's theory may also apply in how economics affects school policy; the school board, or polity of the school system, seems to act as the intermediary between educational and economic systems.

Alternatively, the finding that schools in districts with lower median household incomes use corporal punishment more often lends some support to hypotheses suggesting that school discipline procedures are reflective of broader social stratification, a finding that may be more readily explained by reproduction theory. Reproduction theorists would argue that curriculum, discipline, and other classroom procedures used in schools not only help produce the values and belief system of the larger community but serve to reaffirm and thus sustain these larger social values (Anyon, 1980, 1981a, 1981b, 1981c; Bowles & Gintis, 2002, 1976; Willis, 2003, 1981). For example, in observing schools of different socioeconomic levels, Anyon found that schools in lower socioeconomic areas are dominated by routine, mechanical curricula and those curricula are designed to prepare students for the same types of procedures characteristic of blue-collar occupations.

Consequently, the mechanisms through which school districts maintain classroom order may be reflective of this larger process as well. School boards in low socioeconomic status, blue-collar areas may allow the use of coercive discipline procedures that demand conformity and compliance, not only as a method of reproducing the values of the lower socioeconomic community, but also as a method of preparing students to accept those values and reproduce them in the next generation. The cyclical nature of this process and the lack of counter-forces make change difficult and slow.

Because we could not identify the direction of the income-school corporal punishment relationship, it is also possible that corporal punishment legitimates the stratification mentioned above and grooms children to accept not only the hard-nosed values of the working class, but their place in the working class. School corporal punishment is even more powerful because it adds to the stratification effects of corporal punishment in the home evidenced in previous research (e.g., Straus & Donnelly, 2001). Thus, some children are receiving the message from their family and their school that corporal punishment is suitable for them, but not other children.

Finally, these findings support Owen's (2005) extension of Durkheim's theory of cultural involvement to school corporal punishment. Although median household income had the highest correlation with school corporal punishment, bivariate correlations showed that median household income, poverty rate, educational attainment, and voter turnout were almost statistically inseparable. Thus, these findings support the idea that social capital may also be linked to school corporal punishment. Future research should further explore this issue.

On the other hand, the use of corporal punishment had only a weak association with those variables that would represent the culture of a county. The religious, political, labor, and geographic type of a county did not have a significant impact on its use of corporal punishment. It appears that the characteristics one would associate with a mechanical society (conservative, literalist, blue-collar, rural, racially homogenous) did not predict the use of school corporal punishment. Likewise, indicators of physical aggression (abuse and crime rates) had only a mild relationship with school corporal punishment. Thus, neither the explanation of corporal punishment as a characteristic of mechanical societies nor the explanation of corporal punishment as a result of a "culture of violence" was supported.

The evidence reviewed above suggests that use of corporal punishment in school seems to create a cycle where it shapes and is shaped by: (1) economic stress, (2) broader stratification, and (3) social capital. Thus, the implications of this study focus on how to slow down or stop this cycle. In our view, this change can include forces both within and outside the educational system.

First, by choosing not to use corporal punishment in school, teachers can create a ripple effect in their students that reduces not only its use in the home, but also the negative social effects of its use in the home and the school. As Bowles and Gintis (2002) suggest, the school system is a unique entity in that students are exposed to individuals (teachers) who are often unrepresentative of the parental population and these people occupy "privileged positions" in the school system. Thus, when a teacher decides to use a form of punishment other than those to which the student has been exposed at home, some children may break out of the reproductive cycle of corporal punishment by choosing to use other forms of punishment with their own children (or, in extraordinary cases, convince their parents of the efficacy of alternative forms of punishment). These children often continue to live in (and become influential members of) the next generation in that community, perhaps occupying positions as school board members and teachers. These "privileged" positions then give these former students the power to make change in their own communities.

Second, in order to reduce corporal punishment in school, change must also occur outside the classroom. This includes improving broader social systems; however, it also includes improving the knowledge and discussion among educational policy makers at the school board and state level. Wauchope and Straus (1990) review research that suggests that peer pressure may have the greatest influence on punishment among parents. Exposure to differing forms of punishment often prompts discussions between parents about the effectiveness and morality of the forms they use. Knowing that there are other forms of punishment that may be more effective (and that there are negative effects of corporal punishment) is often the first step in stopping its use. Theoretically, this same idea should work among policy makers as well. If school board members, superintendents, and legislators from districts that do not allow the use of corporal punishment were to have frank, informed discussions about the effectiveness, morality, and justifications of the punishments they use, these discussions might lead them to reconsider their discipline policies and implement those policies that best serve the student and the school. Most states have both an association that represents school boards and one that represents superintendents; these discussions could be fostered through these organizations or even through the legislative process. Although some districts may not change their discipline policies, they will have at least been exposed to alternative punishments and given the best information possible about the ones they use. This, in turn, might influence school board policy in the future.

It is important to note that this study is not without limitations. First and foremost, the data used this study regarding the prevalence and incidences of corporal punishment were derived from officially reported data from the schools. This fact may have introduced a "social desirability bias," as school administrators may under-report the incidence of corporal punishment in their schools to the Kentucky Center for School Safety (as a police agency may under-report crime) in order to improve its image in the community. Secondly, although socioeconomic strain, social capital, and the use of corporal punishment are related, the data considered here do not allow for a causal link to be drawn between any variables in this study. Instead, we have identified four variables (median household income, poverty rate, educational attainment, and voter turnout) that co-vary with both one another and with the use of school corporal punishment. Establishing a linear pattern of interaction between these variables was not possible given the limitations of the data. However, demonstrating that these variables co-vary is a first step in determining the existence and direction of a causal link between them or if there is a common cause for all three phenomena, and serves as a springboard for future research.

In order to establish a causal link between corporal punishment and any of the four variables mentioned above, future research should follow two guidelines. First, researchers should use longitudinal data to match trends in a given variable to trends in school corporal punishment. This effort may help separate the variables that were so closely related in this study and identify any linear relationships with corporal punishment. An added benefit of longitudinal research would be its propensity to measure the effectiveness of school corporal punishment, as researchers would be able to match trends in corporal punishment use with trends in problem behavior. Second, it is important that this research be extended to the district and individual level. School districts should be analyzed because some districts in the same county differ greatly in their social and demographic characteristics and in their corporal punishment use. Also, district level data may provide more direct measures of the concepts used in this study.

Finally, while research at the aggregate level may identify strong predictors of a county or district's use of corporal punishment, counties and school districts are not living, breathing entities. Superintendents and school board members who establish district policy, however, are. Asking these policy-makers why they use, do not use, or have stopped using corporal punishment in their district would help determine the predictors of corporal punishment as a policy at the individual level.

References

Agnew, R. (2005). *Why do criminals offend? A general theory of crime and delinquency.* Loa Angeles: Roxbury.

American Religion Data Archive. (2000). *Religious congregations & membership maps and reports* [Data file]. Retrieved August 9, 2014 from the American Religion Data Archive Web site, http://www.thearda.com/rcms2010/

Anyon J. (1980). Social class and the hidden curriculum of work. *Journal of Education, 162*(1), 67–92.

Anyon, J. (1981). Elementary schooling and distinctions of social class. *Interchange, 12*(2–3), 118–132.

Anyon J. (1981). Schools as agencies of social legitimation. *International Journal of Political Education, 4,* 195–218.

Anyon, J. (1981). Social class and school knowledge. *Curriculum Inquiry, 11*(1), 3–37.

Arcus, D. (2002). School shooting fatalities and school corporal punishment: A look at the states. *Aggressive Behavior, 28,* 173–183.

Benatar, D. (1998). Corporal punishment. *Social Theory and Practice, 24*(2), 237–260.

Bowles, S., & Gintis, H. (1976). *Schooling in capitalist America: Educational reform and the contradictions of economic life.* New York: Basic Books.

Bowles, S., & Gintis, H. (2002). Schooling in capitalistic America revisited. *Sociology of Education, 75*(1), 1–18.

Bronfenbrenner, U. (1958). Socialization and class through time and space. In E.E. Maccoby, T.M. Newcomb, & E.L. Hartley (Eds.) *Readings in social psychology* (pp. 400–425). New York: Henry Holt and Company.

Bryan, J.W., & Freed, F.W. (1982). Corporal punishment: Normative data and sociological and psychological correlates in a community college population. *Journal of Youth and Adolescence, 11*(2), 77–87.

Crandall, J. (2002). *Support for spanking: Most Americans think corporal punishment is OK,* November 2. Retrieved February 10, 2006 from http://abcnews.go.com/sections/us/DailyNews/spanking_poll021108.html

Crouch, J.L., & Behl, L.E. (2001). Relationships among parental beliefs in corporal punishment, reported stress, and physical child abuse potential. *Child Abuse & Neglect, 25,* 413–419.

Durkheim, E. (1973). *Moral education: A study in the theory and application of the sociology of education.* (Transl.). New York: Free Press (Original work published 1925).

Durkheim, E. (1933). *The division of labor in society* (G. Simpson, Trans.). New York: Free Press. (Original work published 1895).

Ellison, C.G., Bartowski, J.P., & Segal, M.L. (1996). Conservative Protestantism and the use of corporal punishment. *Social Forces, 74*(3), 1003–1028.

Ellison, C.G., & Sherkat, D.E. (1993). Conservative Protestantism and support for corporal punishment. *American Sociological Review, 58,* 131–144.

Grasmick, H.G., Morgan, C.S., & Kennedy, M.B. (1992). Support for corporal punishment in the schools: A comparison of the effects of socioeconomic status and religion. *Social Science Quarterly, 73*(1), 177–187.

Hyman, I.A., & Wise, J.H. (1979). *Corporal punishment in American education.* Philadelphia: Temple University Press.

Ingraham v. Wright, 430 U.S. 651 (1977).

Kentucky Cabinet for Health and Family Services Division of Epidemiology and Health Planning. (2000). *Kentucky county health profiles, 2000.* Frankfort, KY: Author.

Kentucky Center for School Safety. (2005). [Worksheet 8—Disciplinary actions for school board violations in Kentucky]. Unpublished raw data.

Kentucky Legislative Research Commission. (2002). *KY Congressional districts.* Retrieved July 12, 2005 from http://www.lrc.ky.gov/pubserv/gis/maps.htm

Kentucky State Board of Elections. (2004). *Commonwealth of Kentucky-State board of elections: Voter turnout for the 11/02/04 general election* [Data file]. Available from Kentucky State Board of Elections Web site, http://elect.ky.gov/stats/turnout.htm

Kentucky State Police. (2001). *Crime in Kentucky: 2000 crime report.* Frankfort, KY: Author.

Knoke, D., Bohrnstedt, G.W., & Mee, A.P. (2002). *Statistics for social data analysis* (4th ed.). Belmont, CA: Wadsworth.

McCoy-Simandle, L., May, D.C., & Chen, Y. (2005). *Kentucky 2005: Safe schools data project.* Richmond, KY: Kentucky Center for School Safety.

Merton, R. K. (1938). Social structure and anomie. In F.T. Cullen & R. Agnew (Eds.). *Criminological theory: Past to present* (pp.176–185). Los Angeles: Roxbury.

Messner, S.E., & Rosenfeld, R. (2001). *Crime and the American dream.* Belmont, CA: Wadsworth-Thompson.

National Center for Education Statistics (2000). Table 14.-Percentage of public schools reporting that specified actions other than removals, transfers and suspensions were available as disciplinary actions, by selected school characteristics: 1999–2000. *Crime and Safety Surveys.* Retrieved November 24, 2005 from http://nces.ed.gov/

surveys/ssocs/tables/table_14.asp.

Owen, S. S. (2005). The relationship between social capital and corporal punishment in schools: A theoretical inquiry. *Youth & Society, 37*(1), 85–112.

Regaldo, M., Sareen, H., Inkelas, M., Wissow, L.S., & Halfon, N. (2004). Parents' discipline of young children: Results from the national survey of early childhood health. *Pediatrics, 113*(6), 1952–1958.

Sears, R.R., Maccoby, E.E., & Levin, H. (1957). *Patterns of child rearing.* Oxford, England: Row, Peterson, & Company.

Straus, M.A., & Donnelly, D.A. (1993). Corporal punishment of adolescents by American parents. *Youth & Society, 24* (4), 419–442.

Straus, M.A., & Donnelly, D.A. (2001). *Beating the devil out of them: Corporal punishment in American families and its effects on children.* New Brunswick, NJ: Transaction.

Straus, M.A., & Stewart, J.H. (1999). Corporal punishment by American parents: National data on prevalence, chronicity, severity, and duration, in relation to child and family characteristics. *Clinical Child and Family Psychology Review, 2*(2), 55–70.

The Center for Effective Discipline. (2010). *Corporal punishment in U.S. public schools.* Canal Winchester, OH: Center for Effective Discipline. Retrieved June 27, 2014 from http://www.stophitting.com/index.php?page=statesbanning.

U.S. Census Bureau (2000). *Decennial census data, 2000* [Data file]. Retrieved August 9, 2014 from U.S. Census Bureau Website, http://www.census.gov/mp/www/cat/decennial_census_2000/

U.S. Department of Education Office for Civil Rights. (2014). *Civil rights data collection: 2009–2010 national and state estimations.* Washington D.C.: Author. Retrieved June 28, 2014 from http://ocrdata.ed.gov/StateNationalEstimations/Projections_2009_10

U.S. Department of Education Office for Civil Rights (2005). Projected Data. *OCR Elementary and secondary school survey: 2002.* Retrieved November 24, 2005 from http://vistademo.beyond2020.com/ocr2002r/wdsdata.html

Wauchope, B.A., & Straus, M.A. (1990). Physical punishment and physical abuse of American children: Incidence rates by age, gender, and occupational class. In M. A. Straus & R. J. Gelles *Physical Violence in American Families: Risk Factors and Adaptations to Violence in 8,145 Families* (pp. 133–149). Piscataway, NJ: Transaction Publishers.

Willis, P. (2003). Foot soldiers of modernity: The dialectics of cultural consumption and the 21st-century school. *Harvard Educational Review, 73*(3), 390–415.

Willis, P. (1981). Cultural production is different from cultural reproduction is different from social reproduction is different from reproduction. *Interchange, 12*(2–3), 48–67.

Xu, X., Tung, Y., & Dunaway, R.G. (2000). Cultural, human, and social capital as determinants of corporal punishment: Toward an integrated theoretical model. *Journal of Interpersonal Violence, 55*(6), 603–630.

Chapter 7

Evaluating the Effectiveness of a Bullying Prevention Program: Evidence from a Quasi-Experimental Design

David C. May, Carly Cornelius, Ethan Stokes, Christy Rogers, and April Walters

Many people, even as adults, remember their own personal experiences with bullying at school, whether they were a victim, witness, or the actual bully. When the word "bullying" is mentioned, it often conjures images or memories of physically large and scary boys who beat up smaller or weaker peers for lunch money, homework, or personal possessions. For others, memories of bullies include relentless taunting and teasing. For years, adults responded to reports of such events with, "It's just kids being kids" or recommended that the victim stand up for himself by fighting back. Bullying was (and often still is) deemed a childhood rite of passage that had to be tolerated.

Several recent studies have demonstrated, however, that there are other tactics or strategies that one can use when faced with bullying that result in more favorable outcomes for both bully and victim. More specifically, the school-based bullying prevention programs that empower students to take action to reduce bullying behaviors may be a promising strategy to reduce bullying in schools. In this chapter, we examine the effectiveness of one of those programs in a rural school district in Kentucky. We begin with a discussion of bullying followed by an examination of several evaluations of bullying prevention programs. After a discussion of our current findings, we close with ideas and recommendations for future research.

Literature Review

Definition of Bullying

The most commonly accepted definition of bullying is offered by Olweus (1993), who defined bullying as being exposed, repeatedly and over time, to negative actions on the part of one or more other students. These negative actions typically are thought of as physical acts; however, they can also be defined as unpleasant gestures, spreading rumors, or intentional exclusion from a group.

Olweus (1997) also noted that there are three core characteristics of bullying. One of these characteristics is *aggressive behavior*. Aggressive behavior, as defined in a bullying situation, includes hostile and proactive behaviors, both indirect and direct, that are repeatedly targeted at an individual or group perceived as weaker (Elinoff, Chafouleas, & Sassu, 2004). The second core characteristic of bullying is that the behaviors occur *over time* (Olweus, 1997). True bullying incidents do not occur once or twice. They continue to happen over and over again. The third core characteristic of bullying involves an *imbalance of power*. A student who is being targeted by a bully often has difficulty engaging in self-defense, as they may be physically or mentally weaker, thus increasing the disparity between the power levels of the bully and their victim.

Definitions of Bullies, Victims, and Bystanders

According to Olweus (1994, 1997), a distinctive characteristic of bullies is their aggression toward others. This aggression is not only targeted at peers, but towards adults as well. Olweus (1993, 1995) noted that bullies also tend to be hot-tempered, impulsive, and exhibit a low frustration tolerance. Bullies display a strong need to dominate other people and have little empathy toward their victims.

A commonly held myth suggests that bullies have low self-esteem and target their victims in order to increase their own self-esteem. In fact, studies have shown that bullies do not suffer from poor self-esteem and actually think highly of themselves (Olweus, 1981, 1984, 1986; Pulkkinen & Tremblay, 1992) and demonstrate low levels of anxiety or insecurity. Several studies have also shown that bullies can be described as having average to slightly below average popularity (Olweus 1973, 1978; Pulkkinen & Tremblay, 1992) and appear to be popular amongst other children in early grades (Pellegrini, 1998). Their popularity appears to decrease in the higher grades, yet never seems to reach the low level of popularity seen by most victims (Olweus, 1994, 1997).

Victims are defined as the recipients of peer abuse (Smokowski & Kopasz, 2005). The typical victims are more anxious and insecure than other students (Ortega et al., 2012; Schneider et al., 2012; Olweus, 1994, 1995, 1997). They are often more cautious and quiet and frequently react to attacks from other students by crying or withdrawing. Victims also tend to suffer from low self-esteem and have a negative view of themselves and their environment. Other negative consequences of bullying include an increased chance to commit suicide (Olweus, 1993) and an increased likelihood of being involved in school shootings (Leary et al., 2003; Kärnä et al., 2011). Boys are typically bullied by other boys, while girls are bullied by both boys and girls (Boulton & Underwood, 1992; Olweus, 1991, 1993; Whitney & Smith, 1993).

Victims of bullying can be divided into two categories: *passive victims* and *provocative victims* (Olweus, 1994, 1995, 1997). Passive victims display behaviors that may signal that they are insecure, worthless, and will not retaliate if they are attacked or victimized. Passive victims are characterized by a submissive or anxious reaction pattern. Male passive victims are also generally physically weaker, which may lead to a fear of getting hurt and a negative attitude toward violence (Smokowski & Kopasz, 2005).

Provocative victims exhibit both anxious and aggressive reaction patterns (Olweus, 1994, 1995, 1997). They typically have difficulty with concentration and often behave in ways that may cause irritation for those around them. Some provocative victims may also have difficulties with hyperactive behaviors as well. These victims often display behaviors that provoke negative reactions from those around them. Olweus (1995) determined that provocative victims are difficult to identify. These students may react with hostility toward students who accidentally "provoke" them (Pellegrini, 1998). These students are often the recipients of negative responses from other students and school staff (Andreou, 2001; McNamara & McNamara, 1997). Teachers may even feel that provocative victims deserve their victimization because of their own actions.

Age appears to impact the likelihood of being a passive or provocative victim. The likelihood of being bullied tends to decrease with age, with primary school-age children being more likely to experience bullying than secondary school-age children (Boulton & Underwood, 1992; Charach et al., 1995; Olweus, 1991, 1993; Whitney & Smith, 1993). These findings suggest that bullying likely peaks as children approach adolescence (Boulton & Underwood, 1992; Charach et al., 1995; Hoover et. al., 1992).

In addition to consideration of the bully and the victim in a bullying event, another role that must be considered is that of the *bystander*. O'Connell, Pepler, and Craig (1999) found that bystander behaviors can be divided into three categories. Some bystanders are deemed to be "reinforcing" (54% of group) because they stay and passively watch a bully victimize a victim. Others are categorized as "modeling" (21% of group) when they actively join in the bullying. The third type is "intervening" bystanders (25% of group); intervening bystanders offer some type of support to the victim. O'Connell et al. (1999) determined that when bystanders intervene in a bullying episode, they are successful in ending the situation 75% of the time.

While considering how bystanders are impacted by bullying, Lodge and Frydenberg (2005) found that "passive bystanders" do not feel that they are affiliated with either the bully or victim and they also experience less emotional distress and apprehension when witnessing bullying incidents. Female bystanders are more likely to feel sad, upset, angry, and disgusted, while male bystanders are more likely to feel indifferent. Regardless of their gender, many bystanders report feeling guilt, anger, confusion, lack of knowledge regarding what to do, and fear of retaliation. Additionally, bystanders report that witnessing bullying incidents is unpleasant and many report being extremely distressed by what they had seen (Nickerson, Mele, & Princiotta, 2008; Hoover & Oliver, 1996; Zigler & Pepler, 1993). These witnesses may often feel intimidated and fear that they will become targets of bullies (Chandler, Nolin, & Davies, 1995). Olweus, Limber, and Mihalic (1999) noted that bullying negatively effects the entire school population, creating an environment that fosters fear and intimidation. After witnessing bullying episodes for a long period of time, many bystanders also report a decreased sense of empathy for other students (Olweus & Limber, 2002).

Effects of Bullying

Many individuals involved in bullying, whether as a bully, victim, or bystander, experience consequences due to their involvement. Victims may experience numerous school-related difficulties, including lower levels of school attachment and increased likelihood of drop-out risk (Card & Hodges, 2008; Forero, McLellan, Rissel, & Bauman,

1999; Sharp, 1995). Victims of bullying may also exhibit chronic absenteeism and minimal school performance (Card & Hodges, 2008; Beale, 2001). Targets of bullies frequently have difficulty concentrating on school work, which often leads to poor academic performance (Nakamoto & Schwartz, 2010; School Crime Report, 2005).

A number of victims are also afraid to go to school and may develop psychosomatic symptoms, such as headaches or stomachaches, prior to or upon arrival at school (Smokowski & Kopasz, 2005). Other studies also suggest that victims may develop severe mental health difficulties such as psychotic symptoms and thoughts of suicide (Schreier et al., 2009; Hay & Meldrum, 2010; Olweus, 1993). Studies have shown that as many as 7% of American eighth-graders stay at home at least once a month due to bullying (Banks, 1997). Bullying victims can experience diminished self-esteem, increased feelings of depression and loneliness, and have difficulty making friends and social and emotional adjustments (Rudolph et al., 2013; OJJDP Fact Sheet, 2001). One-half of former childhood victims of bullying report long-term impacts of being bullied which affect their adult relationships (Cowie, 2013; Hugh-Jones & Smith, 1999). These individuals may also suffer from humiliation and insecurity, which can lead to some type of retaliation (School Crime Supplement, 2005). Bullied students may resort to antisocial responses by carrying a weapon for protection and may be more likely to be involved in physical confrontations at school.

Bullying behaviors are also correlated with many antisocial behaviors in adulthood, including shoplifting, vandalism, fighting, and the use of alcohol and/or drugs (Banks, 1997; OJJDP, 2001; Wolke et al., 2013). Olweus (1993) noted that 60% of male students who were characterized as bullies between sixth and ninth grades had been convicted of at least one crime as an adult, compared with 23% of males who were not deemed to be bullies. Of the population of former bullies, between 35% and 40% have had three or more criminal convictions by age 24, compared with 10% of those who were not bullies. Recent studies also suggest that a number of individuals involved in fatal school shootings had been bullied, persecuted, threatened, or injured prior to the attack, although not all school shooters had been bullied and, certainly, not all bullying victims become school shooters (U.S. Secret Service and U.S. Department of Education, 2004).

Effectiveness of School-Wide Bullying Programs

The research reviewed above documents both the short- and long-term negative consequences of bullying for all those involved in bullying incidents. Because of these negative consequences, a wide variety of bullying prevention programs have been developed and implemented at schools throughout the United States. Despite their wide availability, however, the effectiveness of these programs is still questionable at best. The literature in the school safety area is inundated with anecdotal accounts of programs that increase school safety through a variety of mechanisms; the literature around bullying prevention programs is one of the biggest culprits in this regard.

As the goal of this chapter is to determine the effectiveness of bullying prevention programs, we began our initial review of bullying prevention programs with a goal of including only those recent (published between 2000 and 2010) studies in which a school-wide bullying prevention program was utilized and in which classical experimental designs were used to analyze the effectiveness of the program. Given the difficulty associated with experimental design when implementing programming in schools and the limited number of studies that used experimental design uncovered in our initial literature search, we expanded the criteria to include studies containing quasi-experimental conditions in order to obtain more information regarding possible effects of school-wide bullying prevention programs. Studies meeting these criteria are reviewed below.

Program Components

The specific prevention programs examined that met the previously established criteria included programs implemented in Spain, Ireland, Finland, and the United States (Vreeman & Carroll, 2007; Frey et al., 2005; O'Moore & Minton, 2005; Salmivali, Kaukiainen, & Voeten, 2005; Melton et. al, 1998; Ortega & Lera, 2000,). A brief description of each of the research projects is provided in addition to intervention outcomes, with the exception of one study in which outcomes were not published. Of the specific variables examined in these studies, we attempted to limit our focus to those outcomes deemed beneficial for students. These outcomes included reductions in bullying behaviors and perceptions of victimization, increases in helping behaviors (utilization of prevention and/or interventions strategies), and increases in student perceptions of the program's effectiveness. It should be noted that all variables were not necessarily examined in all of the studies reviewed.

The Seville Anti-Bullying in School Project in Spain was described as a whole-school approach that was developed independently but was based upon concepts from Olweus' prevention program (Ortega & Lera, 2000; Olweus, 1991). While pre- and post-intervention data were collected, the same schools were not included in both data collection samples. Additionally, a control group was not utilized to examine program effects. At the time of the publication, baseline data were available; however, the posttest results were unavailable in the literature. Baseline data obtained from the students prior to program implementation revealed equal percentages (33%) of students who (1) occasionally engage in bullying behaviors and (2) who occasionally experience victimization. Bystander students accounted for 75% of the population; they neither engaged in bullying nor reported victimization by bullying but they did indicate that violence existed among peers at school. Perceptions of the need for intervention among students revealed that more than half deemed bullying prevention as necessary, whereas only 2% felt it unnecessary. Others students either indicated that no solution to bullying existed or they had no opinion about the need for prevention (Ortega & Lera, 2000).

In contrast to the Spanish study, the study in Ireland utilized the same schools in the pre/post analyses; however, this study lacked a control group (O'Moore & Minton, 2005). This nationwide program aimed to prevent and manage bullying behaviors was also based upon Olweus' prevention program. O'Moore and Minton (2005) determined that both the incidence of reported bullying and bullying victimization were significantly reduced after the program was implemented. Bystander students were also significantly more likely to assist a victim of bullying following the intervention. In addition, the findings also revealed a significant reduction in the percentage of students who indicated they would do nothing if they witnessed bullying behaviors. While intervention was found to have positive effects on bullying frequency, victimization, and peer-to-peer assistance, bullying victims were no more likely to report their bullying experience (O'Moore & Minton, 2005).

Vreeman and Carroll (2007) examined ten curriculum interventions, ten school-wide interventions, four social skills intervention groups, a mentoring intervention, and a social worker support intervention. The scholars found that all of the bullying intervention types were successful, in one way or another, in reducing bullying activities amongst children and within schools (Vreeman & Carroll, 2007). While there were multiple intervention strategies that did not report a significant decrease in bullying activities, others were very successful. The most successful anti-bullying intervention approaches were those conducted at the school-wide levels, followed by the mentoring approach and the increase of social workers within schools (Vreeman & Carroll, 2007). It is worth noting that Vreeman and Carroll's (2007) results were not the first time that scholars have observed the whole-school, or school-wide, approach to reducing bullying behaviors.

According to Salmivalli, Kaukiainen, and Voeten (2005), the whole-school program approach used in Finland was based on Olweus' concepts but was independently developed. To conduct comparisons, a "cohort longitudinal design" was used, where sets of cohorts were developed among the students. Posttest scores from students who had received the intervention during one school year were compared with the same grade students during the following school year prior to the introduction of the intervention. In this study, a true control group did not exist. Pretest and posttest scores were obtained from students who were not exposed to the treatment but were in the same grade as the experimental students. The Finland study examined both self-reported and observed incidents of bullying and found that both self-reported bullying and the number of bullying events witnessed were significantly reduced; however, these reductions were not necessarily consistent across grade and age levels (Salmivalii et al., 2005).

Frey and colleagues (2005) evaluated the effectiveness of the school-based bullying program *Steps to Respect*. The primary goals of the program were to reduce bullying and destructive bystander behaviors, to increase pro-social beliefs related to bullying, and to increase social and emotional skills among almost 2,000 students in three matched pairs of elementary schools in the Pacific Northwest. Self-report questionnaires determined that students in the intervention schools were significantly less likely to approve bullying behaviors and were more likely to feel they should intervene on the bullying victim's behalf than those students in the control schools. Additionally, students in the experimental school were significantly less likely to experience bullying victimization. The researchers also used teacher observations of playground behaviors and determined through the teachers' ratings that the program reduced bullying on the playground at the experimental school but did not reduce the likelihood of bystanders joining in the bullying.

Baldry and Farrington (2004) examined the effectiveness of the Bulli & Pupe program in Rome, Italy. The program uses videos and lesson booklets to achieve the goal of teaching empathy among students and, in doing so, reduce bullying and victimization among middle and high school students. There were 131 students in the experimental group and 106 students in the control group. All students came from the same middle and high schools but from 10 different classes that were randomly allocated to either the experimental or control class. Baldry and Farrington determined that, over a four-month period, the program reduced bullying victimization among older (last year middle- and first year high-school) students but increased bullying victimization among younger, middle school students (Baldry & Farrington, 2004).

The final prevention program examined was conducted in South Carolina (Melton et. al., 1998). The program materials were similar to that of Olweus'; however, additional supplemental materials were provided to each of the intervention schools. Because several of the original control group schools received the intervention during the second year of implementation (thus making them treatment groups instead of control groups), findings regarding the long-term impacts of the program that was implemented in those schools were not available following the introduction of the prevention program. Of the findings available for examination after the first year of implementation, a reduction in bullying behaviors was indicated at the intervention school. This change was not sustained following the second year of intervention. The study yielded no significant reductions for student reported victimization (Melton et. al., 1998).

Summary of Existing Evidence about School-Wide Bullying Prevention Programs

Despite the wide variety of studies that exist in the area of bullying, our literature review indicates that few published studies have collected data through experimental or quasi-experimental studies utilizing a pre/post design with control groups to examine the effectiveness of bullying prevention programs (the most valid way to measure the effectiveness of bullying interventions). Even fewer studies have used longitudinal data to do so. To add to this literature, we collected data about the effectiveness of a bullying prevention program from students in the school district where three of the authors worked to examine the long-term effects of a prevention program while utilizing a control group. Using two waves of data collected over a three-year period, in the following section, we examine the impact of a bullying prevention program at a middle school in central Kentucky and compare the trends in that data with a similar middle school where the program was not implemented.

Methods

Program Description

The bullying prevention program that was implemented in the middle school was entitled *Bully-Proofing Your Schools.* The program was simultaneously delivered, twice per month, on a designated day of the week throughout the treatment school. The program was implemented in the study school district in the 2005–2006 school year in an effort to reduce bullying in middle schools in the district.

Sample and Procedure

The pre-test data used in this study were collected as part of a bullying needs assessment by the school district during the fall 2005 semester at two middle schools in a rural school district in Kentucky. The results of that needs assessment were presented to the administrators at each school, and the administrators were given the opportunity to have the program delivered in their school beginning in the 2005–2006 school year. One administrator declined the opportunity (and thus became the control school) while the second administrator accepted the opportunity and thus became the experimental school for this study. Both administrators agreed to collect data to (1) continue to assess the scope of bullying at their school and (2) assist with the evaluation of the bullying prevention program. The treatment school implemented the bullying prevention program twice a month during the 2005–2006 and 2006–2007 school years. The control school had not implemented a school-wide bullying prevention program at the time of this study. The total sample consisted of responses from 2,345 students.

In the treatment school, surveys were completed by all students at the beginning of the school day during their homeroom (first) period (in both the fall 2005 and spring 2007 semesters). Homeroom was extended for the duration of survey completion. Prior to the school day's opening, we arrived at the school and hand delivered the surveys in envelopes to each teacher. The envelopes were labeled with the teacher's name, approximate numbers of students, and general administration instructions. This number of students was verified upon delivery to the teacher.

In the control school, surveys were completed by all students during the last period of the school day during last block (advisory period) in both the fall 2005 and spring 2007 semesters. The advisory period began several minutes early to allow for completion of the survey. The surveys were delivered to the school the day prior to administration and placed in each teacher's mailbox. The envelopes were labeled with the teacher's name, approximate numbers of students, and general administration instructions. A school-wide announcement at the end of that same day instructed teachers to retrieve their respective envelopes and to ensure they had the correct number of copies.

Administration Instructions

The envelopes given to each teacher provided a brief description of the how the survey would be administered. More specifically, the directions for the teacher were to wait for the reader on the school intercom to provide instructions to distribute surveys and begin administration, remain at the front of the room during administration, and assist students with the coding section following completion of the survey. The surveys were then to be collected individually (facedown) from each student, returned to the provided envelope, and sealed in the presence of the students.

Survey Administration

On the day of survey completion, three of the authors arrived early to ensure survey distribution was completed. Following an introduction from the principal, one of the authors read the survey over the school-wide intercom (SWI) and all students completed the questions simultaneously. While the survey was read aloud, the remaining authors walked the hallways to monitor survey completion and assist with any teacher questions/problems. At the control group school, another one of the authors read the survey with a microphone to a group of students in the auditorium due to a limited number of classrooms with SWI capabilities. A total of three classrooms (approximately 75 students) completed the survey in the auditorium setting while seated at the front of the venue within close proximity to the author reading the survey aloud.

Following completion of the survey, the reader provided additional instructions over the SWI to complete the coding section of the survey. Students were instructed to provide the first letter of their first, middle, and last names as well as the day and month only of their birthday. For example: Jane Doe Smith 1/1/06 would be coded as JDS 1/1. Upon completion, the surveys were immediately collected by the researchers.

Survey Instrument

The instrument used to collect the data was a five-page questionnaire adapted from the Colorado School Climate Survey as presented in *Bully-Proofing Your School* (Garrity, Jens, Porter, Sager, & Short-Camilli, 2004). Because the survey was administered as part of the school district's effort to examine the impact of the program in the experimental school, school personnel decided that the research was covered under the parental consent obtained from parents to conduct school-based research with students at the beginning of the year.

The survey used to obtain the data included a series of questions designed to assess the prevalence of bullying, direct and indirect victimization (bystander), types of bullying behaviors (physical, verbal, social, intimidation, sexual harassment, race/ethnicity), locations in which bullying behaviors occurred, actions of peers/adults following bullying incidents, and perceptions of school climate including safety, teacher/adult responsiveness to bullying/victimization, peer acceptance and support, fear of attending school, importance of academic achievement, and the presence of clear school rules/policies. Additional demographic data were collected, including grade level, sex, race, free/reduced lunch program participation, academic achievement, disciplinary suspension/expulsions, and absence from school due to fear of bullying.

Survey Information

Given that the purpose of this effort was to examine the impact of the bullying prevention program on reporting behaviors, we asked respondents to indicate what actions they took when they were either bullied themselves or saw another student being bullied. Possible responses included obtaining assistance from a peer or adult at schools, reciprocating the bullying behavior, avoidance, agreeing with the bullying statements, leaving the sight of the bullying incident, making positive self-statements, using humor, or doing "nothing." Respondents were to indicate any or all behaviors in which they engaged when they witnessed or were victims of bullying.

Ideally, we would have compared responses from Wave 1 to responses from Wave 3 for individual students who participated in both waves. Unfortunately, a large number of students did not complete the identifying information at both Wave 1 and Wave 3, thus precluding us from directly comparing individual responses among the students. Given this limitation, we decided to calculate an average response score for each school for each item and compared the changes in the mean scores for the schools to determine if the bullying prevention program was successful in encouraging reporting among bullying victims and bystanders. The results from that analysis are presented below.

Results

The comparison of mean scores on the willingness to report bullying variables is presented in Table 7.1. The wording of each item is presented in the first column, followed by four columns representing responses to surveys administered at the control and experimental schools in Year 1 (prior to implementation of the prevention program) and Year 3 (two years after the initial implementation). Columns 2 and 3 display the Year 1 and Year 3 scores for the experimental school, respectively; Columns 4 and 5 display the Year 1 and Year 3 scores for the control school, respectively. The mean differences are discussed in detail below.

The results presented in Table 7.1 indicate that, in general, students at the experimental school were more willing to intervene in bullying incidents to assist victims of bullying. The results also suggest that students were much more willing to intervene on the behalf of others than on their own accord. In fact, there were no significant differences between Year 1 and Year 3 at the experimental school for any of the variables representing what students would do on their own behalf. However, for the variables that measured their willingness to help other students who had been bullied, there were a number of significant changes from Year 1 to Year 3. Students who had received the bullying prevention training were significantly more likely to (1) ask the bullying victim to join them to remove the student from the bullying situation, (2) help the bullying victim get away, (3) help the bullying victim come up with ideas about how to handle the bullying incident, (4) get help from an adult at school, and (5) talk to the bullying victim about how they felt. Students receiving the bullying prevention training were also significantly less likely to (1) do nothing when witnessing a student being bullied or (2) tell no one after they witnessed a student being bullied. Conversely, at the control school, students were generally less willing (although not reaching the level of statistically significance) to intervene on behalf of others in Year 3 than in Year 1 and were significantly less likely to stand up to the bully and tell others about the bullying incident. Thus, the bullying prevention training appears to work to help students to become more involved in helping bullying victims other than themselves but does not appear to empower bullying victims to act on their own behalf.

Table 7.1. Mean Differences in Willingness to Report Bullying among Experimental and Control Middle Schools

Variable (Range 0-1)	Experimental Pre-test	Experimental Post-test	Control Pre-test	Control Post-test
When bullied, you:				
Got help from an adult at school	.21	.25	.28	.33
Got help from another student	.28	.32 b	.37	.42
Hit, kicked, or pushed back	.28	.35 b	.42	.46
Teased or called the bully names, etc.	.22	.22 b	.29	.34
Agreed with bully's comments	.08	.09	.13	.14
Avoided the bully	.26	.32	.30	.29
Got help from my parents	.18	.19 b	.27	.31
Ignored the bully or walked away	.46	.49	.49	.50
Told the bully to stop	.41	.47	.53	.51
Tried to stop bully with humor	.10	.16	.16	.15
Said positive things to myself	.15	.17	.24	.21
Did nothing	.19	.19	.24	.16
Told no one	.30	.26	.25	.21
Told a friend	.51	.56	.57	.59
Told an adult at school	.13	.16	.16	.19
Told a parent	.24	.25	.25	.23
Told the bus driver	.02	.04	.03	.01
Told someone else	.11	.08	.13	.08
When I saw bullying, I:				
Did nothing	.58	.49 ab	.55	.59
Asked the victim to join me	.20	.27 ab	.25	.20
Helped the victim get away	.13	.21 a	.24	.19
Worked with victim to solve problem	.16	.25 a	.26	.24
Got help from an adult at school	.06	.11 a	.10	.12
Stood up to the bully	.27	.33 ab	.34	.21 c
Talked with victim about their feelings	.16	.28 ab	.25	.19
Told no one	.50	.42 a	.41	.38
Told my friend	.39	.45	.47	.46
Told an adult at school	.10	.15	.14	.18
Told a parent	.13	.16	.17	.15
Told the bus driver	.01	.03	.03	.02
Told someone else	.09	.11	.14	.08 c

a Significant ($p < .05$) difference between Experimental School Pre-test and Post-test scores
b Significant ($p < .05$) difference between Experimental School and Control School Post-test scores
c Significant ($p < .05$) difference between Control School Pre-test and Post-test scores

The results presented in Table 7.1 also reveal another interesting finding. With limited exceptions, students at the control school were more willing to intervene on their own behalf in both Wave 1 and Wave 3 than students at the experimental school. For example, students at the control school were significantly more likely than students in the experimental school in Year 1 to (1) get help from another student, (2) hit, kick, or push the bully, (3) tease or call the bully names, and (4) get help from their parents. These significant differences were also found in Year 3 for several of the variables. The potential explanations and implications of these findings are discussed below.

Discussion

In this study, we used data collected before and after a bullying prevention program was implemented in a rural Kentucky middle school to examine differences in experimental and control schools on student responses to bullying. We investigated the effectiveness of the *Bully-Proofing Your School* (Garrity et al., 2004) prevention and intervention program on middle school participants over a period of three years. We primarily focused on the personal strategies that bullying victims used to respond to their own bullying victimization and the willingness of students to assist bullying victims when they witnessed those actions (bystanders). The results presented above suggest that, while the program appears to empower students to intervene on behalf of others, it does not motivate them to intervene on their own behalf. The context and implications of those findings are discussed below.

First, it appears that the program was effective with regard to bystander intervention among students who had witnessed bullying. Experimental school participants were more likely to implement strategies such as asking a person who was bullied to join them, were more likely to assist the person who was bullied by helping them to develop ideas to handle the problem, and were more likely to help the person who was bullied to get away in the post-test survey than in the pre-test survey. This suggests that, despite the limitations discussed below, the program was effective in empowering bystanders to intervene on behalf of their peers.

This finding is particularly encouraging given the fact that three of the authors were instrumental in implementing the program and were aware that teachers and staff at the schools did not follow the program designers' recommendations for full implementation of the bullying prevention program. For example, the program recommends: regular meetings of a cadre who are implementing the program; a bus driver and cafeteria staff training component; a systematic approach to documentation of bullying incidents and interventions to address those incidents; and a school-wide student reward program for intervening on behalf of bullying victims. None of these components of the program were consistently implemented. Intuitively, stronger program integrity would increase the likelihood of students exhibiting the desired outcomes. The level of on-going fidelity in the delivery of the program at the school after the initial staff training thus appears to affect the success of the bullying prevention programs.

As part of the initial staff training prior to implementation, information was provided to the schools modeling a number of strategies to assist in the monitoring and sustainability of the prevention program. These strategies included developing a cadre of school staff whose primary focus was to monitor effective program implementation, serve as a voice for the teachers at each respective grade level, and solve problems when implementation problems were discovered. In retrospect, the cadre should have consisted of representatives from each grade-level, school administrators, guidance staff, and other related areas. This cadre should have met consistently to ensure that the program was being implemented effectively and should have served as vehicle of communication for all teachers and staff involved in the bullying prevention program throughout the year.

Second, the results also indicate that the program had limited success with regard to motivating individual victims of bullying to stand up for themselves, a key component of the *Bully-Proofing Your School* curriculum. These results imply that school participants were more likely to empathize with others than to take action to protect themselves from bullying, a finding supported by several studies that indicate the importance of empathy in responding to victimization (see Malti, Perren, & Buchmann, 2010). This finding may also be due to the limited program integrity described above. Future efforts should closely monitor program implementation to determine if the lack of change in responding to bullying victimization is due to limitations of the program or limitations of the program's implementation.

Third, the fact that students at the control school were significantly more likely to take action on their own behalf may stem from a variety of sources. First, students at the control school may not report their own victimization from bullying to adults because they (1) fear retaliation from the bully if an adult intervenes, (2) previous requests for assistance from adults did not deter the bully from reoffending, and/or (3) adolescents, in general, rely less on adult support for social issues than in previous years (Garrity et al., 2004). Additionally, the physical structure and design of the control school was such that there were a number of areas where active adult supervision is limited or nonexistent. Consequently, students at the control school may have been aware that they needed to protect themselves at greater levels than the experimental school, whose building had a physical design that allowed for better adult supervision throughout the building.

A third explanation could be the fact that students at the control school had not been educated about the possible support that could come from student peers acting as bystanders. Without this knowledge, the student may have been more likely to intervene on their own behalf than students who knew that peers could be relied on for support in bullying instances. Finally, there was a history of significant administrative turnover at the control school; thus, the expectations of the school administrators were constantly changing, resulting in students and teachers finding it difficult to be cognizant of the school's expectations and making it more difficult to build rapport with the administrators. These factors may have combined to urge control students to look to themselves or peers for assistance at levels greater than in the experimental school.

Limitations

In addition to the concerns discussed above, there are at least three limitations of this research. First, as with any self-report survey, this research relies on student self-reports of their own behaviors. This may be a particular concern with this study because of the nature of the *Bully-Proofing Your Schools* program. Given that the program teaches students to intervene on behalf of other students and themselves when they are bullied, this program has the potential to introduce an additional social desirability bias at the experimental school (but not at the control school) because students at the experimental school were now aware they are supposed to intervene on behalf of bullying victims.

An additional limitation is that a small number of students at the control school may have been briefly introduced to the bullying prevention program during their prior elementary school experience. Because the program was being introduced at the elementary level in select schools in the district, a small number of students may have had one year of exposure to the program prior to entering the control school. Nevertheless, given the small number of students affected and the fact that there was little change in the control school over the evaluation period, we feel that this factor likely had little impact on the results of this study.

A third limitation of this study involves the level of measurement utilized. Optimally, a quasi-experimental design would have used pre-test and post-test data from the same individual students, rather than using school-level measures of these variables. Despite our best efforts, we were unable to match an acceptable number of students from one wave to another with any degree of confidence because teachers did not ensure that the students completed the identifying information on the surveys correctly when the data were collected originally. A possible explanation for this may be the survey wording, measurement limitations, and design of the self-report survey given to the students. We used the survey provided by the bullying prevention program, which, in our opinion, could have been more succinct and logical, thus making it easier for students to complete and understand. Add to this the fact that the identifiers were not completed correctly on at least half of the student surveys, we were forced to use school-level measures of bullying intervention. Future research efforts should ensure that a large enough research team is used so that classroom teachers are not required to administer the surveys to the students while also utilizing a redesigned survey to collect the data.

Future Directions

This research has revealed a number of potentially important areas of future research in bullying prevention. First, the findings uncovered suggest that future research may need to closely examine how bullying prevention programs are implemented, particularly in the area of teacher and staff responses to reported bullying victimization. As discussed above, we are not entirely confident that the program was implemented in the experimental school in the manner outlined by the program designers. In fact, there were a number of specific instances where the authors noted teacher and staff failures to comply with the intended program design, including failure to train new staff in bullying prevention in the second and subsequent years of the program and a failure to provide consistent refresher training on the bullying prevention program. This failure to comply with the program design may have limited the effectiveness of the program at the experimental school. Future research efforts need to ensure that regular, consistent monitoring of the program implementation is occurring.

This need for monitoring of the program's implementation is evidenced by Hirschstein, Van Schoiack Edstrom, Frey, Snell, and MacKenzie (2007) who examined the importance of program integrity in the *Steps to Respect* program. In their findings, they determined that when teachers adhered closely to the program, successful peer interaction among the students increased. Our experience with the implantation of this program suggests that program integrity is highest when a trained cadre (whose purpose is to make sure that the program is implemented as designed) is empowered by school administrators to implement the program correctly to reduce bullying behaviors.

A second recommendation for future research involves the area of bullying program evaluation. The literature reviewed for this paper suggests that limited research is available that uses a quasi-experimental design with control and experimental schools. Additionally, like most other studies of which we are aware, we were unable to measure whether students who intervened in bullying situations perceived their actions as effective in reducing bullying. Until these specific areas are examined, confidence in effectiveness of school-wide bullying prevention programming will remain limited.

Conclusion

The findings from this research suggest that properly designed and implemented bullying prevention programs work to empower students to intervene in bullying situations on behalf of others. Thus, these programs should continue to be explored and evaluated as a means of intervention in schools aspiring to reduce bullying. Increased program integrity during implementation may also increase the willingness of students to act on their own behalf when faced with bullying victimization.

Our experience with this research effort also suggests the necessity of gaining acceptance from staff charged with implementing the program beginning at the discussion level when considering implementing bullying prevention programming. Additional research examining perceived need for intervention by students may also be beneficial when selecting schools in which to implement prevention programming. Without this "buy-in" and forethought, the program will have limited integrity and will be less effective than it could be.

References

Andreou, E. (2001). Bully/victim problems and their association with coping behavior in conflictual peer interactions among school-age children. *Educational Psychology, 21,* 59–66.

Baldry, A.C., & Farrington, D.P. (2004). Evaluation of an intervention program for the reduction of bullying and victimization in the schools. *Aggressive Behavior, 30,* 1–15.

Banks, R. (1997). Bullying in schools. *ERIC Clearinghouse on Elementary and Early Childhood Education, April 1997.*

Beale, A. V. (2001). Bullybusters: Using drama to empower students to take a stand against bullying behavior. *Professional School Counseling, 4,* 300–306.

Boulton, M. J. & Underwood, K. (1992). Bully/victim problems among middle school children. *British Journal of Educational Psychology, 62*, 73–87.

Card, N. A., & Hodges, E. V. (2008). Peer victimization among schoolchildren: Correlations, causes, consequences, and considerations in assessment and intervention. *School Psychology Quarterly, 23*(4), 451–461.

Chandler, K., Nolin, M. J., & Davies, E. (1995). *Student strategies to avoid harm at school.* Retrieved January 8, 2008, from http://nces.ed.gov/pubs95/web/95203.asp.

Charach, A., Pepler, D., & Ziegler, S. (1995, Spring). Bullying at school: A Canadian perspective. *Education Canada*, 12–18.

Cowie, H. (2013). The immediate and long-term effects of bullying. In I. Rivers & N. Duncan (Eds.), *Bullying: Experiences and Discourses of Sexuality and Gender*, (pp. 10–18). New York, NY: Routledge.

DeVoe, J.F., Kaffenberger, S., & Chandler, K. (2005). *Student reports of bullying: Results from the 2001 school crime supplement to the national crime supplement to the national crime victimization survey.* Washington D.C.: U.S. Department of Education, 2005.

Elinoff, M. J., Chafouleas, S. M., & Sassu, K. A. (2004). Bullying: Considerations for defining and intervening in school settings. *Psychology in the Schools, 41*(8), 887–897.

Forero, R., McLellan, L., Rissel, C., & Bauman, A. (1999). Bullying behaviour and psychosocial health among school students in New South Wales, Australia. *British Medical Journal, 319*, 344–348.

Frey, K.S., Hirschstein, M.K., Snell, J.L., Van Schoiack Edstrom, L., MacKenzie, E.P., & Broderick, C.J. (2005). Reducing playground bullying and supporting beliefs: An experimental trial of the Steps to Respect program. *Developmental Psychology, 41*(3), 479–491.

Garrity, C., Jens, K., Porter, W., Sager, N., & Short-Camilli, C. (2004). *Bully-proofing your school (3rd ed.).* Longmont, CO: Sopris West.

Hay, C., & Meldrum, R. (2010). Bullying victimization and adolescent self-harm: Testing hypotheses from general strain theory. *Journal of Youth and Adolescence, 39*(5), 446–459.

Hirschstein, M.K., Van Schoiack Edstrom, L., Frey, K.S., Snell, J.L., & MacKenzie, E.P. (2007). Walking the talk in bullying prevention: Teacher implementation variables related to initial impact of the Steps to Respect program. *School Psychology Review, 36*(1), 3–21.

Hoover, J. H., Oliver, R., & Hazier, R. J. (1992). Bullying: Perceptions of adolescent victims in the Midwestern USA. *School Psychology International, 13*, 5–16.

Hoover, J. H., & Oliver, R. (1996). *The bullying prevention handbook: A guide for principals, teachers, and counselors.* Bloomington, IN: National Educational Service.

Hugh-Jones, S., & Smith, P. K. (1999). Self-reports of short-and-long-term effects of bullying on children who stammer. *British Journal of Educational Psychology, 9*, 141–158.

Kärnä, A., M. Voeten, T. Little, E. Poskiparta, E. Alanen, & C. Salmivalli. (2011). Going to scale: A nonrandomized nationwide trial of KiVa Antibullying Program for grades 1–9. *Journal of Consulting and Clinical Psychology*, *79*(6), 796–805.

Leary, M., R. Kowalski, L. Smith, & S. Phillips. (2003). Teasing, rejection, and violence: Case studies of the school shootings. *Aggressive Behavior*, *29*, 202–214.

Lodge, J. & Frydenberg, E. (2005). The role of peer bystanders in school bullying: Positive steps toward promoting peaceful schools. *Theory into Practice, 44*(4), 329–336.

Malti, T., Perren, S., & Buchmann, M. (2010). Children's peer victimization, empathy, and emotional symptoms. *Child Psychiatry and Human Development, 41*, 98–113.

McNamara, B. & McNamara, F. (1997). *Keys to dealing with bullies*. Hauppague, NY: Barron's.

Melton, G.B., Limber, S., Flerx, V., Cunningham, P., Osgood, D.W., Chambers, J., Henggler, S., & Nation, M. (1998). *Violence among rural youth: Final report to the Office of Juvenile Justice and Delinquency Prevention.* Washington D.C.: Office of Juvenile Justice and Delinquency Prevention.

Nakamoto, J., & D. Schwartz. (2010). Is peer victimization associated with academic achievement? A meta-analytic review. *Social Development, 19*, 221–242.

Nickerson, A. B., Mele, D., & Princiotta, D. (2008). Attachment and empathy as predictors of roles as defenders or outsiders in bullying interactions. *Journal of School Psychology*, 46(6), 687–703.

O'Connell, P., Pepler, D., & Craig, W. (1999). Peer involvement in bullying: Insights and challenges for intervention. *Journal of Adolescence, 22*, 437–452.

Olweus, D. (1973). *Victims and bullies: Research on school bullying*. Stockholm: Almqvist & Wicksell.

Olweus, D. (1978). *Aggression in the schools: Bullies and whipping boys*. London: Hemisphere.

Olweus, D. (1981). Bullying among school-boys. In N. Catwell (Ed.), *Children and violence* (pp. 97–131). Stockholm: Akademilitteratur.

Olweus, D. (1984). Aggressors and their victims: Bullying at school. In N. Freude & H. Gault (Eds.), *Disruptive behaviour in schools* (pp. 57–76). New York: Wiley.

Olweus, D. (1986). Aggression and hormones: Behavioral relationship with testosterone and adrenaline. In D. Olweus, J. Block, & M. Radke-Yarrow (Eds.), *Development of antisocial and prosocial behaviour* (pp. 51–72). New York: Academic Press.

Olweus, D. (1991). The bullying/victim problems among school children: Basic facts and effects of a school-based intervention program. In K.H. Rubin & D.J. Pepler (Eds.), *The development and treatment of childhood aggression* (pp. 411–448). Hillsdale, NJ: Erlbaum.

Olweus, D. (1993). *Bullying at school: What we know and what we can do*. Cambridge, MA: Blackwell Publishers.

Olweus, D. (1993b). Victimization by peers: Antecedents and long-term outcomes. In K. H. Rubin & J. B. Asendorf (Eds.), *Social withdrawal, inhibition, and shyness* (pp. 315–341). Hillsdale, NJ: Erlbaum

Olweus, D. (1994) Annotation: Bullying at school: Basic facts and effects of a school based intervention program. *Journal of Child Psychology and Psychiatry and Allied Disciplines, 35*, 1171–1190.

Olweus, D. (1995). Bullying or peer abuse in school: Fact and intervention. *Current Directions in Psychological Science, 4*, 196–200.

Olweus, D. (1997). Bully/victim problems in school: Facts and intervention. *European Journal of Psychology of Education, 12*, 495–510.

Olweus, D., Limber, S., & Mihalic, S. F. (1999). *Blueprints for violence prevention. Book nine: Bullying prevention program.* Boulder, CO: Center for the Study and Prevention of Violence.

Olweus, D., & Limber, S. (2002). *Bullying prevention program (Blueprints for violence prevention)*. Washington, DC: Center for the Study of Prevention of Violence, Institute of Behavioral Science, University of Colorado at Boulder.

O'Moore, A., & Minton, S. (2005). Evaluation of the effectiveness of an anti-bullying programme in primary schools. *Aggressive Behavior, 31*(6), 609–622.

Ortega, R., & Lera, M.J. (2000). The Seville anti-bullying in school project. *Aggressive Behavior, 26*(1), 113–123.

Ortega, R., Elipe, P., Mora-Merchán, J. A., Genta, M. L., Brighi, A., Guarini, A. & Tippett, N. (2012). The emotional impact of bullying and cyberbullying on victims: a European cross-national study. *Aggressive behavior, 38*(5), 342–356.

Pellegrini, A. D. (1998). Bullies and victims in school: A review and call for research. *Journal of Applied Developmental Psychology, 19,* 165–176.

Pulkkinen, L., & Tremblay, R. E. (1992). Patterns of boys' social adjustment in two cultures and at different ages: A longitudinal perspective. *International Journal of Behavioral Development, 15,* 527–553.

Rudolph, K. D., Lansford, J. E., Agoston, A. M., Sugimura, N., Schwartz, D., Dodge, K. A., & Bates, J. E. (2013). Peer victimization and social alienation: predicting deviant peer affiliation in middle school. *Child Development, 85*(1), 124–139.

Salmivalli, C., Kaukiainen, A., & Voeten, M. (2005). Anti-bullying intervention: Implementation and outcome. *British Journal of Educational Psychology, 75*(3), 465–487.

Schneider, S. K., O'Donnell, L., Stueve, A., & Coulter, R. W. (2012). Cyberbullying, school bullying, and psychological distress: A regional census of high school students. *American Journal of Public Health, 102*(1), 171–177.

Schreier, A., Wolke, D., Thomas, K., Horwood, J., Hollis, C., Gunnell, D., et. al. (2009). Prospective study of peer victimization in childhood and psychotic symptoms in the nonclinical population at age 12 years. *Archives of General Psychiatry, 66,* 527–536.

Sharp, S. (1995). How much does bullying hurt? *Educational and Child Psychology, 12,* 81–88.

Smokowski, P. R. and Kopasz, K. H. (2005). Bullying in school: An overview of types, effects, family characteristics, and intervention strategies. *Children & Schools, (27)2,* 101–110.

U.S. Secret Service & U.S. Department of Education. (2004). *The final report and findings of the safe school initiative: Implications for the prevention of school attacks in the United States.* Washington D.C.: Authors. Retrieved June 29, 2014 from http://www2.ed.gov/admins/lead/safety/preventingattacksreport.pdf

Vreeman, R., & A. Carroll. (2007). A systematic review of school-based interventions to prevent bullying. *Archives of Pediatrics and Adolescence Medicine, 161,* 78–88.

Whitney, I., & Smith, P. K. (1993). A survey of the nature of extent of bullying in junior/middle and secondary schools. *Educational Research, 35,* 3–25.

Wolke, D., Copeland, W. E., Angold, A., & Costello, E. J. (2013). Impact of bullying in childhood on adult health, wealth, crime, and social outcomes. *Psychological Science, 24*(10), 1958–1970.

Ziegler, S. & Pepler, D. J. (1993). Bullying at school: Pervasive and persistent. *Orbit, 24,* 29–31.

Chapter 8

Reducing Disproportionate Minority Contact in Schools: Stemming the School to Prison Pipeline

David C. May and Ethan Stokes

Over the years, there have been many efforts made to reform public schools through policy changes (e.g., *No Child Left Behind Act* of 2001) that have resulted in a growing standardization of public schools across the nation. Nevertheless, these efforts to broaden and strengthen the U.S. educational experience in primary and secondary schools have not always been successful. In fact, in numerous public school districts throughout the United States, the state's department of education has taken over the day-to-day operations of failing school districts and there remains a large portion of students across the country that only have access to low-quality public education (Howard, 2013). These areas are overwhelmingly areas where students of color and lower socioeconomic status reside.

Because of the poorer quality of education in these schools, graduates (or, even worse, those students that drop out) from these schools have limited chances of educational and economic success. This, coupled with the fact that the overall well-being of racial minorities (especially African American males), is at risk because of reduced likelihood of good health, employability, and economic income, makes it highly unlikely that these groups will obtain equality with white males in the United States (Noguera, 2009). As with many minority groups, black males are stereotyped by the larger society and modern cultural norms that often hinder their individual capabilities (Noguera, 2009; Townsend, 2000).

Thus, the status of African Americans in the United States has a lot of room for improvement. This room for improvement is particularly evident in the area of school discipline. In 1973, only 6% of all African American students received out-of-school suspension; by 2006, this percentage had risen to 15% (Osher et al., 2012) and, by 2010, one in four (24.3%) black students were suspended compared to less than 1 in 10 (7.1%) white students (Losen & Martinez, 2013). During the 2009–2010 school year, using data from approximately 26,000 middle and high schools across the United States, over two million students were suspended at least once (Losen & Martinez, 2013). What is most troubling is that Losen and Martinez (2013) found that the overwhelming majority of school suspensions result from less-serious violations of school policies such as class disturbance, arriving late to class, and violating the school dress code (all of which are non-violent and non-criminal behaviors). The numbers from the 2010 school year indicate black students were three times more likely to receive a suspension than white students in U.S. high schools. These findings force us to consider why the rates of suspension for black students have increased in the modern era.

Whenever a group of people is represented in a particular area at levels greater than their representation in the general population, they are said to have disproportionate representation in that area. According to the 2010 census data, 13% of the population in the United States is black (U.S. Census, 2014). Thus, whenever more than 13% of the population of students is suspended, this becomes known as disproportionate suspensions of black students. Given the data presented earlier and discussed later in this chapter, most school districts in the United States have disproportionate suspensions of black students. Nevertheless, the problem of disproportionate minority suspensions is not restricted to African American students alone, nor is the disproportionality limited to suspensions in the education system. In the United States, public schools also experience disproportionate minority dropouts and disproportionate minority expulsions. According to the National Center for Education Statistics (NCES), Hispanic students had the highest dropout rates (28%) when compared to African American (13%) and white (7%) students in the year 2000 (NCES, 2003). In the 2005–2006 academic year, black students were nearly four times more likely to be expelled from school than white students (OCR, 2008). In 2009, the NCES reported that the rates of suspension and expulsion in U.S. schools surpassed more than double the rates of suspension and expulsion in the mid-1970s (NCES, 2009). Suspension and expulsions are not limited to any level of school; in other words, the problem of disproportionate minority suspensions impacts elementary, middle, and high school kids. To assume that the problem of disproportionality in school discipline is primarily a teenage problem is certainly not the case.

Causes

Perhaps one of the most prevailing arguments against acknowledging the disproportionate suspensions and other disciplinary actions taken against racial minorities is the notion of personal responsibility of the student. Some individuals point fingers at the parents of students who frequently encounter discipline issues within schools, arguing that they cannot control their children and have not "raised them right," and thus they are the problem. However, to solely emphasize personal and parental responsibility and ignore larger societal factors that impact disproportionality is to disregard numerous larger social structures that have a profound impact on a student's attitudes and behaviors about life, school, and obedience (Hirschfield, 2008). The factors we consider as prominent causes to deviant behavior in the classroom are socioeconomic status, the relationship between teachers and students, and the role of parents in a student's life.

Socioeconomic Status

The socioeconomic background of a student can have a lasting effect on the student's behavioral and academic outcomes, not to mention the type of school that the student attends. Students who come from low-income families and low-income neighborhoods with high crime rates are more likely to fall behind in the classroom and are more likely to engage in deviant behaviors at school (Gregory et al., 2010). If a child lives in an impoverished area, the quality of school and educational attainment is much more likely to be poor. Davis and Welcher (2013) define the quality of a school by considering the academic conditions within the classrooms. In their opinion, high quality schools have increased likelihood and frequencies of good behavioral conduct within the schools (i.e. obeying school and classroom policies), more functional structural amenities offered within the school building, and teachers who care about their students. Poor children are thus less likely to attend high quality schools.

Farmer and colleagues argue that, "Antisocial behavior and youth violence is particularly high in the South" (Farmer et al., 2004: p. 318). Therefore, Farmer et al. (2004) studied minority youths from rural areas of the country with a history of low-income minority families to analyze various behavioral and disciplinary problems within schools. However, due to the small sample size of this study, the findings were not generalizable. Nonetheless, this study's focus on rural areas with high poverty rates and high populations of racial minorities should be replicated nationally to gain a better understanding of the relationship between race, poverty, community-type, and disproportionate school suspensions.

Another component of socioeconomic status that one must consider is the misperceptions about African Americans, and especially poor African Americans, by the larger society. Many news outlets jump at the opportunity to cover stories of young black males engaging in deviant and criminal activity without providing critical discussions of the economic and social hardships, as well as the inferior social status of African American males, that can have profound and detrimental impacts on an individual (Alexander, 2010; West, 2011). These prevalent false portrayals in the media reinforce the stereotypes of black males from areas of high poverty and high crime. However, one must consider the possibility that socioeconomic status is not the sole determining cause of the disproportionate suspension of racial minorities.

Davis and Welcher (2013) found that, "Black students in the highest SES quintile attend schools with lower school quality scores than whites in the lowest SES quintile" (p. 478). Similarly, Wallace et al. (2007) report that the socioeconomic status of an individual did not have an effect on the disproportionate suspension rates of racial minorities. Additionally, Skiba et al. (2002) found that race and gender, more than socioeconomic status, were primary indicators of punitiveness within schools. In other words, nonwhite students and boys were significantly more likely to receive disciplinary actions at school, regardless of their socioeconomic status (Skiba et al., 2002). Given this evidence, one must consider other possible causes of the suspension gap.

Teacher/Student Relationship

The maintenance of stable relationships between children and their families, peers, and teachers is essential to sustaining appropriate conduct and obedience in school. Two primary factors in maintaining good behavior and maximizing the academic benefits of students within schools are (1) a stable familial environment where parental support is evident and (2) a teacher's positive perceptions and positive treatment of their students' educational work and their students' behavior at school (Hinojosa, 2008).

Teachers play a key role in ensuring that their students are getting the most out of their educational experience and learning to their full potential. However, various factors such as biases toward or against students, inconsistency in handling challenging students, and poor classroom management skills often contribute to the school discipline gap. Skiba et al. (2002) found that black male students were much more likely to be punished for classroom violations that were less serious and subjective to the teacher's discretion than their white counterparts. Thus, an important component of the gap between black and white students in suspensions may be a "culture mismatch" between the largely white public school teachers and black students in their classes.

Teachers who have difficulties in teaching students with educational challenges can be problematic and can also contribute to the discipline gap. Students with learning disabilities are liable to encounter disciplinary issues due to their difficulty in adapting to classroom learning environments, and race also plays a role among students with disabilities. Krezmien et al. (2006) found that African American students with disabilities were more likely to be suspended than any other racial group. The ability to manage the day-to-day routines of a classroom (both academically and disciplinary) is vital for teachers to maximize their students learning outcomes. Poor behavioral management by teachers over their classrooms is another explanation as to how these disproportionate suspensions of racial minorities can occur. When teachers perceive the classroom environment as being chaotic and, seemingly, out of their control, school discipline policies are often enforced on the students without proper consideration of the negative effects that the policies may have on the students (Fenning & Rose, 2007).

Another factor that has the potential to increase disproportionate suspensions of black students is zero tolerance policies. Zero tolerance policies are those district and school policies that mandate predetermined, often harsh, punishments for rule violations. Zero tolerance policies are most prevalent in the area of firearms and other weapons, drugs, alcohol, and tobacco (National Association of School Psychologists, 2001). Krezmien et al. (2006) found that the use of "zero-tolerance" policies as disciplinary measures in schools is problematic because these policies do not reduce suspensions and problematic behavior. The reality is that "zero-tolerance" policies within schools eliminate the administrators' and teachers' ability to choose less-serious punishments for the students (Hirschfield, 2008; Hoffman, 2014). Sustaining these zero-tolerance policies continues to increase disproportionate suspensions of racial minority students, especially African American males (Hoffman, 2014; Krezmien et al., 2006).

Familial Support

Students who experience punitiveness from school policies are often stigmatized as the "bad kids," and this stigma, combined with a lack of support from families, teachers, and/or peers, often results in an increase of student dropout rates (Wald & Losen, 2003). Black and Hispanic students have dropout rates twice the amount of white students (Carpenter & Ramirez, 2007). Additionally, Carpenter and Ramirez (2007) found that minority students who come from single-parent homes (Hinojosa, 2008) and who have peers and siblings that have dropped out of school are far more likely to dropout themselves.

Beck and Muschkin (2012) analyzed school administrative records in North Carolina and determined that the most influential factors predicting the likelihood of schoolchildren behaving/misbehaving are familial support and demographic characteristics of each student (e.g. race, gender, and socioeconomic status). Furthermore, students whose parents have attained higher levels of education are much more likely to do well in the classroom both academically and behaviorally (Beck & Muschkin, 2012). These literatures suggest that there is much consensus that the familial support of a student has a lasting and profound impact on the student's academic life.

Consequences

Academic Productivity and Learning Capabilities

As demonstrated above, schools, particularly school discipline strategies, often have profound impacts on the lives of students. One of the most important skills that a child can obtain from their primary and secondary education is the fundamental ability to read and write. Winn and Behizadeh (2011) argue that literacy is a civil right that should not be hindered by larger institutional structures. Perhaps it seems ironic to claim that schools are preventing many of their students (especially racial minorities) from learning how to read and write, but the truth of the matter is that the disproportionate suspensions and exclusionary punitive practices against black students often prevent these students from learning basic skills in order to become functional members of society.

There is a direct correlation between those who do not excel in the classroom and those who experience the majority of punitiveness in schools (Yang, 2009). Students who struggle with their schoolwork are often pressured to the point that they become discouraged and insecure in their academic abilities. Many cope with these emotional issues by disengaging from their schoolwork and engaging in deviance at school (Gregory et al., 2010; Miles & Stipek, 2006). Research continually shows that White and Asian Americans have higher scores on achievement tests than Latino, African American, and Native American students (Gregory et al., 2010). The inability to read and write in a proficient and critical-thinking manner inevitably results in a difficulty to actively engage in the larger social, political, cultural, and economic contexts of adulthood (Winn & Behizadeh, 2011). Furthermore, disproportionate suspension of minority students often leads to an increase in absenteeism and, even if the student finishes their secondary education, significantly affects the likelihood of the student attending and finishing college because of the habits they formed (or did not form) while receiving their K–12 education (Milner, 2013).

School Suspensions and Dropouts of Minorities

The demographics of any given student population have an effect on frequencies of deviance and, subsequently, disciplinary actions addressing deviance. Lee et al. (2011) found that schools with the highest levels of dropout rates were also the schools that had the highest levels of minority students. Furthermore, schools that report higher levels of suspension rates also report higher levels of dropout rates of their students (Lee et al., 2011; Milner, 2013). The frequency and severity of punishments that result from school suspensions, combined with the inconsistency of suspensions by race, are indicators of possible systemic and individual racism on the part of school districts, administrative leaders, and schoolteachers (Milner, 2013).

Losen and Gillespie (2012) argue that the fact that disproportionate suspensions of poor and minority students occur raises an issue of civil rights violations and systemic discrimination on many levels. Nonetheless, suspension rates, especially by race, differ from state to state. From their sample of data, Losen and Gillespie (2012) found that Illinois had the highest percentage of suspending African Americans (25%), North Carolina had the highest percentage of suspending Native Americans (18%), and Connecticut had the highest percentage of suspending Hispanic Americans (14%). In many of the country's largest school districts, suspension rates were nearly 20% of the entire district's student population (Losen & Gillespie, 2012). Wallace et al. (2007) found that white and Asian students were slightly less likely than their African American, Hispanic, and American Indian peers to be sent to the office for minor classroom infractions and were significantly less likely than their racial minority peers to be suspended or expelled from school because of disciplinary issues.

Perhaps one of the biggest problems facing young African American males in schools is that the rates of suspensions and dropouts have been, and remain, so prevalent that this behavioral expectation has become the norm in many U.S. schools (Noguera, 2009). This stereotypical norm even resonates within the minority group, where many African American youths consider their failure in the education system just part of the African American experience. Thus, the idea that because a student is black, particularly a black male, they will not be successful in school becomes a self-fulfilling prophecy. The disproportionate rates of school suspensions by race are reflective of larger issues such as the often-repeated stereotypes of African American males and the poor (Monroe, 2005; Noguera, 2009). Especially in regard to black males, the social and cultural norms and expectations of this group often result in a failure to break free of these predetermined perceptions and, thus, stigmatization of the group and individuals is inevitable (Noguera, 2009).

Method

In March 2014, the U.S. Department of Education Office of Civil Rights released their *Data Snapshot: School Discipline, Issue Brief #1* (U.S. Department of Education Office of Civil Rights, 2014). Because these data (from the 2011–2012 school year) were the most recent national data available at the time of this writing, we felt that these data would best demonstrate the topic of discussion for this chapter. The tables below are derived from that data, as is much of the discussion around those tables.

To obtain the data analyzed here, the U.S. Department of Education's Office of Civil Rights (OCR) obtains data from public schools in all 50 states and the District of Columbia that serve students for at least 50% of the day. These data thus include data from traditional public schools but also include data from long-term secure juvenile justice agencies, alternative schools, and schools for the blind and deaf. These data are collected every two years. For the 2011–2012 data collection, the OCR had a response rate of 98.4% of public school districts, which encompassed 99.2% of all public schools in the United States (U.S. Department of Education Office of Civil Rights, 2014).

For the purposes of comparison by race, school districts reported data categorized into seven racial categories: (1) Hispanic/Latino, (2) White, (3) Black/African-American, (4) Asian, (5) Native Hawaiian/Other Pacific Islander, (6) American Indian/Alaska Native, and (7) Two or More Races. Thus, the tables included below categorize the race of the students using those seven categories.

In Table 8.1, we present the three most well-known disciplinary actions (in-school suspension, out-of-school suspension, and expulsion) by race. Additionally, we include a fourth category that represents those students that received multiple out-of-school suspensions during the 2011–2012 school year. The results presented in Table 8.1 indicate that, although African American students comprise only 16% of the total enrolled students in the United States, one in three students that received an in-school suspension (32%), out-of-school suspension (33%), or expulsion (34%) was African American. Additionally, almost half (42%) of those students receiving multiple suspensions in 2011–2012 were African-American. Thus, the problem of disproportionate suspensions and expulsions of African American students continues in the most recent year for which data are available.

The results presented in Table 8.1 also reveal a number of other important pieces of information. Neither Hispanic, Native Hawaiian, Asian, nor multi-racial (students of two or more races) students were disproportionately represented in these disciplinary actions. On the other hand, American Indian students were represented at four times greater than their rate in the enrolled population for out-of-school suspensions (2% of all students that received out of-school suspensions were American Indian, compared to only 0.5% of the students in the general enrolled population) and six times greater for expulsions (3% of the total expelled population). What has long been a problem for African American students now also appears to be a problem for American Indian students as well.

The results presented in Table 8.2 depict the percentage of total students by race/gender category that received an out-of-school suspension in 2011–2012. Although about 1 in 16 white males (6%) received an out-of-school suspension in 2011–2012, one in five (20%) black males received an out-of-school suspension. Thus, black males

Table 8.1. Students Receiving Suspensions and Expulsions, by Race and Ethnicity

	Percent of Total Enrolled Students	Percent of Total In-School Suspensions	Percent of Total Out-of-School Suspensions (Single Offense)	Percent of Total Out-of-School Suspensions (Multiple Offenses)	Percent of Total Expulsions
White	51.0	40.0	36.0	31.0	36.0
Black/African American	16.0	32.0	33.0	42.0	34.0
Hispanic/Latino of any race	24.0	22.0	23.0	21.0	22.0
Native Hawaiian/Other Pacific Islander	0.5	0.2	0.4	0.3	0.3
Asian	5.0	1.0	2.0	1.0	1.0
American Indian/Alaska Native	0.5	0.2	2.0	2.0	3.0
Two or more races	2.0	3.0	3.0	3.0	3.0

This table was created by the authors using data presented in charts from the United States Department of Education Office of Civil Rights available at http://www2.ed.gov/about/offices/list/ocr/docs/crdc-discipline-snapshot.pdf3.

Table 8.2. Percentage of Total Students by Racial Category Receiving Out-of-School Suspensions by Gender

	Males	Females
White	6	2
Black/African American	20	12
Hispanic/Latino of any race	9	4
Native Hawaiian/Other Pacific Islander	7	3
Asian	3	1
American Indian/Alaska Native	13	7
Two or more races	11	5

were more than three times as likely as white males to receive an out-of-school suspension in 2011–2012. In fact, with the exception of Asian males (3%), males from each of the nonwhite categories were more likely than whites to be suspended.

The results presented in Table 8.2 portray a similar picture for females. Although only 1 in 50 white females were suspended (2%), approximately 1 in 8 black females were suspended (12%). Thus, black females were six times as likely as white females to be suspended in 2011–2012. Again, with the exception of Asian females (1%), females from each of the nonwhite categories were more likely than whites to be suspended.

As Tables 8.1 and 8.2 clearly demonstrate, black males and females are significantly more likely than white males and females to receive out-of-school suspensions. Nevertheless, the data presented in those tables do not allow the reader to determine the types of behaviors in which students were engaging that caused them to receive that out-of-school suspension. In 2011, the lead author for this chapter was employed as the Kentucky Center for School Safety Research Fellow. As part of that role, we released a report entitled *Kentucky 2010: Eleventh Annual Safe Schools Data Project* in which we compared the types of behaviors for which students received disciplinary actions by racial category. In that report, we examined racial differences for all disciplinary actions (instead of only out-of-school suspensions as presented in Tables 8.1 and 8.2). Because we did not collect data on In-School Suspensions, however, 97.3% of the disciplinary actions for board violations (61,236 out 62,917 disciplinary actions) were out-of-school suspensions and 96.4% of the disciplinary actions for law violations were out-of-school suspensions (4,840 out of 5,019). The Kentucky Department of Education assumed data reporting responsibilities upon the completion of that report and thus this report is the last one publicly available with the level of detail needed for this analysis.

In the tables below, we present disciplinary actions for 8 board violations (Table 8.3) and 10 law violations (Table 8.4) by race of the student receiving the disciplinary action. In the Appendix to this chapter, we have included a definition of each of the types of violations under consideration in those tables. In general, board violations are actions in which students engage that violate some policy created by the school board prohibiting that action (e.g., tardiness, failure to attend detention, tobacco violations) while law violations are those actions in which students engage that violate a statutory law prohibiting that action.

The results presented in Table 8.3 depict the proportions of students receiving disciplinary actions for board violations in the state of Kentucky in 2009–2010. In 2009–2010, black students comprised approximately 10% of the student enrollment in public schools in Kentucky (May & Chen, 2011). Thus, with the exception of disciplinary actions for tobacco violations, black students are disproportionately represented in disciplinary actions for all board violations. For each of the seven remaining board violations, the proportion of students receiving disciplinary actions for board violations is at least twice the proportion of black students found in the typical student population. Furthermore, for defiance of authority, disturbing class, inappropriate sexual behavior, and threat/intimidation, the proportion of students receiving disciplinary actions that are black is three times higher than the proportion found in the general student enrollment. In general, these board violations are those for which teachers and administrators have the most discretion. This finding will be discussed in detail below.

Table 8.3. Total Students by Racial Category Receiving Disciplinary Actions for Board Violations in Kentucky (2009–2010)

	Whites N (%)	Blacks N (%)	Others N (%)
Defiance of Authority	8262 (64)	3931 (30)	769 (6)
Disturbing Class	8327 (64)	3947 (30)	725 (6)
Failure to Attend Detention	1073 (72)	310 (21)	117 (8)
Fighting	10661 (66)	4616 (29)	896 (6)
Inappropriate Sexual Behavior	425 (59)	254 (35)	38 (5)
Profanity or Vulgarity	3092 (73)	937 (22)	234 (5)
Threat/Intimidation	4322 (57)	2845 (37)	422 (6)
Tobacco Violations	1687 (94)	67 (4)	38 (2)
Dangerous Instruments	584 (71)	175 (21)	59 (7)

* In 2009–2010, 82.5% of the student population was white, 10.6% was black, and 6.8% were of race/ethnicities other than White or Black (May & Chen, 2011).

The results presented in Table 8.4 depict the proportions of students receiving disciplinary actions for the six most serious law violations (with the exception of forcible rape and murder, for which there were no disciplinary actions in 2009–2010) and the four most frequently occurring less serious law violations in the state of Kentucky in 2009–2010. As with board violations, Blacks are disproportionately represented in disciplinary actions for law violations as well. The greatest disproportionality occurs for robbery (70% of students receiving disciplinary actions were black) and motor vehicle theft (60%). Blacks were least likely to receive disciplinary actions for drug abuse violations (18%) and aggravated assault (18%).

Discussion

In this chapter, we have discussed the disproportionate representation of minorities in general, but particularly African American students, in disciplinary actions in schools. Research at the national level suggests that black students (and, to some extent, Native American students) receive a disproportionate amount of out-of-school suspensions each year. As reviewed above, these suspensions have serious consequences for students in general, but particularly students of color. Educational success, coupled with family, social, and economic support, are key to being successful in the United States. When students are suspended, they become more likely to have poor educational outcomes and more likely to drop out of school; thus, any disproportionality that occurs in suspensions or other disciplinary actions disproportionately impacts those groups that receive the disciplinary actions.

Table 8.4. Total Students by Racial Category Receiving Disciplinary Actions for Part I and Select Part II Law Violations in Kentucky (2009–2010)

	Whites N (%)	Blacks N (%)	Others N (%)
Arson	29 (64)	14 (31)	2 (4)
Aggravated Assault	27 (82)	6 (18)	0 (0)
Burglary	13 (62)	8 (38)	0 (0)
Larceny-Theft	53 (56)	36 (38)	5 (5)
Motor Vehicle Theft	2 (40)	3 (60)	0 (0)
Robbery	6 (22)	19 (70)	2 (7)
Drug Abuse	1808 (76)	433 (18)	149 (6)
Simple Assault	364 (56)	245 (37)	45 (7)
Disorderly Conduct	194 (56)	127 (37)	24 (7)
Terroristic Threatening	193 (68)	74 (26)	18 (6)

* In 2009–2010, 82.5% of the student population was white, 10.6% was black, and 6.8% were of race/ethnicities other than White or Black (May & Chen, 2011).

One of the most controversial consequences of disproportionate suspensions is what has become known as the "school-to-prison" pipeline. According to Wald and Losen (2003), nearly 68% of state prison inmates in the late 1990s did not finish their high school education. This suggests that dropping out of school leads to criminal involvement and supports the concept of the "school-to-prison pipeline." The American Civil Liberties Union (ACLU) defines the school-to-prison pipeline as "the policies and practices that push our nation's schoolchildren, especially our most at-risk children, out of classrooms and into the juvenile and criminal justice systems. This pipeline reflects the prioritization of incarceration over education" (2013: p. 1). The students who are "most at-risk" are primarily poor, racial minorities that live in areas with high-crime rates and have unstable familial support. Overall, minority students (specifically African Americans and Latinos) are much more likely to be funneled through the school-to-prison pipeline than their white peers (Alexander, 2010; Hirschfield, 2008; Wald & Losen, 2003).

The school-to-prison pipeline drastically affects a youth's outlook on life and, thus, seemingly normalizes the expectation of deviance. Furthermore, those who are prone to falling victim to the pipeline lose self-worth and hope for their future in learning that their lives are dispensable (Winn & Behizadeh, 2011). As Noguera (2009) notes, African American males are ten times more likely to go to prison than any other group in the United States. Therefore, one can gather that the substantial increase in the likelihood of black males going to prison when compared to other races, combined with the pessimistic outlook on life that is common amongst those who have experienced school failure, leads to a better understanding of the attitudinal and behavioral consequences that can result from dire situations.

Education plays a vital role in determining if an individual is likely to experience the pipeline. One of the key predictors to becoming a part of the school-to-prison pipeline is having subpar literacy skills or no literacy skills at all (Winn & Behizadeh, 2011). The lower one's educational attainment, the more likely they are to be arrested and incarcerated as adults (Pettit & Western, 2004; Wald & Losen, 2003). Ewert and Wildhagen (2011) explain that the adult correctional population is more likely to have a GED and less likely to have more than a high school education than the general population. In fact, the average prisoner is less educated than both the population of general households and the population of low socioeconomic households in the United States (Ewert & Wildhagen, 2011).

Conclusions and Policy Implications

The data presented in this chapter are enlightening for a number of reasons. Perhaps the most enlightening data were presented in Tables 8.3 and 8.4. Recall that most of the disciplinary actions experienced by public school students in Kentucky in 2009–2010 (and by most students in public schools everywhere in the United States at any time), involved disciplinary actions for student behavior that violated school board policies, not state statutes. In other words, most students that receive disciplinary actions (whether white, black, or of some other ethnicity) are disciplined for violations of school board policies that involve a tremendous amount of discretion on the part of teachers and administrators.

To illustrate this point, consider the following situation. David, a ninth grade student attending Mr. Jones' American History class, "talks back" to Mr. Jones when Mr. Jones tells him to remove his hat and open his textbook. Mr. Jones has a variety of options at this point, one of which is to send the student to the principal's office for defiance of authority. This office referral, coupled with one or more previous office referrals for David from Mr. Jones or some other teacher, may be enough to warrant an out-of-school suspension for David.

However, Mr. Jones has a variety of other options he could use to avoid that office referral and subsequent suspension. In fact, it may be that another student that Mr. Jones thinks highly of did not want to open his textbook either. In that case, Mr. Jones asked the student to step outside, understood from the student that he was having personal issues at home, and reasoned with the student to avoid any further confrontation.

Our belief is that the vast majority of public school educators are in the trade because they love children and feel education is important for everyone. However, teachers, particularly those with relatively little experience interacting with other cultures, may be particularly defensive about student behaviors that undermine their authority. A famous quote (often attributed to Dan Brown in his book *The Lost Symbol*) states that "we all fear what we do not understand." Thus, teachers that do not understand the impetus for a student's "disrespect" (or vulgarity, or tardiness, or dozens of other behaviors that occur in schools daily) may fear that behavior will lead to further misbehavior or even violence. Thus, they may act harshly when other options could be just as effective but have not been considered.

To reduce disproportionate disciplinary actions of black students, we agree with Fenning and Rose (2007) who suggest that schools should consider disciplinary policy changes by: (1) examining data around disciplinary infractions and the racial and class proportions of those infractions, (2) constructing a team of decision-makers to collectively decide on punitive policies that are progressive and fair to all students, (3) making improvements in programs that emphasize school-wide development for both the students and their parents, and (4) developing discipline policies within schools that are more progressive and stress the importance of positive reinforcement to support good behavior. School discipline should be data-driven. As mentioned in the next chapter, schools regularly rely on out-of-school suspension as a primary disciplinary action, even when they know that out-of-school suspension does not deter future misbehavior and has serious negative consequences for future success. There are a number of alternatives that should thus be considered.

A more macro-level approach may be needed as well. In addressing policies for consideration, we believe that a collective and systemic overhaul may be helpful in solving a clearly broken system. Similar to Davis and Welcher's (2013) argument, we argue that policies must be implemented to address the racial inequalities in access to adequate resources to improve the overall quality of these schools. Losen (2011) suggests that the concept of "school efficacy" should be determined through multiple factors and one of those factors should be the rate of out-of-school suspensions. Another policy consideration is for lawmakers to incentivize systemic and school policy improvements at the state, district, and local school levels (Losen, 2011). We further join Stincomb et al (2006) who suggests that policies be implemented to abandon the practices of "zero-tolerance" in disciplining students. In the modern U.S., "three-strikes" policies have been common throughout the criminal justice system, even though they are demonstrably ineffective, and that may be a cause for the harshness and disproportionality of punitive measures within schools. Most states are now moving away from three-strikes policies; schools should join them in that move away from zero tolerance.

In addition, Losen and Skiba (2010) recommended three policies to consider as possibilities. First, they suggest better use of school disciplinary records and, especially, an increase of this information separated by demographics (e.g., race, gender, and socioeconomic status), (2) a heightened awareness of, and a need to provide direct administrative assistance to schools and school districts with the highest suspension rates, and (3) an increased openness to allow the U.S. Department of Education Office for Civil Rights (OCR) to investigate incidents of punitiveness that might be considered unlawful or discriminatory (Losen, 2011; Losen & Skiba, 2010).

Krezmien et al. (2006) further suggested that experts in the areas of special education and other leaders in administrative positions should be leaders in developing discipline policies for students with learning disabilities (and from lower socioeconomic status) because of their expertise and training in those areas. On the other hand, Beck and Muschkin (2012) argue that the gap of success in schools between white and black students would be dramatically reduced if socioeconomic levels were more equally distributed amongst the students by race. Another factor that could result in the improvement of school quality for racial minorities could be taken at the community-level where improvements in social, political, economic, and infrastructural conditions are addressed. Strategies that are more culturally aware and sensitive to the backgrounds of many racial minorities are also needed (Townsend, 2000). Improvement in classroom and behavioral management skills of teachers is another priority for reducing the discipline gap (Losen, 2011). As Monroe (2005, 2006) suggests, the best way to address the disproportionate rates of school suspensions is to develop approaches that prepare teachers and administrative officials to be race-conscious and to consider larger social structures (e.g., poverty) that may have an effect on student behavior.

Perhaps one of the most effective ways to alleviate this problem is to adopt the philosophy of restorative justice when making policy decisions about school punitiveness. The restorative justice approach is characterized by individuals who share similar beliefs in restoring and converting deviant students into productive and well-equipped students in order to assimilate them back into the school population and their local communities (Stincomb et al., 2006). Through this holistic approach toward reducing disproportionate suspensions of racial minorities, and particularly African American students, we believe the outcomes will be the most beneficial and effective for the entire student population.

Appendix*

Board Violations

Dangerous instruments include objects (other than firearms or deadly weapons) that are brought on school grounds by a student to be used as a weapon.

Defiance of authority includes any action in which a student engages that undermines the authority of teachers, administrators, or staff at the school. Examples include cheating, dress code violations, skipping class or school, tardiness, truancy, etc.

Disturbing class includes any activity that disrupts the educational process activity. This would include disruptive behavior on the bus.

Failure to attend detention occurs when a student does not attend a mandatory detention given to the student by the school administration.

Fighting includes student-to-student fighting or student-to-staff fighting.

Inappropriate sexual behavior includes sexual behaviors deemed inappropriate by school administrators.

Threat/Intimidation includes bullying, harassment, and threats made to students or staff.

Tobacco violations include possession, distribution, or use of tobacco products on school grounds.

Law Violations

Aggravated assault: Assault with intent to cause serious bodily injury.

Arson: Any intentional burning or attempt to burn, with or without intent to defraud, a dwelling house, public building, motor vehicle, or aircraft.

Burglary: A person is guilty of burglary when, with the intent to commit a crime, he knowingly enters or remains unlawfully in a building. A building, in addition to its ordinary meaning, means any structure, vehicle, watercraft or aircraft where any person lives or where people assemble for purposes of business, government, education, religion, entertainment or public transportation. Thus, breaking into a bus and stealing something from the bus would be counted as burglary.

Disorderly conduct: Committing a breach of the peace. In Kentucky, a person is guilty of disorderly conduct when in a public place and with intent to cause public inconvenience, annoyance or alarm, or creating a risk thereof, he: (a) Engages in fighting or in violent, tumultuous or threatening behavior; or (b) Makes unreasonable noise; or (c) Refuses to obey an official order to disperse issued to maintain public safety in dangerous proximity to a fire, hazard or other emergency; or (d) Creates a hazardous or physically offensive condition by any act that serves no legitimate purpose.

Drug abuse: Possession and/or distribution of alcohol or an illegal or unauthorized prescription drug on school property or at a school-sponsored function.

Larceny/Theft: The intentional taking of the property of another.

Motor vehicle theft: The theft or attempted theft of a motor vehicle.

Robbery: The taking or attempting to take anything of value from the care, custody, or control of a person or persons by force or threat of force and/or putting the victim in fear.

Simple assault: Assault with intent to cause bodily injury.

Terroristic threatening: Intentionally (1) making false statements that he or she has placed a bomb on school property, (2) placing a counterfeit bomb on school property, or (3) threatening to commit an act likely to result in the death or serious injury to any student group, teacher, volunteer worker, or school employee, volunteer, or person with a right to be on school property.

* Definitions for both Board and Law violations were derived from an internal document provided as part of training to educators by the Kentucky Center for School Safety.

References

Alexander, M. (2010). *The new Jim Crow: Mass incarceration in the age of colorblindness.* New York, NY: The New Press.

American Civil Liberties Union. (2013). *Annual report 2013.* Retrieved February 27, 2014 from https://www.aclu.org/sites/default/files/assets/aclu_annual_report_2013.pdf.

Anderson, E. (2011). *Against the wall: Poor, young, black, and male.* Philadelphia, PA: University of Pennsylvania Press.

Beck, A. N., & Muschkin, C. G. (2012). The enduring impact of race: Understanding disparities in student disciplinary infractions and achievement. *Sociological Perspectives, 55*(4), 637–662.

Carpenter, D.M., and Ramirez, A. (2007). More than one gap: Dropout rate gaps between and among Black, Hispanic, and White students. *Journal of Advanced Academics, 19*(1), 32–64.

Davis, T.M., & Welcher, A.N. (2013). School quality and the vulnerability of the Black middle class: The continuing significance of race as a predictor of disparate schooling environments. *Sociological Perspectives, 56*(4), 467–493.

Ewert, S., & Wildhagen, T. (2011). Educational characteristics of prisoners: Data from the ACS. In *Annual Meeting of the Population Association of America, Washington, DC.*

Farmer, T.W., Goforth, J.B., Man-Chi, L., Clemmer, J.T., & Thompson, J.H. (2004). School discipline problems in rural African American early adolescents: Characteristics of students with major, minor, and no offenses. *Behavioral Disorders, 29*(4), 317–336.

Fenning, P., & Rose, J. (2007). Overrepresentation of African American students in exclusionary discipline: The role of school policy. *Urban Education, 42*(6), 536–559.

Gregory, A., Skiba, R. J., & Noguera, P. A. (2010). The achievement gap and the discipline gap: Two sides of the same coin? *Educational Researcher, 39*(1), 59–68.

Hinojosa, M.S. (2008). Black-White differences in school suspension: Effect of student beliefs about teachers. *Sociological Spectrum, 28*(2), 175–193.

Hirschfield, P. J. (2008). Preparing for prison? The criminalization of school discipline in the USA. *Theoretical Criminology, 12*(1), 79–101.

Hoffman, S. (2014). Zero benefit: Estimating the effect of zero tolerance discipline policies on racial disparities in school discipline. *Educational Policy, 28*(1), 69–95.

Howard, T. C. (2013). How does it feel to be a problem? Black male students, schools, and learning in enhancing the knowledge base to disrupt deficit frameworks. *Review of Research in Education, 37*(1), 54–86.

Krezmien, M.P., Leone, P.E., & Achilles, G.M. (2006). Suspension, race, and disability: Analysis of statewide practices and reporting. *Journal of Emotional and Behavioral Disorders, 14*(4), 217–226.

Lee, T., Cornell, D., Gregory, A., & Fan, X. (2011). High suspension schools and dropout rates for Black and White students. *Education and Treatment of Children, 34*(2), 167–192.

Losen, D. (2011). Discipline policies, successful schools, and racial justice. *National Education Policy Center*. Retrieved June 10, 2014 from http://escholarship.org/uc/item/4q41361g#page-1.

Losen, D. J., & Gillespie, J. (2012). Opportunities suspended: The disparate impact of disciplinary exclusion from school. *The Civil Rights Project*. Retrieved June 10, 2014 from http://escholarship.org/uc/item/3g36n0c3#page-1.

Losen, D. J., & Martinez, T. E. (2013). Out of school and off track: The overuse of suspensions in American middle and high schools. *The Civil Rights Project*. Retrieved June 10, 2014 from http://civilrightsproject.ucla.edu/resources/projects/center-for-civil-rights-remedies/school-to-prison-folder/federal-reports/out-of-school-and-off-track-the-overuse-of-suspensions-in-american-middle-and-high-schools.

Losen, D. J., & Skiba, R. J. (2010). Suspended education: Urban middle schools in crisis. *The Civil Rights Project*. Retrieved February 25, 2014 from http://escholarship.org/uc/item/8fh0s5dv#page-4.

May, D.C., & Chen, Y. (2011). *Kentucky 2010: Eleventh annual safe schools data project*. Richmond, KY: Kentucky Center for School Safety and Kentucky Department of Education. Retrieved June 30, 2014 from http://www.kycss.org/data10.php.

Miles, S.B., & Stipek, D. (2006). Contemporaneous and longitudinal associations between social behavior and literacy achievement in a sample of low-income elementary school children. *Child Development, 77*(1), 103–117.

Milner, H. R. (2013). Why are students of color (still) punished more severely and frequently than white students? *Urban Education, 48*(4), 483–489.

Monroe, C.R. (2005). Why are "bad boys" always black? *Clearing House, 79*(1), 45–50.

Monroe, C.R. (2006). African American boys and the discipline gap: Balancing educators' uneven hand. *Educational Horizons, 84*(2), 102–111.

National Association of School Psychologists. (2001). *Zero tolerance and alternative strategies: A fact sheet for educators and policymakers*. Retrieved June 30, 2014 from http://www.nasponline.org/resources/factsheets/zt_fs.aspx

National Center for Education Statistics. (2003). *Status and trends in the education of Hispanics*. Retrieved June 10, 2014 from http://nces.ed.gov/pubs2003/hispanics/Section3.asp.

National Center for Education Statistics (2009). *Contexts of elementary and secondary education.* Retrieved June 10, 2014 from http://nces.ed.gov/programs/coe/2009/section4/indicator28.asp.

Noguera, P. A. (2009). *The trouble with black boys: ... And other reflections on race, equity, and the future of public education.* San Francisco, CA: Jossey-Bass.

Osher, D., Coggshall, J., Colombi, G., Woodruff, D., Francois, S., & Osher, T. (2012). Building school and teacher capacity to eliminate the school-to-prison pipeline. *Teacher Education and Special Education: The Journal of the Teacher Education Division of the Council for Exceptional Children, 35*(4), 284–295.

Pettit, B., & Western, B. (2004). Mass imprisonment and the life course: Race and class inequality in U.S. incarceration. *American Sociological Review, 69,* 151–169.

Skiba, R. J., Michael, R. S., Nardo, A. C., & Peterson, R. L. (2002). The color of discipline: Sources of racial and gender disproportionality in school punishment. *The Urban Review,* 34(4), 317–342.

Stinchcomb, J. B., Bazemore, G., & Riestenberg, N. (2006). Beyond zero tolerance: Restoring justice in secondary schools. *Youth Violence and Juvenile Justice, 4*(2), 123–147.

Townsend, B. L. (2000). The disproportionate discipline of African American learners: Reducing school suspensions and expulsions. *Exceptional Children, 66*(3), 381–391.

U.S. Census. (2014). *Annual estimates of the resident population by sex, race, and Hispanic origin for the United States, states, and counties: April 1, 2010 to July 1, 2013.* Washington D.C.: Author. Retrieved June 30, 2014 from http://factfinder2.census.gov/faces/tableservices/jsf/pages/productview.xhtml?src=bkmk.

U.S. Department of Education Office of Civil Rights. (2008). *2006 data collection.* Retrieved June 10, 2014 from http://ocrdata.ed.gov/ocr2006rv30/.

Wald, J., & Losen, D. J. (2003). Defining and redirecting a school-to-prison pipeline. *New Directions for Youth Development, 2003*(99), 9–15.

Wallace, J. M., Goodkind, S., Wallace, C. M., & Bachman, J. G. (2007). Racial, ethnic, and gender differences in school discipline among U.S. high school students: 1991–2005. *The Negro Educational Review, 59*(1–2), 47–62.

Winn, M. T., & Behizadeh, N. (2011). The right to be literate: Literacy, education, and the school-to-prison pipeline. *Review of Research in Education, 35*(1), 147–173.

Yang, W.K. (2009). Discipline or punish? Some suggestions for school policy and teacher practice. *Language Arts, 87*(1), 49–61.

Chapter 9

Exploring Alternatives to Out-of-School Suspension: A Quasi-Experimental Study Examining the Effectiveness of Community Service Work

David C. May, Ethan Stokes, Ashlee Oliver, and Timothy McClure

Creating a safe school environment is an important goal for all school officials. One of the most widely used methods to assist with this goal is punishing misbehavior through use of out-of-school suspension. However, over the years, the use of out-of-school suspension to address student misbehavior, especially when used alone, has been shown to negatively impact schools, students, and communities (Brownstein, 2010; Costenbader & Markson, 1998; Garibaldi, 1980; Losen & Martinez, 2013; Morgan-D'Atrio, Northrup, LaFleur, & Spera, 1996; Raffaele-Mendez, Knoff, & Ferron, 2002; Toby & Scrupski, 1991).

To address these concerns, many districts have developed alternatives to suspensions including in-school suspension, alternative school placement, cognitive skills training, and specialized programming. While these are some of the most popular alternatives used by school administrators, the use of community service as both a punishment and learning experience is an emerging method for curbing high suspension rates. Proponents claim that community service is a way to get kids involved in their communities and reduce suspensions.

In this chapter, we explore the effectiveness of community service work as an alternative to suspension by conducting a quasi-experimental design experiment. In this experiment, we compare 17 schools that utilized a community service work program with 17 matched schools that did not to examine the impact of community service work as an alternative to suspension for board and law violations over a 12-year period. The results from this study suggest that community service work reduces the number of out-of-school suspensions for both board and law violations and, when properly implemented, may have a dramatic effect in this area.

Out-of-School Suspensions

Schools across the nation have increased their use of out-of-school suspensions in recent years to serve as punishment for disciplinary actions, even though there is no evidence to demonstrate that suspensions are effective in changing the behavior of the students (Brownstein, 2010; Henderson & Friedland, 1996). In fact, there is research to support the idea that suspension rarely benefits the student being disciplined. Concerns raised by use of out-of-school suspension include: (1) out-of-school suspensions alone are ineffective in changing student behavior (Costenbader & Markson, 1998; Garibaldi, 1980; Losen & Martinez, 2013; Morgan-D'Atrio et al., 1996; Raffaele-Mendez et al., 2002; Toby & Scrupski, 1991); (2) time out of school is often unproductive as many youth are unsupervised, placing the student and community at risk, and negating the penalty involved with the out-of-school suspension; (3) students who are suspended are more likely to fall behind academically, increasing the possibility that schools will not meet their academic goals or that the student will dropout (Christle, Jolivette, & Nelson, 2007; Council on School Health, 2013; DeRidder, 1991; Morgan-D'Atrio et al., 1996); and 4) the number of minority students suspended and expelled is disproportionate to their overall numbers in the student population (Barnhart et al., 2008; Costenbader & Markson, 1998; Dupper, 1994; Radin, 1989; Raffaele-Mendez et al., 2002; Uchitelle, Bartz, & Hillman, 1989). Out-of-school suspension thus hinders the educational process by causing students to fall behind their peers academically due to loss of instructional time and may differentially impact minority students (Dupper, 1994; Henderson & Friedland, 1996; Mattison, 2004; Radin, 1989; Raffaele-Mendez et al., 2002; Uchitelle et al., 1989).

Out-of-school suspension also reduces the support that students are given in the school environment because their teachers, administrators, and peers are not present—this reduced support increases the likelihood of a student dropping out of school altogether (Brownstein, 2010; Henderson & Friedland, 1996). Repeated removal through out-of-school suspensions may also make a student frustrated with school, distancing them from positive school interaction and a sense of belonging in their school environment. Out-of-school suspension thus may drive the at-risk student away instead of helping them to cope with and resolve the underlying problems that led to the suspensions (Christenson & Thurlow, 2004; Neeld, 1999).

Alternatives to Suspension

As noted earlier, many districts are using alternatives to out-of-school suspension. The most popular of these programs is in-school suspension. Normally, an in-school suspension would precede an out-of-school suspension or expulsion. In an in-school suspension (ISS) program, students report to an isolated room where they work on their assignments from their regular teachers. Students typically do not leave until the end of the day; lunch is often brought to the room. The adult supervising the student answers questions related only to the student's assignments and does not engage in other forms of conversation with the student. This program does isolate disruptive students from their classmates, but does so in a school setting and keeps the offending students off the streets and in school. ISS programs can be effective if designed and implemented properly (Morris & Howard, 2003; Radin, 1989).

A key component of ISS is the person that is assigned to monitor the program. This monitor can attempt to establish personal connections with the students, encourage them, and express to them that they have a worthwhile place in society. Many researchers believe that the monitor should have counseling, special education, and social work experience. Other important elements the program should possess are: isolation from the student population, operative procedures for student assignments, and professional intervention by a counselor. ISS programs accomplish the goal of removing the student from the classroom setting but do not reward the students for bad behavior by giving them a vacation from school (Vanderslice, 1999). In-school suspension programs have proven to be successful in reducing suspensions because out-of-school suspensions often result in the further resentment of conforming to school rules by those students who were suspended from school property (DeRidder, 1991; Morris & Howard, 2003).

Another type of program that has emerged as an alternative to suspension is Saturday School. One Saturday School program in Franklin, Tennessee required students to arrive in a punctual manner, complete academic exercises, write essays on discipline, and participate in behavior improvement activities (Winborn, 1992). Saturday School programs can include features such as physical labor, academic work, counseling, and detention. Some Saturday Schools have been established as a way to deal with suspensions without losing revenue through Average Daily Attendance (ADA) funds. Students in this specific program were assigned to Saturday School by the principal or assistant principal, not by classroom teachers. Parents are also made aware of the fact that their child had been assigned Saturday School so arrangements could be made to ensure the child's attendance. The program lasts for three hours on Saturday morning and includes two hours of academic work and one hour devoted to behavior improvement. This behavior improvement information comes in the form of discussion, role-playing, viewing a video, or completing worksheets. Data from research pertaining to suspensions show that Saturday School programs have a positive effect on reducing the number of suspensions in a school (Winborn, 1992).

Some alternative to suspension programs target a more specific area of interest, serving one population of students that violate a specific disciplinary action. One specific alternative to suspension program like this is a Tobacco Education Program. This program targets students who have gotten in trouble for one specific offense: the use of tobacco products. One such program is formed by a partnership between a children's hospital, the local school district, and a county tobacco free coalition in Florida. The Tobacco Alternative to Suspension (TATS) program is a three-hour course that is designed to enhance the student's knowledge of the effects of tobacco products. This program is used for first-time offenders caught using tobacco on or within 1,000 feet of school grounds. Rules for this class are similar to those of in-school suspension and Saturday School programs. The student must arrive on time, participate in all activities, abide by the Student Code of Conduct, and must not act disruptive during the class or they will be removed. The students are given a completion form once they have attended the class. Programs like TATS can be effective, but mostly assist in providing discipline for the specific area of violation (Neeld, 1999).

Another popular alternative to suspension is an alternative education center. In some districts, students are given the choice between out-of-school suspension and alternative school attendance. The student's decision to attend alternative school often gives the student a feeling of ownership and commitment to the school because they made the choice to go there. This type of alternative to suspension is often successful because it focuses more on social, emotional, personal, and academic development. There are fewer students in an alternative setting, allowing for more individual attention than a regular school setting. The teachers are an important part of the alternative school structure, because they have the ability to develop warm, caring relationships with the students. Ideally, alternative schools also encourage a supportive peer culture so that students will not only be encouraged by teachers, but will encourage each other as well (Christenson & Thurlow; 2004; Radin, 1989).

Teachers in these programs have expanded roles, serving as advisors, mentors, and counselors in addition to their educational roles. There are smaller classes in alternative schools, thus facilitating the greater individual attention mentioned previously. Counseling is an important part of the alternative education curriculum, helping students deal with problems they may have in their lives at school or away from school. Teachers are given flexibility in crafting strategies to meet the needs of their students. Another important feature in alternative education centers is parent and community involvement (Christle et al., 2007). These types of environments contribute widely to student success. At-risk students often seek out these types of environments that they do not get to experience in the regular school setting.

Some programs created as alternatives to suspension strive to provide alternatives to all types of suspension, including in-school suspension. The Student Advisory Center (SAC) concept is one brought about by the National Association of Elementary School Principals (NAESP). The NAESP believes that both in-school and out-of-school suspension programs do very little to actually change the student's attitudes and behaviors that resulted in his or her placement in the program in the first place. The SAC concept focuses on supporting the students and helping them learn how to make positive changes in their behavior. This program also aspires to promote academic success, as well as build the self-esteem of the student. The SAC model focuses on positive reinforcement and teaching students to acknowledge responsibility for their own actions. Students in SAC receive counseling and one-on-one instruction, much like that provided in an alternative center (Sanders, 2001). This SAC model developed by the NAESP could be beneficial to a school district in developing an alternative to suspension program. Staff members and students work together in the SAC to set behavioral goals and objectives for their time in the program and develop an action plan for success. The goal of this SAC is to help students improve their academic skills as well as their behavioral skills in an effort to make them a successful and productive citizen of their school and community (Sanders, 2001).

Although there are many types of alternative to suspension programs, there are certain components that are essential to make each alternative to suspension program a success. According to MacWilliams (1992), the development of additional problem-solving levels to be imposed prior to an out-of-school suspension include: time-out areas, group counseling, therapeutic discipline, in-school suspension, or combinations of each. These strategies provide a continuum of strategies to bring improvement to student behavior rather than merely identifying and punishing unacceptable behaviors (MacWilliams, 1992; Osher et al., 2010).

Community Service Work Programs

Community service is another potential alternative that can be used to alleviate some of the problems of out-of-school suspension. In these programs, students may either be required to participate in community service or required to do so in place of suspension or in addition to another alternative punishment. Community service work is a supervised and structured work experience for youth designed to meet community needs and foster the student's responsibility for personal actions. Some, like Toby and Scrupski (1991), have advocated the use of community service programs since the late 1980s, pointing to its potential to punish the student, remove him or her from the classroom, and provide a learning experience at the same time. However, it is not certain how widespread community service is in the school system. Few studies have directly evaluated the effectiveness of community service programs.

We were able to uncover only two examples of programs in the literature that use or have used community service as a disciplinary procedure. The first used community service as part of an alternative school program (Denner, Coyle, Robin, & Banspach, 2005). In this program, community service was used as a learning tool for students placed in an alternative school. Denner and colleagues (2005) focused on one aspect of the program: the use of community service in AIDS organizations to supplement HIV and pregnancy prevention curriculum. Their conclusions about the effectiveness of the program, however, described the effects of participation in a wide variety of community service activities, including working with the elderly and creating a mural in the community. The authors noted that the students, teachers, and organizations all benefited from the various types of community service in general and concluded that a community service component can be assimilated into a HIV/pregnancy prevention program. However, they were not able to present any empirical evidence ascertaining whether or not the program actually prevented HIV and pregnancy (Denner et al., 2005).

A second program that used community service to replace out-of-school suspension was mentioned briefly in an article describing a review of a school's discipline policies (Malesich, 1994). In this review, students, teachers, parents, and administrators collaborated to design policies that used alternatives to suspension including community service, Saturday school, and a youth court as discipline procedures. Nevertheless, there was no indication in this article or any other available articles regarding the effectiveness of community service as an alternative to suspension program (Malesich, 1994).

Despite the lack of research on the effectiveness of community service as a discipline policy, there is limited empirical evidence that community service helps promote prosocial attitudes and personal growth. Youniss, Mclellan, Su, and Yates (1999) found that involvement in community service predicted avoidance of deviant behaviors such as marijuana use in a nationally representative sample of high school students. Another study noted community service participants' experienced behavioral, cognitive, and emotional growth as a result of their service. However, there was no quantitative evidence of higher than normal self-esteem or social interest (Middleton & Kelly, 1996).

Consequently, despite limited evidence that community service may foster personal growth and prevent deviance, it is uncertain if the same results will occur as the result of community service when used as a disciplinary technique. Thus, more evaluative research is needed to resolve this uncertainty. This research begins an effort to fill that void. In this study, we seek to determine whether or not the implementation of community service programs in 17 schools in six districts in the state of Kentucky resulted in a successful reduction in the number of suspensions over a 12-year period. Furthermore, we use a quasi-experimental design to determine whether schools in these districts had greater reductions in out-of-school suspensions over a 12-year period than a sample of matched schools that did not implement community service as an alternative to suspension.

Based on the preceding review, we expected to find that the schools that implemented community service will have significantly fewer out-of-school suspensions than their counterparts that did not because the districts have now been given an alternative to suspending students, which we believe will result in a reduction of the number of suspensions (in their districts) over that time period.

Method

In the spring of 2003, the Kentucky Center for School Safety (KCSS) was contracted by the Kentucky Department of Education to solicit proposals from Kentucky school districts to explore the use of community service as an alternative to suspension. After a competitive grant process, six school districts in Kentucky were selected to receive funding for a Community Service Work Program in which students were required to perform community service in lieu of being suspended from school. These schools implemented community service in lieu of suspension in the 2003–2004 and 2004–2005 school years. According to the funding criteria, students in the program also had to complete homework assignments and receive counseling from the school counselor as part of the program. The aim of this program was to give districts an opportunity to reduce suspension rates and increase their average daily attendance (ADA) revenue.

While each program varied in its design by district, students typically spent half of each day engaged in community service work and the other half on academic assignments and working closely with the school counselor to discuss the causes and consequences of their misbehavior that led to the student's involvement in the program. For students to take part in the program, their parents had to allow them to volunteer for the program. Students who completed the programs received both academic and attendance credit. Each individual district designated the actual community service tasks. Some districts had students who stayed to work on school grounds, while others sent students to work with outside agencies including soup kitchens, animal shelters, Goodwill stores, and care centers for children or adults. Students that participated in these programs did not receive a suspension mark on their records and they also were not counted as absent for that school day.

Data Collection and Experimental Design

Despite our recommendations, none of the school administrators chose to randomly assign some of the students who committed infractions that qualified them for out-of-school suspension to community service; as such, the optimal experimental design (using random assignment and control and experimental groups) was impossible to conduct. Instead, we chose to use the most valid "quasi-experimental design" available. The design that we used is referred to as the "control-series" design (Nachimas & Nachimas, 1982), one of a series of interrupted time series analyses. In this design, a group similar in composition to the group receiving the intervention is used as a control in both pretest and posttest observations. Use of a control group helps to eliminate alternative explanations for the relationship between the treatment (in this case, the community service work program) and the effect (in this case, reductions in out-of-school suspensions). If those receiving the intervention show greater improvement than the control group in the phenomenon under study, then we can have some confidence that intervention was successful.

To begin the experiment, we identified the schools in each district that used community service as an alternative to suspension. Among the six districts, 17 middle and high schools used the community service work program. This group of schools served as the experimental group. We then had to establish a control group of schools that did not receive the intervention to compare with the group of experimental schools that actually used community service. To establish our control group, we first identified the enrollment numbers of each school that used community service. Then, using Kentucky census data, we determined the population size of the counties in which each school was located. Next, we found districts/counties from areas in Kentucky with similar demographics (e.g., percent nonwhite, median household income) and, within those districts, selected schools with comparable enrollments as those of the 17 schools under study. These 17 schools became the control group.

Dependent Variables

The dependent variables used in this research were variables representing the change in suspensions for both board and law violations over a 12-year period. To begin our analysis, we collected the number of suspensions for each school in both our experimental and control groups. Using Kentucky Safe Schools Data collected for each year between the 2000–2001 and 2011–2012 school years, we were able to calculate the number of suspensions reported by each school for each school year during that time frame. These data were collected by the Kentucky Department of Education from individual schools throughout the state and provided to the Kentucky Center for School Safety (KCSS) at the end of each school year to be reported in the Kentucky Safe Schools Data Report. Suspensions at each school are reported to the KCSS based on two separate types of violations: a law violation or a board policy violation. A law violation occurs when a law is broken (assault, rape, robbery, etc.) whereas a board policy violation occurs where a "rule" set by a school board has been violated (defiance of authority, cheating, dress code violation, fighting, etc.). We thus ran two sets of analyses to examine differences between experimental and control groups, one to address suspensions due to law violations and one to address suspensions due to board policy violations.

To begin our quasi-experimental evaluation, we coded the experimental groups (those schools that utilized community service in lieu of suspension) as 1 and the control groups as 0. Next, we calculated the changes in suspensions for board and law violations at each school from 2000–2001 to 2011–2012. Then, using the Statistical Package for Social Scientists (SPSS), we conducted an independent sample t-test to determine if the changes in suspensions from 2000–2001 to 2011–2012 for board violations and the law violations were significantly different between the experimental and control schools.

We next examined whether the changes in suspension over the time period were contingent on the level of school (e.g., middle v. high school). To determine whether there was a significant change in the suspensions of board and law violations between middle school group and high school group, we coded the middle schools as 0 and the high schools as 1 and then ran an independent sample t-test. From these tests, we were able to determine the reduction or increase of suspensions for each group.

Results

Shown in Table 9.1 are the mean changes in suspensions for board violations from the 2000–2001 school year to 2011–2012 school year for both control and experimental schools. The results presented in Table 9.1 indicate that schools using community service had a mean decrease of 149.06 suspensions for board policy violations while schools that did not use community service (the control group) actually had a mean increase of 61.59 suspensions for board violations over the 12-year period. The results suggest that the difference in suspensions between experimental and control schools was statistically significant ($t=4.032$; $p<.001$). Thus, over the 12 year period under study, those schools that implemented community service in lieu of suspension in the 2003–2004 and 2004–2005 school years had significantly fewer suspensions than control schools after its implementation than the control schools.

Table 9.1 Changes in Board Violation Suspensions from 2000–01 to 2011–12

School Group	N	Mean Change in Suspensions	Std. Deviation
CSW Schools	17	−149.06	174.40953
Control Schools	17	61.59	126.38684

t-value	df	p-value	Mean Difference	Std. Error Difference	95% confidence interval of the difference Lower	Upper
4.032	32	0.000	210.64706	52.23945	104.23879	317.05533

In Table 9.2, we compare the number of schools that saw a reduction/increase in the number of board violation suspensions between the control and experimental schools. Fourteen of the CSW schools showed a reduction in suspensions, three saw an increase, and none of the schools remained the same from the 2000–2001 to the 2011–2012 school year; in other words, 82.4% of the schools that were using community service saw a reduction in suspensions over 12 years. On the other hand, only two schools in the control group saw a reduction in suspensions over the 12-year period, while 13 saw an increase, and the number of suspensions in two schools remained the same. The control group thus showed only an 11.8% reduction in suspensions, compared to an 82.4% reduction in the experimental group.

Table 9.2 Comparison of Number of Schools by Change in Board Violations

	Saw a reduction	Saw an increase	Remained the same
CSW Schools	14	3	0
Control Schools	2	13	2

In Table 9.3, we compare the mean changes in suspensions for law violations from the 2000–2001 school year to 2011–2012 school year for both control and experimental schools. The results presented in Table 9.3 indicate that schools using community service had a mean decrease of 28.06 suspensions for law violations while schools that did not use community service (the control group) actually had a mean increase of 2.94 suspensions for law violations over the 12-year period. The results presented in Table 9.3 further suggest that the difference in suspensions between experimental and control schools was statistically significant ($t=3.279$; $p<.001$). Thus, over the 12 year period under study, those schools that implemented community service in lieu of suspension in the 2003–2004 and 2004–2005 school years had significantly fewer suspensions for law violations than control schools.

Table 9.3 Changes in Law Violation Suspensions from 2000–01 to 2011–12

School Group	N	Mean Change in Suspensions	Std. Deviation
CSW Schools	17	–28.06	33.99903
Control Schools	17	2.94	19.07705

t-value	df	p-value	Mean Difference	Std. Error Difference	95% confidence interval of the difference Lower	Upper
3.279	32	0.003	31.0	9.45537	11.74005	50.25995

In Table 9.4, we present a comparison of the number of schools that saw an increase or decrease in law violations. Fifteen of the experimental group schools saw a reduction in suspensions for law violations, two saw an increase, and no school remained the same from the 2000–2001 to the 2011–2012 school year. These results are similar to those found for board violations. Thus, 88.2% of the schools in the experimental group saw a reduction in law violation suspensions over the 12-year period. On the other hand, ten schools (58.8%) in the control group saw a reduction in suspensions for law violations, five saw an increase, and two schools remained the same. Thus, control group schools were much more similar to experimental schools in their changes in law violations over the 12-year period than they were for board violations.

Table 9.4 Comparison of Number of Schools by the Change in Law Violations

	Saw a reduction	Saw an increase	Remained the same
CSW schools	15	2	0
Control schools	10	5	2

To determine whether differences in board suspensions varied by the level of the school under consideration, we estimated independent sample t-tests in SPSS separately for middle schools and high schools. The results are depicted in Table 9.5. Among middle schools, there was a mean decrease of 204.75 suspensions for board violations in the experimental group, while there was a mean increase of 62.25 for the control group. Among high schools, there was also a mean decrease in board violation suspensions for the experimental group (–99.56), while there was an increase in the mean for the control group (61.0). These differences were statistically significant for the middle schools ($t = 2.778$; $p < .05$) and the high schools ($t = 3.227$; $p < .01$).

Table 9.5 Percentage Changes for Board Violation Suspensions from 00–01 to 11–12

School Type	School Group	N	Mean of the Percentage Changes	Std. Deviation
Middle Schools	CSW Schools	8	–204.7500	213.43634
	Control Schools	8	62.2500	168.30393
High Schools	CSW Schools	9	–99.5556	122.95641
	Control Schools	9	61.0000	84.62269

School Type	t-value	df	p-value	Mean Difference	Std. Error Difference	95% confidence interval of the difference	
						Lower	Upper
Middle School	2.778	14	0.015	267.000	96.09974	60.88655	473.11345
High School	3.227	16	0.005	160.55556	49.75415	55.08147	266.02964

To determine whether these differences in law suspensions varied by the level of the school under consideration, we estimated independent sample t-tests in SPSS separately for middle schools and high schools. The results are depicted in Table 9.6. Among middle schools, there was a mean decrease of 37.38 suspensions for law violations in the experimental group, while there was a mean decrease of 3.38 suspensions for law violations in the control group. Among high schools, there was also a mean decrease in suspensions for law violations for the experimental group (–19.78), while there was an increase in the mean number of suspensions for law violations in the control group (8.56). The difference in suspensions for law violations was statistically significant for the high schools ($t = 2.903$; $p < .05$) but not for the middle schools ($t = 2.041$; $p = .061$).

Table 9.6 Percentage Changes for Law Violation Suspensions from 00–01 to 11–12

School Type	School Group	N	Mean of the Percentage Changes	Std. Deviation
Middle Schools	CSW Schools	8	–37.38	44.03225
	Control Schools	8	–3.38	16.78381
High Schools	CSW Schools	9	–19.78	21.24722
	Control Schools	9	8.56	20.15013

School Type	t-value	df	p-value	Mean Difference	Std. Error Difference	95% confidence interval of the difference	
						Lower	Upper
Middle School	2.041	14	0.061	34.00000	16.66034	–1.73288	69.73288
High School	2.903	16	0.010	28.33333	9.76088	7.64120	49.02547

Discussion

The results presented in this chapter suggest that the community service projects implemented in lieu of suspension in the selected Kentucky schools were successful in reducing out-of-school suspensions for both board and law violations in the experimental schools. This impact was greater for board violations than for law violations, although there was a statistically significant difference between experimental and control schools for both types of violations. This impact was greater in high schools than in middle schools; when we separated the sample by school level, the difference in reductions in suspension for law violations between the control and experimental groups was not statistically significant. Thus, by and large, the results presented here suggest that community service in lieu of suspension reduces suspensions and should be considered as one strategy to increase instructional time while maintaining a positive, safe, school environment.

To our knowledge, this is the first study that uses a quasi-experimental design to examine the effect of using community service in lieu of out of school suspensions as a form of discipline. As presented earlier, there are a wide variety of alternatives to suspension programs available. We recommend that community service be added to that "toolbox" of strategies that principals can use to discipline students.

Limitations and Suggestions for Future Research

Nevertheless, before accepting that recommendation on its own merit, there are a number of limitations and suggestions for future research that should be considered. First, analysis of out-of-school suspensions in Kentucky public schools over the time period under consideration here shows that there was a 19.5% decrease in suspensions across the state during the time period, dropping from 75,442 during 2000–01 to 60,744 during 2011–12 (McCoy-Simandle & May, 2002; Division of Student Success, 2012). Thus, part of the effectiveness of the community service program may have been due to an overall culture, climate, or behavior change occurring in Kentucky public schools during that time frame. Nevertheless, the fact that the reduction in out-of-school suspensions was significantly greater in the experimental schools than the control schools suggest that at least part of that difference may have been due to the community service program.

A second limitation of this study is that we have little information about the types of community service in which students were involved at the school level. Our interviews with the staff responsible for supervising the program during 2003–04 and 2004–05 school years indicated that some students were working with nonprofits in the community (e.g., American Red Cross, the local humane society) while others were engaged in community service on the local school campus. We suspect that those programs in which students work with community nonprofits will be more effective in changing behavior than those programs where students work on-campus. At this point, however, that is purely conjecture. Consequently, in addition to comparing differences between schools using community service and schools using traditional out-of-school suspension programs, future research should explore differences in the type of programs used to determine if some community service programs are more effective than others.

A third limitation of this research is also worth mentioning. Based on these results, we are confident that community service reduces the number of out-of-school suspensions. However, we do not know *why* it does. It could be that, as part of their community service work or the counseling that is part of that program, students realize something about themselves or their situation that inspires them to change their attitude and behaviors and make them less likely to misbehave in the future than they were in the past. It could also be, however, that students do not want to take part in a program where they actually have to talk to a counselor *and* perform out-of-class labor, some of which may be physical labor. Answers to these questions are beyond the scope of this study but certainly should be considered in future research replicating these efforts.

A fourth limitation revolves around the sample studied here. In total, we examined the impact of community service as an alternative to suspension in 17 schools in one Midwestern state. Thus, the generalizability of the findings presented here is limited at best. Nevertheless, we believe that this exploratory effort is an important contribution, not only because of the results presented here, but because of the questions raised for future research. We hope that this research will serve as a foundation for more generalizable research in the future.

The final limitation of this study involves our limited ability to control for spurious variables that may have contributed to the reduction in out-of-school suspensions in the treatment schools, or conversely, may have contributed to an increase in out-of-school suspensions in the control schools. The research question we attempted to answer in this chapter was whether or not community service used in lieu of out-of-school suspension reduced the number of suspensions in the schools that used it and whether that reduction was greater in those schools than in similar schools that did not use community service. The results presented here suggest that the answer to that question is a qualified yes. Nevertheless, as highlighted earlier, we still do not know why community service reduces suspensions. Furthermore, we cannot argue definitively that it does (1) without further information about the students and programs at the individual schools using community service or (2) without the ability to control for other spurious factors that might have caused reductions in suspensions were the community service program not in place. To some extent, the use of a control group of schools offsets this concern but future research should improve on this design by closely following schools using community service over an extended period of time to provide further credence to the findings presented here.

Conclusions and Policy Impact

The controversy surrounding use of out-of-school suspension continues to plague schools and their administrators. One option to reduce those concerns may be community service. Community service is a valuable tool in finding an alternative to suspension for students that may commit an offense warranting suspension. Government, in the complex and modern society we live in today, must delegate substantial amounts of discretion to agencies allowing them to deal with certain issues such as suspension in public schools. They must also, however, ensure that effective legal constraints will be placed on those administrators making decisions on certain issues without depriving them of the necessary flexibility to efficiently implement certain policies that will be beneficial in making schools safer places to learn and work. Alongside the legal constraints placed on them by the State, administrators must also be given latitude in determining which policies would best help in reducing board and law violations. This includes giving them alternatives other than suspension. Community service is one such viable alternative that should be more widely available.

From the findings presented in this study of community service and its effect on suspensions in schools, it is clear that public school administrators can use this as a tool to reduce suspensions and thereby increase funding that schools received based on their average daily attendance (ADA). We would encourage public school administrators to seek additional funding from government agencies and private foundations to allow them to provide these community service programs in additional schools in the future. In the analyses presented here, only 17 schools in 6 school districts were able to participate in these valuable programs to reduce suspensions. Based on their effectiveness in reducing suspensions demonstrated in this study, we recommend that community service be considered as an alternative to out-of-school suspension to provide a more effective way to address student misbehavior.

In reality, community service in lieu of out-of-school suspension serves at least three important functions. First, and most importantly, rather than forcing a student out of school (often to an unsupervised setting), community service programs provide students the ability to spend that time working on their school assignments, talking with a trained professional about the causes and consequences of their behavior, and assisting their community or school by providing service to those that need it. Intuitively, each of these components of community service is an improvement on out-of-school suspension. Secondly, by maintaining supervision of the student during the school day, the student is no longer counted as absent (as they would be in an out-of-school suspension), thus allowing the school to retain the funding for that student rather than lose funding for the time the student is absent because of the suspension. In reality, in schools with high numbers of out-of-school suspensions, the funding retained by allowing these students to stay under the school's supervision would fund one or more licensed counselors to be responsible for the administration of the program (e.g., counseling with students, arranging work with agencies and transportation of students to those agencies, coordinating homework assignments with teachers). Finally, community service provides school administrators with one more option to avoid out-of-school suspensions. Any effort to keep students in school that does not increase school misbehavior or decrease academic performance or school safety, in our opinion, is an effort worthy of consideration.

References

Barnhart, M., Franklin, N., & Alleman, J. (2008). Lessons learned and strategies used in reducing the frequency of out-of-school suspensions. *Journal of Special Education Leadership, 21*(2), 75–83.

Brownstein, R. (2010). Pushed out. *The Education Digest, 75*(7), 23–27.

Christenson, S. & Thurlow, M. (2004). School dropouts: Prevention considerations, interventions, and challenges. *Psychological Science, 13*(1), 36–39.

Christle, C., K. Jolivette, & Nelson, C.M. (2007). School characteristics related to high school dropout rates. *Special Education, 28*(6), 325–339.

Costenbader, V., & Markson, S. (1998). School suspension: A study with secondary school students. *Journal of School Psychology, 36*(1), 59–82.

Council on School Health (2013). Out-of-school suspension and expulsion. *Pediatrics, 131*(3), e1000-e1007.

Denner, J., Coyle, K., Robin, L., & Banspach, S. (2005). Integrating service learning into a curriculum to reduce health risks at alternative high schools. *Journal of School Health, 75*(5), 151–156.

DeRidder, L. M. (1991). How suspension and expulsion contribute to dropping out. *Education Digest, 56*(6), 44–47.

Division of Student Success. (2012). *Kentucky Department of Education 2011–12 Safe Schools Annual Statistical Report.* Frankfort, KY: Kentucky Department of Education. Retrieved June 17, 2014 from http://education.ky.gov/school/sdfs/Documents/2011-12%20Safe%20Schools%20Annual%20Statistical%20Report.pdf.

Dupper, D.R. (1994). School dropouts or "pushouts?": Suspensions and at-risk youth. *UIUC School of Social Work Newsletter, 7*(1).

Garibaldi, A. (1980). *In-school alternatives to suspensions: An exploratory analysis of four sites.* Paper presented at the Annual Meeting of the American Educational Research Association: Boston, MA.

Henderson, J., & Friedland, B. (1996). *Suspension, a wake-up call: Rural educators' attitudes toward suspension* [Electronic Version]. 1–9. Retrieved August 9, 2014 from files.eric.ed.gov/fulltext/ED394749.pdf.

Losen, D., & Martinez, T. (2013). Out of school & off track: The overuse of suspensions in American middle and high schools. *Civil Rights Project.* Retrieved August 10, 2014 from http://www.childrensdefense.org/child-research-data-publications/archives/school-suspensions-are-they-helping-children.html.

MacWilliams, C. (1992). *Positive measures.* Retrieved August 10, 2014 from http://www.summit-ed.com/f-posint.html.

Malesich, R. F. (1994). Making schools safe for students: Solutions to discipline problems. *Schools in the Middle, 3*(3), 38–40.

Mattison, R. (2004). Universal measures of school functioning in middle school special education students. *Behavioral Disorders, 29*(4), 359–371.

McCoy-Simandle, L., & May, D.C. (2004). *Kentucky 2003: Safe schools data project annual report.* Kentucky Center for School Safety, Eastern Kentucky University.

McCoy-Simandle, L., & May, D.C. (2002). *Kentucky 2002: Safe Schools Data Project.* Richmond, KY: Kentucky Center for School Safety. Retrieved June 17, 2014 from http://www.kycss.org/pdfs-docs/clearpdf/analys03pdfs/02finalreport.pdf.

Middleton, E.B., & Kelly, K.R. (1996). Effects of community service on adolescent personality development. *Counseling & Values, 40*(2), 132–143.

Morgan-D'Atrio, C., Northrup, J., LaFleur, L., & Spera, S. (1996). Toward prescriptive alternatives to suspensions: A preliminary evaluation. *Behavioral Disorders, 21*, 190–200.

Morris, R., & Howard, A. (2003). Designing an effective in-school suspension program. *The Clearing House, 76*(3), 156–159.

Nachmias, D., & Nachmias, C. (1982). *Research methods in the social sciences (2nd ed.)*. New York: St. Martin's Press.

Neeld, R. (1999). *District-wide administrator assistance: Decreasing suspension rates through clear reporting and utilization of discipline alternatives* [Electronic Version]. Retrieved August 10, 2014 from files.eric.ed.gov/fulltext/ED430279.pdf

Osher, D., G. Bear, J. Sprague, & W. Doyle. (2010). How can we improve school discipline? *Educational Researcher, 39*(1), 48–58.

Radin, N. (1989). School social work practice: Past, present, and future trends. *Children & Schools, 11*(4), 213–225.

Raffaele-Mendez, L. M., Knoff, H. M., & Ferron, J. M. (2002). School demographic variables and out-of-school suspension rates: A quantitative and qualitative analysis of a large, ethnically diverse school district. *Psychology in the Schools, 39*(3), 259–277.

Sanders, D. (2001). A caring alternative to suspension. *Education Digest, 66*(7); 51–54.

Toby, J., & Scrupski, A. (1991). Community service as alternative discipline. *School Safety*, 12–15.

Uchitelle, S., Bartz, D., & Hillman, L. (1989). Strategies for reducing suspensions. *Urban Education, 24*, 163–176.

Vanderslice, R. (1999). *Developing effective in-school suspension programs* [Electronic Version]. Retrieved August 10, 2014 from files.eric.ed.gov/fulltext/ED444257.pdf.

Winborn, J. (1992). *A study of the effectiveness of a Saturday school in reducing suspension, expulsion, and corporal punishment.* Retrieved August 10, 2014 from files.eric.ed.gov/fulltext/ED355663.pdf.

Youniss, J., Mclellan, J. A., Su, Y., & Yates, M. (1999). The role of community service in identity development normative, unconventional, and deviant orientations. *Journal of Adolescent Research, 14*(2), 248–261.

Chapter 10

School Resource Officers: Effective Tools When Properly Used?

*David C. May, Brianna Wright, Gary Cordner, and Stephen Fessel**

School Resource Officers

In the United States, sworn law enforcement officers (officers bestowed with arrest powers by the state in which they work) assigned to schools are commonly referred to as school resource officers (SROs). An SRO was officially defined by Part Q of Title I of the Omnibus Crime Control and Safe Streets Act of 1968 and amended in 1998 as "a career law enforcement officer, with sworn authority, deployed in community-oriented policing, and assigned by the employing police department or agency to work in collaboration with school and community-based organizations" (United States Department of Justice, 1999, p. 1). More commonly, an SRO is a sworn police officer employed by the local police department who "provides a variety of security, law enforcement, correctional, and educational services" to students, families, and administrators involved with the school (Girouard, 2001; Brown, 2006; Kim & Geronimo, 2009; Petteruti, 2011). SRO programs range from prevention-based, collaborative community policing models to reactive, enforcement-based traditional policing models (and everything between the two) (Brown, 2006; Finn, 2006; U.S. Department of Justice, 1999).

The number of SROs working in schools in the United States is difficult to estimate accurately (Kim & Geronimo, 2009; May et. al, 2004; Ruddell & May, 2011). Current research efforts to establish the number of SROs are limited for a variety of reasons. First, SRO assignments are typically school-year specific; in other words, many SROs begin their assignments in August, end that rotation in the following June, and then are replaced by another officer at the beginning of the next school year. Thus, in some jurisdictions, a new team of SROs rotates in at the beginning of each school year, resulting in a high turnover rate, and little consistency from one year to the next. Second, SRO funding is not uniform across all jurisdictions. In some cases, school districts fund the SRO program and the SRO is contingent on the school budget from one year to the next. In other districts, the local police department funds the SRO and funding for that position may also vary from one year to the next. In other cases, SROs are grant-funded;

* The information presented in this chapter is largely drawn from an article I coauthored with two colleagues that appeared in print elsewhere. The citation for this article is included below:
May, David C., Gary Cordner, and Stephen B. Fessel. (2004). School Resource Officers as Community Police Officers: Fact or Fiction? *Law Enforcement Executive Forum, 4*(6), 173–188.

consequently, the SRO position expires when the grant expires. There are a number of other scenarios for funding as well. These means include, but are not limited to, private sources, fund-raising events, and donations (Finn, 2006). Typically, SROs are city or county law enforcement officers employed by police departments or sheriff's offices assigned to work specifically in one or more schools. Although SROs may be funded fully or partly by the school district that they serve, they typically remain employees of their respective law enforcement agency (Moore, 2001). Consequently, enumerating SROs in the United States, or even the agencies that provide SROs, is a difficult task because that number changes from one school year to the next.

Nevertheless, the most accurate estimate of the number of active SROs probably is that offered by the Bureau of Justice Statistics (Reaves, 2011). In the 2007 census of state and local law enforcement agencies (CSLLEA), researchers with the Bureau of Justice Statistics reported that 13,056 officers were deployed in public school districts (Bureau of Justice Statistics, 2007; Reaves, 2010, p. 28), a decrease from 14,337 officers in 2003 (Bureau of Justice Statistics, 2003). More recent estimates suggest that there are approximately 17,000 SROs assigned to schools throughout the United States (Brown, 2006; Wald & Thurau, 2010). Although there are likely SRO programs of some form in each of the 50 states, estimates suggest that most schools in the United States do not use SROs. In fact, less than one-third of the 132,656 elementary and secondary schools in the U.S. in 2007–2008 had a daily police presence (Snyder & Dillow, 2010, p. 19).

Although SROs perform a wide variety of tasks in schools, the primary task of SROs is to provide law enforcement (Brown, 2006; Kim & Geronimo, 2009; Petteruti, 2011; Ruddell & May, 2011; May & Higgins, 2011). According to Canaday, James, and Nease (2012), under the NASRO model, SROs are also responsible for patrolling school grounds, supervising traffic at the beginning and end of the school day, assisting with the control of disruptive students, attending parent/faculty meetings, providing intelligence support to criminal justice officials, assisting with delinquency programs (e.g., D.A.R.E.), and serving as a positive role model to students.

Consequently, the job of an SRO is multi-faceted. An SRO is expected to: (1) address crime and disorder problems, gangs, and drug activities affecting or occurring in or around an elementary or secondary school; (2) develop or expand crime prevention efforts for students; (3) educate likely school-age victims in crime prevention and safety; (4) develop or expand community justice initiatives for students; (5) train students in conflict resolution, restorative justice, and crime awareness; (6) assist in the identification of physical changes in the environment that may reduce crime in and around the school; and (7) assist in developing school policy that addresses crime and recommended procedural changes.

SROs are also required to act as a liaison between the school, the community, and the police, to teach law-related education classes, and to counsel students (United States Department of Justice, 2001). These three roles are commonly referred to as the triad model: law enforcement officer, counselor, and teacher (Hickman & Reeves, 2003; Petteruti, 2011). Although the triad may be an accurate concept to describe the role of SROs, the components of the triad for SROs are not equilateral. In other words, for most SROs, law enforcement activities subsume more of the SROs' time than counseling and education. Recent estimates by Petteruti (2011) determined that SROs spend approximately 20 hours per week on law enforcement activities, 10 hours on advising and mentoring, 5 hours on teaching, and 6–7 hours on other activities.

Although a number of researchers have examined the ways that SROs spend their time in schools, there are a number of components of the SRO role that are not as well understood. One of these areas where further research is needed revolves around the training and procedures used by SROs. As of 2009, many SROs were not provided with any formal standards of procedure to provide sufficient expectations and uniform tasks prior to, during, or after employment in schools (Kim & Geronimo, 2009). In their white paper on this topic, Kim and Geronimo argue for a standardized documentation of the goals and expectations of the SRO program. They explain that SROs should be responsible for providing daily activity reports, which would include, for example, the number of student searches, citations, and arrests.

Research on the effectiveness of SROs in reducing crime at school also renders mixed results. The overall analysis is that SROs are generally effective in reducing violence and crime in schools (Brown, 2005; Center for the Prevention of School Violence, 2001; Jennings et. al, 2011; Johnson, 1999; Trump, 2001; Virginia Department of Criminal Justice Services, 2001). Johnson's 1999 research on 18 SROs in a southern city determined that the amount of crimes in high schools and middle schools decreased with the introduction of SROs. This research found that the number of school suspensions decreased as well (Johnson, 1999). In 2001, NASRO surveyed 689 SROs and concluded that two-thirds of SROs had prevented assault on a teacher or staff member and almost all respondents felt that their work and presence contributed to and increased school safety (Trump, 2001). The Virginia Department of Criminal Justice Services conducted research in 2001 via content analyses of reports from 78 SRO programs in Virginia. This research also concluded that SROs were effective in reducing school crime and violence. Four in five (82%) staff and 37.2% of SROs reported a reduction in fighting in their schools (Virginia Department of Criminal Justice Services, 2001). In 2001, the Center for Prevention of School Violence conducted an analysis of SRO effectiveness in North Carolina. The results determined that the school was safer because of the law enforcement presence (Center for Prevention of School Violence, 2001).

The extant research also suggests that school administrators are satisfied with the SROs who work in their schools. May, Fessel, and Means (2004) determined that the majority of principals in schools where SROs were assigned valued the SROs and felt that the SROs reduced crime and violence in their schools. They also noticed a decrease in the amount of fighting (May et al., 2004). In 2005, research was conducted on students in Browsville, Texas; two thirds of the students also agreed that the SROs kept the schools safe (Brown, 2005). In 2011, a survey was distributed to collect data from 954 schools to determine the effectiveness of SROs from a large, nationally representative sample of high schools. The research determined that the presence of SROs might serve to reduce serious crime. It also found that the positive relationship between police and students that results from SRO presence might help to reduce violent crime (Jennings, Khey, Moskaly, & Donner, 2011).

Nevertheless, the presence of SROs in schools is still controversial. Theriot (2009) suggests that the presence of SROs in schools increases the number of students arrested for less serious offenses, thus widening the reach of the criminal justice system. Other research has also questioned the effectiveness of SROs in reducing crimes in schools.

Using data from the 1993 National Household and Education survey, Schreck et al. (2003) determined that the presence of security guards (not specifically SROs) had no relationship to school violence. Barnes (2008) evaluated the North Carolina School Resource Officer program and also determined that school safety was not significantly impacted by SROs (Barnes, 2008). More recently, research was conducted on a nationally representative, longitudinal sample of 470 schools. Unlike the research before it, this study looked at the reporting of crimes instead of perceptions of school safety. This study concluded that the use of SROs did not increase school safety and that more crimes were reported with the introduction of SROs (Na & Gottfredson, 2013).

Although a number of studies have examined SROs from a variety of approaches, little is known about the characteristics and attitudes of the officers who serve as SROs or their actual role on the school grounds. Finally, while many authors have suggested that SROs are a natural "fit" for community police officers, limited evidence exists regarding whether this is actually the case. Thus, in this chapter we use responses from 119 SROS to examine: (1) the daily activities of SROs and whether or not these activities fit in the community policing model; and (2) whether a typology of SRO styles might be identifiable.

Community Policing

Just a few decades ago, the unquestioned ideal model of good policing was the professional model—police officers who were well trained, well equipped, and tightly managed and who enforced the law in a professional manner, as epitomized by the popular images of the FBI and the Los Angeles Police Department. In the heyday of this model (the 1960s and 1970s), however, crime rates escalated and police-community relationships soured (Kelling & Moore, 1988). In addition, evaluation research indicated that the central operational strategies of the professional model—motorized preventive patrol, rapid response, and follow-up investigations—were largely ineffective.

Starting in the 1980s a more community-oriented approach to policing began. Police departments began employing foot patrol as a central component of their operational strategy, implemented crime prevention programs that were reliant on civilians and volunteers (e.g., neighborhood watch programs, community patrol, and Crime Stoppers programs), and made permanent assignment of officers to geographic areas a fixture in their departments. This came to be called community policing, entailing a substantial change in police thinking, "one where police strategy and tactics are adapted to fit the needs and requirements of the different communities the department serves, where there is a diversification of the kinds of programs and services on the basis of community needs and demands for police services and where there is considerable involvement of the community with police in reaching their objectives" (Reiss, 1985, p. 63).

Research on the effectiveness of community policing has yielded mixed results. Foot patrol seems to make citizens feel safer (Police Foundation, 1981) and reduces fear of crime and disorder (Chicago Community Policing Evaluation Consortium, 2003; Pate, Wycoff, Skogan, & Sherman, 1986; Cordner, 1986), but may have minimal effect on the amount of crime (Police Foundation, 1981).

It is difficult to describe community policing because it has remained a rather vague and broad concept. One widely recognized community policing framework presents nine elements—three philosophical, three strategic, and three tactical (Cordner, 2001). These elements include: (1) a shift in departmental philosophy to place more value on citizen input; (2) a broad view of the police function rather than a narrow focus on crime fighting or law enforcement (Kelling & Moore, 1988), recognizing the kinds of non-law enforcement tasks that police already perform and seeking to give them greater status and legitimacy (e.g., order maintenance, social service, and general assistance duties); (3) tailored policing based on local norms and values and individual needs, where officers and their supervisors are asked to consider the "will of the community" when deciding which laws to enforce under what circumstances; (4) less reliance on the patrol car and more emphasis on face-to-face interactions through reoriented operations and strategies such as foot patrol, directed patrol, door-to-door policing, and other alternatives to traditional motorized patrol; (5) permanent assignment of officers to a geographical area with a shift in patrol accountability from time of day to place by establishing a 24-hour responsibility for individual officers for smaller areas; (6) emphasis on a more proactive and preventive orientation, in contrast to the reactive focus that has characterized much of policing under the professional model; (7) an increase in positive interactions between officers and the citizens they serve, with a focus on building familiarity, trust, and confidence on both sides; (8) a spirit of cooperation and collaboration with the community to build partnerships between police and the citizens they serve (Bureau of Justice Assistance, 1994); and (9) a departmental transition from incident-based to problem-oriented policing, seeking customized solutions to specific community problems (Cordner, 2001).

Community Policing, Schools, and School Resource Officers

Schools are often referred to as microcosms of the community in which they are located and, much like the larger community, are affected by crime, fear of crime, and victimization (Atkinson, 2002). Consequently, if community policing is effective in reducing crime and fear of crime in communities, it should be able to reduce these phenomena in schools as well. In fact, one program (Community Outreach Through Police in Schools) that combines the efforts of law enforcement officers and child clinicians to provide weekly sessions to middle school students has decreased feelings of worry and concern about the future and death and has improved emotional functioning in general of the students who participate in the program (U.S. Department of Justice Office for Victims of Crime, 2003).

Nevertheless, not all research supports the idea that problem solving is effective in a school setting. Kenney and McNamara (2003) attempted to implement problem-solving strategies at schools in Kentucky using models similar to those of Kenney and Watson (1998). Their results were somewhat discouraging. They determined that the student-based problem solving models used in the three experimental schools in Kentucky "... had little or no effect on student fears or attitudes ..." (p. 57). Kenney and McNamara argue, however, that this lack of significant impact may have been a result of problems in implementation experienced at the schools, namely resistance from both the school administration and the teachers in implementing the student problem-solving model.

Despite the resistance on the part of some administrators and teachers, however, the number of partnerships between schools and law enforcement agencies has increased dramatically throughout the country (Atkinson, 2002). The most visible of these partnerships is the SRO, typically funded through the Office of Community Oriented Policing Services (COPS) in the U.S. Department of Justice. The COPS statute (Omnibus Crime Control and Safe Schools Act of 1968, as amended in 1998, Title 1, Part Q) defines an SRO as:

> ... a career law enforcement officer, with sworn authority, deployed in community oriented policing, assigned by the employing police department or agency to work in collaboration with schools and community organizations to: (1) address crime and disorder problems, gangs, and drug activities affecting or occurring in or around an elementary or secondary school; (2) develop or expand crime prevention efforts for students; (3) educate likely school-age victims in crime prevention and safety; (4) develop or expand community justice initiatives for students; (5) train students in conflict resolution, restorative justice, and crime awareness; (6) assist in the identification of physical changes in the environment that my reduce crime in and around the school; and (7) assist in developing school policy that addresses crime and recommended procedural changes (COPS, 2003: p. 47).

If SROs are performing their duties as COPS officers, then their duties should consist primarily of those functions listed above. Nevertheless, no empirical assessment of these duties has been performed. Using data from 117 School Resource Officers in Kentucky, we attempt to determine whether SROs *really are* COPS officers or whether they are some other type of officer.

SROs in Kentucky

The first School Resource Officer (SRO) program in Kentucky began in Jefferson County in 1977. The program has grown rapidly since the mid-1990s due primarily to the availability of grants through the federal Community Oriented Policing Services (COPS) Office in the U.S. Department of Justice.

SROs were first referenced in Kentucky statutes with the passage of the Safe Schools Act in 1998. Kentucky Revised Statute 158.441 defines an SRO as "*a sworn law enforcement officer who has specialized training to work with youth at a school site. The officer shall be employed through a contract between a local law enforcement agency and a school district.*" The statutory language was extremely important to the development of the SRO program for three reasons: (1) it required SROs to have specialized training; (2) it recognized the importance of having a written contract between the two agencies to clarify the duties of the officer; and (3) it formally recognized SROs as a specialized field of law enforcement. Notably, though, this Kentucky legislation does not make any direct or indirect reference to community policing.

The Kentucky Center for School Safety (KCSS) began in 1998 as a clearinghouse and resource to assist legislators, school administrators, teachers, law enforcement, and parents in reducing school violence in Kentucky. As part of that effort, the KCSS maintains an SRO database to ease communication with SROs about relevant programs and issues that assist them in the performance of their job. In 2002, this database listed 193 SROs in the commonwealth of Kentucky. In most cases, the officers were employees of a city or county law enforcement agency. A few school districts in the state have created their own special law enforcement districts and, in these cases, the officers are employees of the local boards of education.

Data Collection

In the summer of 2002, in conjunction with the second annual SRO conference in Kentucky, the KCSS conducted the second phase of a panel study examining the attributes of SROs throughout Kentucky. A postcard was mailed to all SROs included in the aforementioned database indicating that a questionnaire would be arriving in two weeks. A questionnaire and cover letter explaining the importance of the project were then mailed two weeks later. After three weeks, a second letter and questionnaire were mailed to those who did not respond to the original questionnaire. A final questionnaire and letter were mailed to nonrespondents three weeks later. Of the 193 SROs who received a questionnaire, 119 SROs provided responses (two of which were later deemed unusable) for a response rate of 61.7 percent. Thus, more than three in five SROs in the state of Kentucky provided data for this report.

The final SRO survey was eight pages long and required approximately 40 minutes to complete. SROs were asked a wide variety of demographic, contextual, and attitudinal questions regarding their perceptions of school safety, their role in school safety, and their impact in increasing safety at the school where they were assigned.

Results

The vast majority of survey respondents (see Table 10.1) were white (84.6 percent) and male (84.6 percent), over the age of 35 (70.9 percent), and with six or more years of law enforcement experience (79.5 percent). One in three officers had been SROs for only one year, while approximately equal percentages of the remaining SROs had been SROs for two years, three years, and four years or more. Three in four SROs had attended at least some college, with about one in four graduating from college and seven percent with some postgraduate education.

Table 10.1. Descriptive Statistics for SRO sample

Race	N	Percent of Sample
White	99	84.6
Black	15	12.8
Other	2	1.7
Gender		
Male	99	84.6
Female	18	15.4
Age		
23 to 29	14	12.0
30 to 34	20	17.1
35 to 39	23	19.7
40 to 44	19	16.2
45 to 49	21	17.9
50 to 54	14	12.0
55 and over	6	5.1
Years of Law Enforcement Experience		
1 year or less	3	2.6
2 to 5 years	21	17.9
6 to 10 years	24	20.5
11 to 15 years	20	17.1
16 to 20 years	24	20.5
More than 20 years	25	21.4
Years of SRO Experience		
1 year or less	39	33.3
2 years	21	17.9
3 years	25	21.4
4 years	19	16.2
5 or more years	9	7.7
Missing	4	3.4
Education		
High School Graduate	27	23.1
Some College	52	44.4
College Graduate	30	25.6
Some Postgraduate Education	8	6.8

Table 10.2 Respondents' Definition of Their Role as an SRO (N = 101)

	N (%)
TRIAD	32 (31.7)
Role model/school security/teacher	7 (6.9)
Law enforcement/teacher	8 (7.9)
Law enforcement/counselor	10 (9.9)
Ensure school safety	10 (9.9)
Teacher/administrator assistant	5 (5.0)
Law enforcement/disciplinarian	3 (3.0)
Security supervisor	3 (3.0)
Law enforcement	19 (18.8)
Duties not defined by officer	4 (4.0)

Respondents were then asked an open-ended question regarding how they defined their duties and responsibilities as an SRO. For the purpose of this study, we grouped the responses into the ten categories that are presented in Table 10.2. The results are presented in such a way that those duties that most closely match the "ideal" COPS SRO are listed toward the top of the table and those that more closely match the role of traditional law enforcement are found toward the bottom of the table. Almost one in three (31.7 percent) respondents indicated their role was best defined by the TRIAD, indicating that their role was divided into thirds: law enforcement, counseling students, and delivering law-related educational classes. Almost seven percent of the respondents stated that they defined their role as a combination of teacher, role model, and person to ensure school security while a slightly higher percentage (9.9 percent) stated that their role was to ensure school safety. Conversely, almost one in five (18.8 percent) respondents indicated that their role was primarily law enforcement, with some variation of the aforementioned roles interspersed in combination for the rest of the respondents. Four respondents did not respond to the question.

Table 10.3 Distribution of Time of School Resource Officer (N = 111)

	N (%)
More counselor and teacher than LE*	20 (18.0)
50 percent LE/50 percent counselor and teacher	24 (21.6)
More than 50 less than 70 percent LE	15 (13.5)
70–99 percent LE	44 (39.6)
100 percent LE	8 (7.2)

*LE = law enforcement

Respondents were then asked, "How much time do you spend on each of the roles associated with officers who work in schools: law enforcement officer, law-related counselor, and law-related education teaching? When added, your responses should total 100%." The three possible answers were derived from the aforementioned TRIAD concept; we then categorized the respondent's answers into the five categories in Table 10.3. These categories are used to depict the combined roles of the SRO from a community policing perspective. Two in five (39.6 percent) respondents indicated that 70 to 90 percent of their time is spent as a law enforcement officer and 7.2 percent said they

Table 10.4 Four Types of SROs Based on Roles and Time Allocation

	Time Allocation		
Roles	0–50% LE	51–100% LE	Row Total
TRIAD	15 (46.9)	17 (53.2)	32
Role model/school security/teacher	3 (50.0)	3 (50.0)	6
Law enforcement/teacher	6 (75.0)	2 (25.0)	8
Law enforcement/counselor	6 (66.7)	3 (33.3)	9
Ensure school safety	1 (25.0)	7 (87.5)	8
Teacher/administrator assistant	4 (80.0)	1 (20.0)	5
Law enforcement/disciplinarian	1 (33.3)	2 (66.6)	3
Security supervisor	0 (0.0)	2 (100.0)	2
Law enforcement	4 (23.5)	13 (76.5)	17
Duties not defined by officer	1 (12.5)	3 (75.0)	4

*LE = law enforcement

spent all their time performing law enforcement duties. Over one in five (21.6 percent) indicated they spend half their time as a law enforcement officer and the other half of their time was divided between counseling and teaching students. Almost one in five (18.1 percent) indicated that they spend more time as a counselor and teacher to the students than a law enforcement officer.

Table 10.4 combines the responses presented in Tables 10.2 and 10.3, contrasting officers' role conceptions with how they say they actually spend their time. The first category of officers, hereafter referred to as "COPS SROs," consists of the officers who both define their role as primarily TRIAD or some version of law enforcement/counselor or law enforcement/teacher and actually spend at least half of their time performing counselor/teacher duties. About one third of the officers fit the COPS SRO category. A second group of officers, hereafter referred to as "Willing COPS SROs," define their role as primarily TRIAD or some version of law enforcement/counselor or law enforcement/teacher but actually spend more than half of their time performing law enforcement duties. About one quarter fit the Willing COPS SRO typology. The third category of officers, hereafter referred to as "Unwilling COPS SROs," define their role as primarily law enforcement/school safety enforcer yet spend at least half of their time performing counselor/teacher duties. By that definition, 11 officers (11.7 percent) fit the Unwilling COPS SRO category. Finally, a fourth group of officers, hereafter referred to as "Traditional

Table 10.5. School Resource Officer Daily Activities

SRO Activity	Daily	Weekly–Monthly	Never
Monitor parking areas	91 (83.5)	6 (5.5)	12 (11.0)
Monitor lunchroom activities	84 (77.1)	17 (15.6)	8 (7.3)
Clear Hallways	66 (60.6)	22 (20.1)	21 (19.3)
Counsel students	56 (51.4)	49 (44.9)	4 (3.7)
Assist teachers with maintaining classroom order	20 (18.3)	64 (58.7)	25 (22.9)
Writing tardy slips	8 (7.3)	15 (13.8)	86 (78.9)
Teach classes	7 (6.4)	77 (70.6)	25 (22.9)
Transporting suspended students home	6 (5.5)	55 (50.4)	48 (44.0)
Search students not under arrest	5 (4.6)	53 (48.5)	51 (46.8)
Break up fighting students	4 (3.7)	83 (76.2)	22 (20.2)

* Only nonmissing responses are included, and percentage totals do not equal 100 due to rounding.

Law Enforcement SROs," define their role as primarily law enforcement/school safety enforcer and actually spend at least half of their time performing law enforcement duties. By that definition, 28 officers (29.8 percent) fit the Traditional Law Enforcement SRO.

In sum, one in three officers in the sample arguably are COPS SROs, while slightly over one in four SROs have aspirations of being a COPS SRO but their daily activities are primarily law enforcement. Just over one in ten officers aspire to a more traditional law enforcement role as an SRO but mainly engage in COPS duties, while almost one in three officers aspire to be traditional law enforcement SROs and actually engage in mostly law enforcement duties in their role as an SRO.

The results presented in Table 10.5 reflect responses to a series of questions asking the officers how often they performed a number of specific activities at their assigned school. More than three in four SROs indicated that monitoring parking areas and monitoring lunchroom activities were the duties performed most often on a daily basis. Clearing hallways (60.6 percent) and counseling students (51.4 percent) were also identified by the majority of the SRO's as part of their daily activities at the school. At the other end of the spectrum, three-quarters indicated they never wrote tardy slips, and nearly one-half said they never searched students not under arrest or transported suspended students home. Three-quarters reported that they broke up fights and taught classes at least monthly.

The aforementioned results clearly reflect that the SROs in this sample were active in a wide variety of capacities in assisting administrators in maintaining school safety. Nevertheless, there was some disagreement between these administrators and the SROs regarding how effective the SROs actually were in reducing problem behaviors at schools. Using data collected from 128 principals at the schools where SROs were assigned (see

Table 10.6. Comparison of Principal and SRO Responses Regarding Changes in Problem Behaviors at School Since SRO Program Began

Safety Issue at School	Decreased		Stayed the Same		Increased	
	Principals	SROs	Principals	SROs	Principals	SROs
Fighting	62.6	63.6	34.3	24.2	3.1	12.1
Marijuana	46.9	49.5	51.0	30.3	2.1	20.2
Theft	45.4	56.7	51.5	25.8	3.1	17.5
Knife Possession	33.7	65.6	65.1	22.9	1.2	11.5
Bomb Threats	30.1	69.7	67.7	25.8	2.2	4.5
Other Weapon Possession	27.7	66.3	71.3	31.4	1.1	2.3
Illicit Sexual Behavior	26.9	51.8	69.9	36.1	3.2	12.0
Gambling	23.9	56.4	70.4	42.3	6.1	1.3
Dress Code Violations	23.5	39.3	75.0	35.7	1.1	25.0
Methamphetamine	22.5	53.5	76.9	39.4	1.1	7.0
Arson	22.0	59.7	75.3	37.5	2.2	2.8
Handgun Possession	20.9	55.0	71.3	43.8	0	1.3
Other Weapon Use	20.7	67.9	78.2	29.6	1.1	2.5
Cocaine	21.1	54.7	77.8	40.0	1.1	5.3
Knife Use	18.3	61.8	80.6	36.8	1.1	1.3
Handgun Use	13.0	51.4	85.9	47.2	1.1	1.4

* Only nonmissing responses are included, and percentage totals do not equal 100 due to rounding.

May, Fessel, & Means, 2004, for discussion of methodology), the results presented in Table 10.6 reflect that, with the exception of arson and dress code violations, at least half of the SROs felt that they had decreased the amount of those problem behaviors since the program began. Among the principals, however, only for fighting did over half the sample feel that the SRO program had reduced the behavior since its inception. For both fighting and marijuana, the percentage of principals and SROs who thought that the SRO program had reduced that problem behavior were approximately equal; for practically all the other behaviors, twice as many SROs as principals felt that the SRO program had decreased the problem behavior in question. Encouragingly, principals were also far less likely to state that problem behaviors had increased than were SROs (see fighting, marijuana, and dress code violations, for example). Thus, it appears that even though SROs and principals may be working on the same problems in the same schools, communication between the two groups needs to be improved to make the SRO a more effective tool to use in increasing school safety in Kentucky schools.

Discussion

The results presented above reveal a number of interesting findings that have implications for the idea that SROs are an extension of community policing practiced on school grounds. First and foremost, at least in Kentucky, over half of the SROs define their SRO role as one that would flow from the NASRO/COPS model—in other words, part law enforcement, part counselor, and part teacher. Nevertheless, two in five SROs define their role as more traditional law enforcement. This may be due, at least in part, to the statutory definition of an SRO in Kentucky, which makes no mention of the community police officer concept.

The findings from this study further reveal that just over one third (39.6 percent from Table 10.3) of the SROs are arguably practicing community policing in their role as an SRO. In other words, more than one in three officers are spending at least half their time counseling students and teaching classes, in addition to performing their law enforcement duties. Nevertheless, the findings from this study also suggest that almost two in three officers spend most of their time practicing more traditional law enforcement duties, a finding not consistent with the NASRO/COPS model.

The interaction between SROs' conceptions of their role and how they actually spend their time paints an even less rosy picture. Less than one-third of SROs both embrace the COPS role and spend at least half their time as counselor and teacher. This is the group that is both willing to do COPS and actually doing it. Another one-quarter must be somewhat frustrated because they indicate a willingness to do COPS but actually spend over half of their time on more traditional law enforcement duties. An additional ten percent are probably also frustrated, as they profess an enforcement orientation but spend the majority of their time doing counseling and teaching—it is likely that they perform these COPS or TRIAD duties half-heartedly, since their interest is more in enforcement. Finally, one in four SROs must be fairly happy, since they subscribe to enforcement and spend the majority of their time doing just that. This group does not even pretend to embrace TRIAD or COPS.

One explanation for these discrepancies, however, may be found in the data on officers' actual duties at the school. For example, the top two daily activities were monitoring the parking area and monitoring the cafeteria. These two activities are analogous to the patrolling that "regular" police officers perform (and which typically also constitute a substantial amount of their time). While certainly a traditional activity, monitoring or patrolling can be motivated and carried out in different ways—for example, it can be done as watching for violations, in which case it is enforcement oriented and might be characterized by a distant, aloof, monitoring persona or by a more active, aggressive, interventionist style. The same activity, though (monitoring or patrolling) might be accomplished through positive interaction with the public (students) in the form of ordinary conversation, persuasion, and informal counseling. It is quite possible that many officers are using this monitoring time to talk to students, teachers, and staff, and build the relationships that are so essential to effective community policing. Thus, even among those officers who define their role as traditional law enforcement or who report that most of their time is devoted to enforcement, many may be engaging in activities quite consistent with community policing and even TRIAD.

Nevertheless, the findings from this study also reveal that there is work to be done in Kentucky before all SROs engage in community policing. The typology developed in Table 10.4 reveals that a substantial minority of the SROs in Kentucky (29.8 percent) consider themselves Traditional Law Enforcement SROs and spend most of their time engaged in traditional law enforcement duties while an additional one in ten consider themselves traditional law enforcement officers but spend the majority of their time on counseling and teaching duties. Consequently, it appears that, at least in Kentucky, if community policing in schools is the model that is desired, more effort needs to be given to socializing officers who go into SRO roles that the role is one of a community police officer in a school setting. SROs should be taught that practically every activity they engage in might be one where they practice community policing. SROs should be taught that: (1) in the hallways, they should build relationships with students while still performing their monitoring duties; (2) in the cafeteria, they can talk to cafeteria staff, teachers, and students about school safety and how each of these groups can assist them in their role as an SRO in insuring school safety; and (3) an SRO can be a tremendous tool in creating a "positive reporting climate," a climate that so often leads to preventing crimes, particularly serious crimes, before they occur.

An additional COPS-related activity that does not seem to have caught on in many Kentucky schools is school-based problem solving (Kenney & Watson, 1998; Kenney & McNamara, 2003). The picture that emerges from this study is one in which some SROs engage in positive interaction, develop partnerships, and embrace the non-traditional functions of teaching and counseling. However, there is little if any indication that SROs are working collaboratively with students, teachers, staff, and parents to identify, analyze, and respond to the chronic problems and conditions in and around their schools that give rise to crime, disorder, and fear. In other words, Kentucky SROs do not seem to have integrated the community policing element of problem solving into their roles and duties.

Those SROs who have adopted an Officer Friendly role or Teacher/Counselor role clearly have some sense of community policing, but it is a limited and ultimately ineffective understanding of the concept unless it is supplemented by problem solving (Goldstein, 1987; Goldstein, 1990). Without problem solving, community policing tends to be all form and no substance. Also, without problem solving, SROs will always turn to enforcement when confronted with crime and serious disorder issues. Problem solving is the operational component of community policing that leads to a more substantive, proactive, and preventive approach to crime and disorder. Nationally and in Kentucky, it would seem to be the key ingredient missing in the school resource officer phenomenon.

References

Atkinson, A.J. (2002). Guide 5: Fostering school-law enforcement partnerships. In *safe and secure: Guides to creating safer schools.* Northwest Regional Education Laboratory and Office of Juvenile Justice and Delinquency Prevention, NCJ 199508. Retrieved June 30, 2014 from https://www.ncjrs.gov/pdffiles1/ojjdp/book5.pdf.

Barnes, L.M..(2008). Policing the Schools: An Evaluation of the North Carolina School Resource Officer Program. Dissertation submitted to Rutgers University, New Jersey. Retrieved August 10, 2014 from: http://proquest.umi.com/pqdlink?vinst=PROD&attempt=1&fmt=6&startpage=1&ver=1&vname=PQD&RQT=309&did=1607105281&exp=07-30-2016&scaling=FULL&vtype=PQD&rqt=309&cfc=1&TS=1312229020&clientId=3507.

Brown, B. (2005). Controlling crime and delinquency in the schools: An exploratory study of student perceptions of school security measures. *Journal of School Violence, 4*, 105–125.

Brown, B. (2006) Understanding and assessing school police officers: A conceptual and methodological comment. *Journal of Criminal Justice, 34*, 591–604.

Bureau of Justice Assistance. (1994). *Understanding community policing: A framework for action*. Washington, DC: Author.

Canaday, M., James, B., & Nease, J. (2012). *To protect and educate: The school resource officer and the prevention of violence in the school*. Hoover, AL: National Association of School Resource Officers.

Center for the Prevention of School Violence. (2001). *The effectiveness of school resource officers*. Retrieved June 30, 2014 from www.ncdjjdp.org/cpsv/Acrobatfiles/brief4.pdf.

Center for the Prevention of School Violence. (1998). The school as 'the beat:' Law enforcement officers in schools. *Center for the Prevention of School Violence Research Bulletin, 1*(3), 1–5.

Chicago Community Policing Evaluation Consortium. (2003). *Community policing in Chicago, years eight and nine: An evaluation of Chicago's alternative policing strategy and information technology initiative*. Springfield, IL: Illinois Criminal Justice Information Authority.

Cordner, G. (1986). Fear of crime and the police: An evaluation of a fear-reduction strategy. *Journal of Police Science and Administration, 14*, 223–233.

Cordner, G. (2001). Community policing: Elements and effects. In R.G. Dunham and G.P. Alpert, eds., *Critical Issues in Policing: Contemporary Readings, 4th edition*. (pp. 493–510) Prospect Heights, IL: Waveland Press.

Finn, P. (2006). School resource officer programs. *FBI Law Enforcement Bulletin, 75*(8), 1–7.

Girouard, C. (2001). *School resource officer training program*. Washington D.C.: U.S. Department of Justice—Office of Juvenile Justice and Delinquency Prevention, www.ncjrs.gov/pdffiles1/ojjdp/fs200105.pdf.

Goldstein, H. (1987). Toward community-oriented policing: Potential, basic requirements and threshold questions. *Crime & Delinquency, 33*(1), 6–30.

Goldstein, H. (1990). *Problem-oriented policing*. New York: McGraw-Hill.

Hickman, M. J., & Reaves, B. A. (2003, January). *Local police departments, 2000* (NCJ 196002). Washington, D.C.: U.S. Department of Justice, Office of Justice Programs, Bureau of Justice Statistics.

Jennings, W.G., Khey, D.N., Maskaly, J., & Donner, C.M. (2011). Evaluating the relationship between law enforcement and school security measures and violent crime in schools. *Journal of Police Crisis Negotiations, 11*(2), 109–124.

Johnson, I. M. (1999). School violence: The effectiveness of a school resource officer program in a southern city. *Journal of Criminal Justice, 27*, 173–192.

Kelling, G., & Moore, M. (1988). The evolving strategy of policing. *Perspectives on Policing*. Washington, D.C.: National Institute of Justice.

Kenney, D., & Watson, S. (1998). *Crime in the schools: Reducing fear and disorder with student problem solving*. Washington, D.C.: Police Executive Research Forum.

Kenney, D., & McNamara, R. (2003). Reducing crime and conflict in Kentucky's schools. *Youth Violence and Juvenile Justice, (1)*, 1, 46–63.

Kim, C., & Geronimo, I. (2009). *Policing in schools: Developing a governance document for school resource officers in K–12 schools*. American Civil Liberties Union.

May, D. C., Fessel, S. B., & Means, S. (2004). Predictors of principals' perceptions of school resource officer effectiveness in Kentucky. *American Journal of Criminal Justice , 29*(1), 75–93.

May, D.C. & Higgins, G.E. (2011). The characteristics and activities of school resource officers: Are newbies different than veterans? *Journal of Police Crisis Negotiations, 11*, 1–13.

Moore, A. (2001). School security staffing part III: School resource officers and off-duty police. *Inside School Safety, (5)*, 11, 3–5.

Na, C., & Gottfredson, D.C. (2013). Police officers in schools: Effects on school crime and the processing of offending behaviors. *Justice Quarterly, 30*(4), 619–650.

National Association of School Resource Officers. (2014). *Introduction to basic school resource officer course*. Retrieved June 30, 2014 from https://nasro.org/basic-sro-course/.

Pate, A.M., Wycoff, M.A., Skogan, W.G., and Sherman, L.W. (1986). *Reducing fear of crime in Houston and Newark: A summary report*. Washington, D.C.: Police Foundation.

Petteruti, A. (2011). *Education under arrest: The case against police in schools*. Justice Policy Institute.

Police Foundation. (1981). *The Newark foot patrol experiment*. Washington. D.C.: Police Foundation.

Reaves, B.A. (2011). *Census of state and local law enforcement agencies, 2008*. Washington D.C.: Bureau of Justice Statistics.

Reaves, B.A. (2010). *Local police departments, 2007*. Washington, D.C.: Bureau of Justice Statistics.

Reiss, A.J., Jr. (1985). Shaping and serving the community: The role of the police chief executive, in W.A. Geller, ed., *Police Leadership in America: Crisis and Opportunity*, (pp. 61–69). New York: Praeger.

Ruddell, R., & May, D. C. (2011). Challenging our perceptions of rural policing: An examination of school resource officers in rural and urban Kentucky schools. *Kentucky Journal of Anthropology and Sociology, 1*, 5–18.

Schreck, C.J., Miller, J.M., & Gibson, C.L. (2003). Trouble in the school yard: A study of the risk factors of victimization at school. *Crime and Delinquency, 49*, 460–484.

Snyder, T. D., & Dillow, S. A. (2010). *Digest of education statistics, 2009*. Washington, D.C.: National Center for Education Statistics.

Theriot, M.T. (2009). School resource officers and the criminalization of student behavior. *Journal of Criminal Justice, 37*, 280–287.

Trump, K. S. (2001). *2001 NASRO school resource officer survey*. Boynton Beach, FL: National Association of School Resource Officers.

United States Department of Justice. (1999). *A national assessment of school resource officer programs*. Washington, D.C.: National Institute of Justice.

United States Department of Justice Office for Victims of Crime. (2003). *Community outreach through police in the schools*. Washington D.C.: U.S. Department of Justice OVC Bulletin.

United States Department of Justice Office of Community Oriented Policing Services. (2003). *COPS in schools grant owner's manual.* Washington D.C.: Government Printing Office.

United States Department of Justice. (2001). *COPS: On the beat.* Washington, D.C.: Office of Community Oriented Policing Services. School Safety Leadership Initiative.

Virginia Department of Criminal Justice Services. (2001). *Second annual evaluation of DCJS funded school resource officer programs: Fiscal year 1999–2000.* Richmond, VA: Crime Prevention Center.

Wald, J., & Thurau, L. (2010). *First do no harm: How educators and police can work together more effectively to keep schools safe and protect vulnerable students.* Retrieved September 6, 2010, from www.modelsforchange.com.

Chapter 11

School-Level Crisis Response Planning

David C. May

Like many other aspects of school safety, crisis management in K–12 schools did not receive much attention until 1999 (after Columbine). Today, if you search "school crisis management" on the Internet, you will find a wide variety of reports, "how to" guides, and example materials about crisis response in schools. However, as the United States Department of Education (2007) report entitled *Practical Information on Crisis Planning: A Guide for Schools and Communities* suggests, "While a growing body of research and literature is available on crisis management for schools, there is little hard evidence to quantify best practices" (pp. 1–4).

Unfortunately, little has changed since that report was published. As I began the research for this chapter, I searched for "crisis response" and "school" in the Mississippi State library database. The search came up with seven book titles, only one of which appeared to be even closely related to school or district crisis management. Other searches, using a variety of search terms including "emergency response," "emergency management," and school, were just as unfruitful. I then went to the library to find the one book that had been identified in the search with the hope that I would be able to identify other books about crisis response on the shelves in close proximity to that book. I found nothing helpful. I then met with a reference librarian and asked for his assistance. His search (using "crisis" then "management" then "school") was able to locate two other books that were in a different section of the library. As I perused those two books, and looked for other books around these two with the hope that I would find other sources, I was struck by the lack of books on this topic. There were literally dozens of books on bullying, counseling students, and classroom management on the adjacent shelves but, again, almost nothing about crisis response.

I then searched the Mississippi State University journal article databases. I searched google scholar and other electronic journal databases and, again, found limited articles about school-wide crisis response. Most of those articles dealt with counseling of troubled students, a very important component of school safety in general, but not exactly what I was looking for. Others dealt with crisis management and crisis response planning for schools, but most were case studies, policy pieces, or theoretical works describing the importance of school-level crisis response planning.

Thus, because of the limited empirical research examining the effectiveness of crisis response planning, this chapter does not include any quantitative data about crisis response planning. In this chapter, I begin with a definition of crisis and crisis response, then provide a discussion of the theoretical background for crisis response planning that has emerged from the extant literature. Next, I recount my own experiences with school-level crisis response planning at one elementary and two middle schools, and close with a "lessons learned" section where I incorporate my own experience with the recommendations of the Bureau of Justice Statistics (2012) to provide examples of ways that schools can incorporate those recommendations into their own crisis response planning.

What Is a Crisis and a Crisis Response?

The ideas of crises and crisis response are not new; in fact, these terms have been used widely in the corporate world for decades. Although a crisis is defined in a wide variety of ways, for the purposes of this chapter, a crisis is any major occurrence that has a potentially negative outcome and can negatively impact a school, its students, parents, or staff, and its reputation (Fearn-Banks, 1996). The term crisis management, in its most general sense, involves planning for any type of event that can negatively impact an organization and its ability to fulfill its mission. Johnson and Johnson's handling of the "Tylenol crisis" (when seven people in the Chicago area died in 1982 after ingesting Extra Strength Tylenol capsules laced with cyanide) is often recognized as an early exemplar in crisis management; their quick recall of Extra Strength Tylenol capsules (and its subsequent replacement with tamper-proof Extra Strength Tylenol caplets) provided a textbook example of how to quickly manage crises and recover from their negative impact (Fearn-Banks, 1996; Fink, 1996).

Most experts in crisis management suggest that there are four stages in the sequence of crisis management: mitigation/prevention, preparedness, response, and recovery. These stages can be clearly seen in school-level crisis management. In the mitigation/prevention stage, school administrators focus on what they can do to reduce loss of life and property in a crisis at their school. The preparedness stage is the process of planning for crises, often preparing for worst case scenarios. The response stage involves the actions school administrators actually take in the case of a crisis. The final stage, recovery, involves those steps school personnel take to return the school to normalcy after a crisis (U.S. Department of Education, 2007).

A detailed discussion of each of the four stages outlined above is beyond the scope of this chapter. Thus, rather than briefly discuss each stage of crisis management, in this chapter I will focus on the second stage: crisis preparedness. In my opinion, the most important step in adequately preparing for a crisis at the school-level involves crisis response planning where a committee of teachers, parents, staff, administrators, students, and emergency response personnel work together to create a crisis response plan for the school. In the following pages, I provide a summary of my personal experience with this process.

My Experience

In July 2008, as part of my role as the Kentucky Center for School Safety (KCSS) Research Fellow at Eastern Kentucky University, I was invited to deliver a presentation about crisis response planning to a group of school administrators as part of their in-service training. As I was preparing the presentation, I was struck by the suggestion that not only do school districts need a crisis response plan, individual schools also need a plan as well. As I was driving two hours to deliver the presentation, it dawned on me that I had children at two separate public schools and, as a parent, I did not have any idea what either school had in place for crisis response. I decided that I would find out.

In the late summer of 2008, I met with the principal at the elementary school where two of my children attended. I asked her what they did about crisis response planning. She said they had a school safety committee a few years ago that put together a plan but she would have to find it (she was not sure that they even had a copy of it). I asked her if she would be willing to let me spearhead the effort to revitalize the school safety committee so we could update the school's plan. I told her I would be doing it as a parent volunteer, not in any official capacity. She willingly accepted the offer and thus began my foray into school-level crisis response planning.

In the fall 2008 semester, we formed a school safety committee whose purpose was to put together a school-level crisis response plan. Following the recommendations of the literature available at the time, we formed a committee comprised of representatives from four outside agencies: law enforcement, fire, emergency management, and the medical community. From the school, we included the principal, guidance counselor, school psychologist, school nurse, custodian, special education teacher, three additional teachers with interests in crisis response, and three students. Together, we met monthly throughout the school year with the primary purpose being that we would develop a school-level crisis response plan.

We decided to follow the National Incident Management System (NIMS) model (Federal Emergency Management Agency, 2014) primarily because (1) that was the model most often referenced in the literature at that time, (2) it was a model that was easy for people to understand, and (3) the KCSS had adopted that model as the recommended model for schools in Kentucky (see KCSS, 2008, for detailed discussion of the model). Before we began our draft of the plan, the principal, the custodian, and I conducted a "hazard hunt," (KCSS, 2008, p. 70), where we walked all over the school property and identified circumstances in the school (or, in some cases, the surrounding community) that "... present unique problems or potential risk to persons or property. These may include materials used in classes, issues specific to your location in the building, situations which may impede evacuation from the building, community issues (factories, airport, water plant, rivers/streams), etc." (KCSS, 2008 p. 70). One tool to assist in this effort is a school vulnerability checklist similar to the one I have downloaded from the Kentucky Center for School Safety website and included in Appendix 11.1. After compiling the list of hazards, we then went back to the committee with the list and discussed strategies to mitigate the hazards.

This process was particularly revealing to the school staff. It was well-known in the community that the school had traffic problems—the hazard hunt revealed the extreme nature of this problem for a crisis. The principal had never considered hazardous chemical storage and labeling; this became a problem that needed an immediate solution. As a parent, I was impressed and encouraged with the attention to detail that the committee gave to this process. They took their job seriously, even when it involved discussion of crises with only a small likelihood of occurring (e.g., school shootings, airplane crashes, kidnapping). Furthermore, these discussions led to consideration of a number of possibilities (no matter how expensive those solutions) of how to mitigate the problems that were identified.

Based on the committee discussions, my graduate assistants and I developed a crisis response plan for the school. In lieu of including the entire template we created (approximately 70 pages that is available for download on the website for this book), I have included some of the most important components from that plan in Appendix 11.2. In that appendix, I have included: (1) two table of contents (one for the overall crisis response plan and one found later in the plan that deals specifically with individual incidents); (2) an example of the general individual responsibilities description for the public information officer and safety officer, two designated roles in the Incident Command System plan; (3) a template for the drill schedule and log; (4) the contents of the emergency team toolbox; and (5) an Accidents with Injuries flowchart. Although the following paragraphs contain a discussion of the items included in Appendix 11.2, I encourage the reader to view and download the template in its entirety on the website for this book.

In general, the template that we created would likely mirror those at many schools throughout the country; however, there are two notable differences. The first improvement we made to the typical crisis response plan was one that originated from one of the school staff assigned to the team. She suggested that it would be a good idea to make an electronic version of the plan, with hyperlinks from the table of contents to each component of the plan. Then, teachers could put the electronic version on their computer desktop, open it in an emergency, and quickly find the appropriate procedure for handling that emergency. We incorporated that idea, one I certainly did not think about, but one that made the plan even better and more user-friendly. Thus, as the reader views the plan, they can click on any part of the table of contents and be taken directly to that part of the plan.

The first document included in Appendix 11.2 is the overall table of contents for the plan. In that table of contents are included the various components of the plan. Rather than discuss each component in detail, I will discuss the contents generally then encourage the reader to examine the entire plan in more detail on the book's website. The plan begins with emergency contact information for teachers, school staff, and local emergency response agencies. Next, we list the lockdown procedure for the school in detail so every teacher knows exactly what they are supposed to do in those cases where a lockdown is necessary. The next section lists the crisis response team members and their responsibilities, then identifies "relief teachers" to take over supervision of students when crisis response team members have to leave to fulfill their duties.

The following section provides information about the general responsibilities of each member of the crisis response team. As examples of these responsibilities, in Appendix 11.2, I have included the responsibilities for the public information officer and the safety officer. At all three schools where we implemented this plan, these roles were filled by teachers who were either level-headed, articulate speakers (public information officer) or had some background in first aid, emergency response, or industrial safety (safety officer). The next sections include a list of students needing special assistance because of physical, mental, or emotional disabilities, a hazard hunt form (referenced earlier) for team members to identify hazards and assign responsibilities and deadlines to deal with those hazards, and a section about plans for moving students off-site when needed.

In Appendix 11.2, I have included an example of the drill schedule and log; this component of the Crisis Response Plan is vital because it serves as a constant reminder that schools need to train and practice crisis response regularly. In the table of contents, the next form is the "Emergency Team Tool Box" checklist, which has also been included in Appendix 11.2. This checklist serves as a reminder of the items that need to be included in a portable "toolbox" that can be used by the crisis response team while dealing with any crisis that may occur. The plan closes with designated crisis response and evacuation responsibilities, a current floor plan, bus assignments (where students are assigned by class to a specific bus to avoid further confusion in cases of a crisis), a list of "teacher pairs," who follow the idea of buddy teams so that all teachers have a colleague checking on the welfare of their classes, and a form to use to identify parts of the crisis response plan that need to be updated annually (which will change from year to year as components are added or removed from the plan).

In the back of the plan, for each crisis included, we included a flowchart of individual actor responsibilities. I have included the table of contents for those flowcharts (labeled Crisis Response Plans Table of Contents), which lists the crises for which we created flowcharts in Appendix 11.2. As an exemplar, I have also included a flowchart for Accidents with Injuries in Appendix 11.2. The genesis for this flowchart idea began during my military career as an Air National Guard Security Forces Supervisor (their version of the military police). In that role, members of my unit had to respond to a variety of emergencies. Because we often had inexperienced airmen working as the dispatcher for the shift, we had a set of emergency protocols located in the command control center. In that set of protocols was included a step-by-step procedure for each emergency that we had dealt with and a set of tasks for each member involved in the crisis response. This made it very easy for the airman to direct responding units on how they were supposed to react and the tasks they were to perform upon arrival at the emergency. I felt this would be a good idea for the school crisis response plan; there was unanimous agreement among the team with the idea so we included that in the template.

The crisis response plan we developed was met with tremendous support by the school. Based on our discussions in the plan, a number of changes (many of which are discussed below) were also made and, as a result, I believe the school is safer today than it was in 2008 when we began the process (although, as mentioned earlier, this is only anecdotal evidence). Based on that process, I was asked to assist two other middle schools in the district. We used largely the same process; my work with both those schools convinced me that every school needs to have a school-specific crisis response plan. While all three schools had some problems that were similar (e.g., hazardous waste storage, unlocked doors), there were also many challenges that were unique to each school. Thus, I would encourage every student, parent, or concerned citizen to visit the schools in their community and ask to see their school crisis response/emergency management plan. If they have one, ask them how often they train the teachers and staff about the plan. If they do not have one, take the necessary steps to ensure that they create one. My experience is that if a parent or concerned citizen is willing to drive the effort at no cost to the school, then the school administrators and staff will do their part to make sure that a plan is created or updated. With persistent pressure from the interested parties, that plan might even be distributed to the teachers and staff, trained, and updated regularly. That process is just one more step in insuring the safety of the school.

Above I have included details of my own experience that resulted in the template included on this book's website. Keep in mind that template is only of many that are available. To make the reader aware of other important considerations, I have included details about developing a crisis response plan from one of the best sources available, the Bureau of Justice Statistics *Guide for Preventing and Responding to School Violence* (Bureau of Justice Statistics, 2012). In the following paragraphs, I provide a review of that document and apply it to school-level crisis response planning.

In the section entitled "Section 4—Crisis Planning and Preparation," (Bureau of Justice Statistics, 2012), the report authors discuss the essential nature of planning in preparing for crises in the school setting. They present 23 points for school administrators, teachers, and staff to consider in crisis response planning. All of those points are presented on pages 20 and 21 of that document; I have included their recommendations verbatim in italics below, then followed their recommendations with comments from my own experience.

1. *Establish a crisis planning team that includes representation from faculty and staff, as well as safety, security, and emergency response providers who are knowledgeable about crisis planning or would help intervene in a school safety crisis.* In my experience, this is perhaps the most important element of crisis response planning. In each of the schools where I was involved in crisis response planning, the school administrators were happy to assign teachers, counselors, and custodians to the team but did not offer any police, fire, or medical providers as initial suggestions for the team. In each case, however, they were open to the idea when I suggested it. In two of the three schools, there were parents of current students employed in these roles and they were happy to help (and good about attending meetings of the team once they began). Additionally, we incorporated the school resource officer and school nurse assigned to the schools into the team. In every case, they were valuable team members.

2. *Establish school crisis management teams at district and site levels using the nationally recognized Incident Command System (ICS).* The template that I created for readers to consider as a model for their own school plan was based on the ICS; in my opinion, it is intuitive and most school personnel understand the design and are often familiar with the terminology. Thus, of the various models that are available, I would join the Bureau of Justice Statistics in recommending this plan.

3. *Have a working knowledge of all available and needed resources for handling and responding to a crisis situation.* No one individual knows everything they need to know about the school and community resources available. In general, I am not a big fan of "group-think"; however, this process is one where group-think is beneficial every time. In my own experience, whenever emergency response personnel work with school personnel, the process of identifying resources expands dramatically beyond what either group would have developed alone. In each case, there were members of the team who had lived in the community for decades. When identifying resources, however, someone made them aware of a resource to deal with crisis response that they had never heard of before.

4. *Include off-site school activities such as stadium events, field trips, and so on, in crisis planning.* Given that practically every child attends at least one field trip or extracurricular activity on behalf of the school, it is important to prepare for these events as well. Because of the wide variety of situations that might be possible off-campus, schools cannot reasonably provide the same detail for each of these situations as they would in their main campus crisis response plan. However, a page dedicated to a protocol for a crisis at a football game will be handy should the situation ever arise.

5. *Assign all faculty and staff to clearly defined roles under the ICS system. Critical assignments must be three deep.* These roles and assignments should be based on the strengths and weaknesses of the teachers and staff. An articulate, extroverted prior military teacher would be a good fit for the public information officer position (described in Appendix 11.2) but not as good a fit as an introverted accounting teacher for the finance/administration chief position. Thus, the crisis response committee should carefully consider teachers for each of the roles, and always assign two back-ups for each position.

6. *Identify and make arrangements now with the mental health professionals who would provide the critical incident stress debriefing immediately after a crisis.* Most school districts have guidance counselors available at all schools; some districts even have school psychologists at each school. Nevertheless, in a time of a death of a student, these resources will quickly become overwhelmed. Thus, it is important to have good working relationships with mental health professionals in the community that are not full-time employees of the school system. In general, these professionals are willing to help and will do so if called on in time of need. Making arrangements beforehand is crucial to activate mental health providers quickly in times of crises.

7. *Identify and train on-site building maintenance staff (primary and backup) and off-site personnel who will take responsibility for dealing with fire alarms, sprinkler systems, gas, and so on.* Unfortunately, in most school buildings, the only person that is familiar with the alarm system may be the custodian (and they may not be entirely aware of all alarm systems). Thus, it is important to identify both a primary and secondary individual to be trained on all school alarm systems. Using a "train the trainer" model, these individuals can then train other teachers and staff about the systems for quick response when a crisis does occur.

8. *Identify personnel who have master keys, codes, and access to secured areas at the site.* In my experience, schools often have a poor key tracking system, which (a) causes them to have a number of keys that are unaccounted for and (b) doesn't allow them to know who has the master keys and codes for access to all school sites. The principal is often relied on for this access in non-crisis situations; however, in a crisis situation, the principal will be busy with the ICS model and will not have time to serve as an access point for emergency response personnel to allow them into school areas. Thus, it is important to have a list of who has been issued master keys to the building; additionally, an exhaustive list of codes and persons who have access to secured areas needs to be readily available in the crisis response kit. This list needs to be updated at the beginning of each semester.

9. *Classrooms should have locks that can be locked from the inside in the case of a crisis …* To most readers, this seems intuitive. Nevertheless, particularly in older buildings, there are a number of classrooms that have locking systems that only allow the door to be

locked from the outside with a key. These locks need to be replaced. The initial expense may seem daunting, but a project such as this is a good fundraising project for a student organization such as the Beta club, the National Honor Society, the Key club, etc. My experience is that community members are willing to help when they see a specific need at the schools. This is one area where that need is easily communicated.

10. *Establish and publicize the chain of command ...* The ICS chain of command should be in the crisis response plan, posted in the office, and readily accessible to teachers and staff members throughout the building. However, just creating and posting the chain of command is simply not enough. Teachers and staff should regularly be reminded of the chain of command and it should be updated at the beginning of every semester because staff turnover is likely to occur. When it does, the chain of command needs to be updated accordingly.

11. *Establish and practice how to protect students with physical, cognitive, or developmental disabilities.* In my experience, this was one of the areas that most of the crisis response team had not considered prior to our first meeting. In the discussions that followed, the school counselor created a list of students that would need assistance in a crisis then identified a student in each of their classes that would be their "buddy" in the time of a crisis to assist them. In addition, they ensured that the teachers of the students with disabilities were cognizant of the fact that they would need assistance during the time of a crisis, and listed the students by name in their crisis response plan. This strategy seemed to be an effective strategy for all involved.

12. *Prepare a dismissal plan in the event students need to be sent home early.* As with any event involving children (particularly in elementary schools), the first response of parents is always to "go get my child." Unfortunately, in many crises, this often causes far more problems (e.g., traffic tie-ups, staff needed in other areas have to deal with parents) than it solves. Thus, it is important to have a dismissal plan in the event students need to be sent home early or students need to be moved to an off-campus site. A U.S. Army ammunitions depot was located within the county where we worked on school-level crisis response plans; a variety of potentially hazardous ammunition was stored on that depot, so each of the schools already had an evacuation plan in place and parents were aware of that plan. Thus, we simply merged our dismissal plan in crises with that evacuation plan. As with any other activity involving students, command and control of the students is essential so we created plans to have one entry/exit point where two teachers would be stationed with a roster of all students. Parents would come to that exit point to check out their children. This allowed the school personnel to maintain control of all children at all times.

13. *Establish and practice lockdown and evacuation procedures, including where students should go during different types of crises ...* This is probably the largest area of failure for most schools that develop crisis response plans. If the school does not practice the plan, then the plan is useless. Additionally, some crises required different responses than other crises. In our plan, we created both an "Orientation and Training Schedule" and a "Drill Schedule and Log" that were included in the plan. It is crucial that the principal and/or other designees plan training and drills prior to the beginning of the school year and let faculty and staff know when both are scheduled. Just as importantly, however, principals need to ensure that they *follow the training and drill schedules.* Time is one of the most valuable commodities in a school setting; thus, these schedules must be

protected and enforced by the principal/assistant principals or the training and drills will be replaced by another activity that someone else deems more important.

14. *Publicize locations to students, parents, school teachers, and staff, crisis team members, and emergency response personnel.* In both of the points above, I discussed the importance of planning and advertising that plan with parents. Revealing the entire contents of the school's crisis response plan is both unnecessary and potentially unsafe. However, all parents need to be regularly reminded of off-campus locations where students will be relocated in crises that require evacuation of the school.

15. *Develop an emergency traffic plan capable of protecting emergency response routes and accommodating the likely traffic and parking needs.* In my experience, whether through intentional or unintentional design, schools are often located in areas that cause natural traffic problems on a "normal" day when there are no crises occurring. Although all three schools with whom I worked to develop a crisis response plan had serious traffic concerns, none of the concerns were identical. Thus, there is a strong likelihood that the school(s) in your local community have traffic problems as well. Development of this plan is essential to handling a crisis situation.

An example of the creativity that may be needed is provided by the first school with whom I worked. At this elementary school, there was one entry/exit point for the entire school that was a nightmare to navigate during morning drop-off and afternoon pickup times. Thus, this was one of the first priorities we discussed as we completed our hazard hunt for the school. At the back of the school lot, a fence separated the school property from a golf course adjacent to that property. Because the golf course was owned by the university where I was employed at the time, we approached the university to gain permission to install a gate at the back of the property to provide an emergency response/evacuation route through the golf course in a crisis. The university agreed to allow the gate, which allowed us to have a second entry/exit point in case of a crisis.

16. *Designate places, depending on the nature of the crisis, for personnel to perform their roles. These include*

a. *A designated media contact location*: It is important to allow the media access to the school; in any crisis, the media have the potential to be either an important ally or a powerful enemy of the school. This location should be close enough to the school where the media can secure limited video footage of the school but far enough away from the school that the media do not interfere with crisis response operations.

b. *A designated place for parents and guardians to congregate*: As mentioned earlier, in any crisis, parents will come to the school. Thus, a designated location for parents and guardians is essential. Like the media contact location, the designated parent location needs to be far enough away that parents do not interfere with crisis but close enough where they can receive regular updates from designated school personnel.

c. *A designated place for clergy* and

d. *A designated place for mental health professionals*: Both clergy and mental health professionals need a dedicated space to work with students, staff, and others affected by the crisis. This area should not be visible to the media or parents and should allow enough privacy that these professionals can perform their duties without worrying about interference from outside sources.

e. *Staging areas for transportation*: Most school administrators do not regularly consider how they would evacuate the entire school from the building in an emergency situation and, in many cases, would not have the buses on-site to evacuate even if they wanted to. Thus, it is important to designate a staging area for transportation of students in the crisis response plan. This area needs to be close enough to the school that children can easily walk/run to the area in a timely manner.

17. *Establish a calling tree or phone tree that allows the crisis management team to be notified immediately.* Every crisis response plan needs a calling tree. The calling tree needs to clearly designate who are the first points of contact, the structure of the process whereby they alert other teachers regarding any crisis that has occurred, and a feedback loop so that the initial person contacted knows that the message has gone all the way through the chain. As a replacement for the calling tree, many schools now use some type of "one call" system, whereby all teachers, students, parents (or select individuals from those groups) can be alerted with one phone call regarding any crisis that has occurred. In reality, this system works far better than a calling tree and, in my experience with both schools and volunteer agencies, is well worth the cost that the organization pays to use that service.

18. *Make alternative response plans known to key personnel who would communicate the nature of the crisis and the appropriate level of response.* In some cases, the initial crisis response plan may be compromised or impossible to execute (e.g., a designated evacuation spot becomes unavailable because of severe weather). To prepare for those situations, alternative response plans need to be created and given to key personnel (the principal, the assistant principal, and a select few others who have key responsibilities in the plan). These individuals can thus turn to the alternate plan (and advise others of that plan) if the situation arises.

19. *Create crisis and evacuation kits and lace them at strategic locations inside and outside the schools.* As mentioned earlier and included in Appendix 11.2, a crisis evacuation kit is essential to assist in response to crises. Schools need to have three or more identical kits available at various locations on the school grounds so that members of the crisis response team will have those resources available even when some area of the school is no longer accessible due to natural or unnatural damages that destroy that kit or make it inaccessible.

20. *Consider using digital technology and computer databases to store photographs and demographic information . . .* I believe it is a good idea to digitize the entire crisis response plan. Digitizing photographs and databases containing important demographic information (e.g., adults allowed to pick up students from school, medicines needed for various students) will make those databases accessible even when hard copies are not available.

21. *Provide copies of all emergency and evacuation plans to local law enforcement, fire, and other emergency response agencies.* These agencies will be important assets in the case of a real crisis. It is important that these agencies be aware of the school's plans for evacuation and other actions included in the response plan. In addition to including members of these agencies as part of the crisis response team, it is important for these agencies to have a copy of the entire plan so they will know what to expect from the school in case of a crisis.

22. *Provide law enforcement, fire, and other emergency response personnel with blueprints, layouts, and floor plans of school buildings and grounds . . .* The initial team(s) of emergency responders may have never visited the school before. Thus, having blueprints, layouts,

and floor plans available to them (ideally, in digitized form) will assist them in their initial response to the crisis and will help them clear various areas in cases of fire or criminal crisis situations.

23. *Consider creating a system of storage boxes outside school buildings ... that provide staff and emergency response personnel with access to keys at any time of the day and night.* In many cases, schools now use some type of alarm system that unlocks doors without a physical key. Nevertheless, just as many schools still use physical keys to gain access into school buildings. If these boxes are not available, there is a real possibility that the person(s) that have keys to those buildings will not be immediately available. Placing keys in storage boxes outside of the school will allow emergency responders, teachers, or school administrators to gain immediate access to a building in time of crisis without waiting on other persons who have been assigned the keys to those buildings.

Conclusions

In this chapter, I have briefly addressed the importance of crisis response planning and discussed my own experiences in creating crisis response plans for individual schools. Hopefully, the discussion and resources provided in this chapter will be helpful to the readers as the engage in crisis response planning in their own local schools.

Nevertheless, crisis response planning is only one component of dealing with crisis situations at the school and district levels. Two excellent resources that succinctly address a wide variety of elements of dealing with crises are the second edition of the *Guide for Preventing and Responding to School Violence* that is available online from the Bureau of Justice Statistics (2012) and *Practical Information on Crisis Planning*, a report also available online from the U.S. Department of Education (2007). Other agencies such as the Kentucky Center for School Safety, the Federal Emergency Management Association, the United States Department of Education, and the National Center for Education Statistics all have a variety of resources available to assist in crisis management in schools.

As with any dynamic topic, the crises facing schools change as new technologies and new social problems are developed. Nevertheless, one of the most important challenges facing individuals concerned about crisis management in schools is the dearth of scholarly research in this area. As I reviewed the literature for this chapter, I was unable to find any research that used experimental or quasi-experimental designs to determine whether those schools using crisis response teams and protocols were better prepared for crises than their counterparts without them. Luckily, the number of serious crises occurring in schools is so limited in number that natural experiments (where similar crises occur in schools with good crisis management planning and schools without crisis management planning) are so rare that it is impractical to expect such studies to appear in the future.

Thus, one method of evaluating the effectiveness of crisis response planning is to use drills with objective evaluators using scoring metrics whereby they provide scores based on readiness and response. Researchers could then compare the scores of schools with crisis response plans to those without crisis response plans; in theory, those with crisis response plans in place, that train and drill the response plans regularly, should score better on those metrics than either schools without crisis response plans or schools with crisis response plans that rarely train those plans. Until this type of research is conducted, I remain hopeful (but not empirically convinced) that crisis response plans make schools safer. At the very least, I believe that crisis response planning builds communication between schools, emergency responders, and community resources. If that is all that it does, it is still a step in the right direction.

Appendix 11.1

K–12 Security & Vulnerability Assessment*

	Area	Y/N	Description/Comments
	School Profile		
	School name:		
	Location:		
	Website address:		
	Principal's name:		
1	# of Students:		
2	# of Teachers:		
3	Student to teacher ratio:		
4	Average # of visitors daily:		
5	Number of buildings:		
6	Approx. square footage:		
7	Year of construction:		
8	Campus style (multi-story building/ multi-building, open, etc)		
9	School environment (urban, suburban, rural)		
	Student Transportation		
10	% traveling by bus:		
11	% traveling by personal vehicle:		
12	% driven by parents:		
13	% traveling by foot or bike:		
	Law Enforcement Relations		
14	School Resource Officer:		
15	How many days/hours is SRO on campus?		
	Social Factors Pertinent to the Student Population		
16	Ethnic and cultural backgrounds:		
17	Languages spoken by students:		
18	Economic conditions:		
19	Single parent households:		
20	Unique characteristics of student body:		
	Documentation Collection		
21	Please provide us with a copy of the following:		
	Campus Map		
	Current Emergency/Crisis Response Plan		

	Area	Y/N	Description/Comments
	Safety Concerns		
22	What would you consider to be the number 1 risk to student safety?		
23	What would you consider to be the number 1 risk to staff safety?		
	Policies and Procedures		
	ID Cards		
24	Are staff and teachers issued ID badges? Is display enforced?		
25	Are employees wearing their badges if made available?		
26	Are students issued ID cards?		
27	Who controls the issuance of ID badges?		
28	Are IDs also used for doorway access control?		
29	Do procedures exist for activation/deactivation of access?		
30	Is there a system in place to provide temporary ID cards to visitors/outside contractors/vendors/janitorial personnel?		
	Visitor/Volunteer/Contractor Protocol		
31	Is there a visitor log book or computerized visitor log-in system in the main office?		
32	Describe the visitor sign-in policy and procedures.		
33	Are visitors and vendors escorted while on campus?		
34	Are volunteers, contractors, temporary personnel, and substitute teachers required to sign in and receive a badge prior to gaining entry to the school?		
35	Do outside contractors/vendors/janitorial personnel check-in before providing services?		
36	Do outside contractors/vendors/janitorial personnel have a routine entry point and route of service?		
37	Are criminal background checks conducted on all employees, outside contractors, outside vendors, and janitorial personnel?		

	Area	Y/N	Description/Comments
	Key Control		
38	Describe key control procedures.		
39	Where are keys stored?		
40	Is the key cabinet properly secured with a lock, or located in the safe of another secure area?		
41	Is a key log maintained?		
42	Do teachers return their keys at the end of the school year?		
43	Who has access to the master keys to the school?		
44	Are contractors or other vendors issued keys?		
45	Do local police and fire departments have access to the master key (e.g., via a key box located on the exterior of the facility)?		
	Temp Personnel/Subs Protocol		
46	Are substitute teachers provided a copy of the school's emergency procedures?		
47	Are substitute teachers issued classroom keys?		
	Money Handling		
48	Is there a safe for money?		
49	Where is the safe located, and who has access to it? Who is responsible for money handling on campus?		
50	Who is responsible for taking money to the bank or school district headquarters?		
	Mail Handling		
51	Is there a designated mail handling facility?		
52	Have any staff members received training in proper mail handling and suspicious package procedures?		
	Special Needs Students and Staff		
53	Does the school have a list of special needs occupants listing their special need and location within the schools?		
54	Are special provisions made to ensure the safety and welfare of the special needs occupants?		
55	Does the school have predetermined evacuation/sheltering staging areas for special needs occupants?		
56	Does the school implement the "buddy system" to ensure that each special needs occupant has a person who is responsible for their safety and welfare?		

	Area	Y/N	Description/Comments
	Off-Premise Procedures		
57	Have those responsible for driving students off school grounds been trained in emergency procedures?		
58	What is the ratio of supervisors/chaperones to students?		
59	Are the supervisors equipped with radios or cell phones? If so, does the main office have a list of staff cell phone numbers?		
60	Do all students/parent fill out an informational form before attending an off-campus activity?		
61	Has staff received training on hazard avoidance and emergency management procedures while off school grounds?		
62	Are staff members required to check-in on a periodic basis while on a trip?		
63	Do staff members carry the necessary forms (permission slip, emergency contact information, special medical needs) while on a trip?		
	After-Hours Emergency Procedures		
64	What type of after-hours activities are conducted at this school?		
65	Is your school used regularly after-hours?		
66	Is the school used during the weekend for church services or other activities?		
67	Who is in charge of the school during after-hours activities? Has this person been trained in the Incident Command System and knows the school's emergency procedures?		
68	Is the after-hours IC authorized and trained on how to evacuate the school or shelter in place?		
69	Are teachers allowed to work at the school in the evening hours without permission?		
70	How many custodians work in the evening and what time does their shift end? Do they have radios in case of trouble?		
	Emergency Procedures		
71	Are the school's safety and security plans updated annually?		
72	Does the school or school district have an anonymous hotline number to report incidents to school administrators?		
73	Are there emergency phone number stickers on all school telephones?		

	Area	Y/N	Description/Comments
	Emergency Procedures (cont.)		
74	Does the school have an automated voice mail system that includes the statement, "Your telephone call may be monitored to ensure safety"?		
75	Has the school designated a PRIMARY location for its emergency operations center?		
76	Has the school designated a SECONDARY location for its emergency operations center?		
77	Has a kit been established for the emergency operations center, including (but not limited to) emergency contact lists, medical considerations list, flashlights, first aid supplies, and radios?		
78	Does the school have a School Safety Committee? How often do they meet?		
79	Do all staff members receive a copy of the school's emergency procedures manual?		
	Emergency Response Plan/Safe School Plan		
80	Does the school's emergency response plan have an "all hazards" approach?		
81	Has an Emergency Response Team (ERT), or equivalent, been developed?		
82	Has the school involved local public safety agencies in developing the school's "all hazards" emergency response plan?		
83	Do local public safety agencies have a copy of the school's Emergency Response Plan and blueprints/drawings for the school?		
84	Has Police and Fire done a walkthrough of the school to familiarize themselves with its layout?		
	Training and Exercising		
85	Do teachers and staff receive emergency management training, regardless of whether they are on the ERT?		
86	Has the school ever conducted tabletop exercises or other exercises to test its emergency preparedness?		
87	Have staff members been trained in how to take a bomb threat phone call?		
88	Has staff received fire extinguisher training?		
89	Describe the school's drill protocol. Is it in line with district/local standards?		
90	Is a drill log maintained and post-drill critique conducted after each drill?		

	Area	Y/N	Description/Comments
	Training and Exercising (cont.)		
91	After an incident, does ERT conduct a post-incident critique? Are lessons learned shared with District Administration?		
92	Has staff been trained in how to recognize signs of drug use, physical abuse, and gang activity among students?		
	Evacuation Procedures		
93	How many evacuation drills are performed?		
94	Has the fire department participated in any drills at the school?		
95	Are evacuation drills conducted between classes, at lunch, or arrival/dismissal?		
96	Have the school's assembly points been established, both on and off campus? Have transportation needs been addressed if all occupants need to be relocated to the off campus assembly point?		
97	How far from the school facilities is the PRIMARY assembly point(s)?		
98	How far from the school facilities is the SECONDARY assembly point(s)?		
99	Are evacuation assembly points near the street?		
100	Does the school have an adequate system to track students evacuating out of the school?		
101	Do you have any mutual aid agreements with other schools or community organizations?		
	Shelter-in-Place Procedures		
102	How many sheltering drills are conducted each year?		
103	Are sheltering drills conducted between classes, at lunch, or arrival/dismissal?		
104	Have sheltering areas been pre-determined and are they clearly marked?		
	Lockdown Procedures		
105	Does the school have a lockdown plan?		
106	How many lockdown drills are conducted each year?		
107	Are lockdown drills performed in between classes, at lunch or arrival/dismissal?		
108	Have the local police department reviewed the school's lockdown procedures for familiarity?		

	Area	Y/N	Description/Comments
	EXTERIOR		
	Neighborhood/Perimeter		
109	Describe characteristics of neighborhood		
110	Are there issues with gang activity, drug activity, or unauthorized use of school grounds?		
111	Are there issues with unsafe conditions regarding traffic in the area?		
112	Describe adjacent land use		
	Fencing		
113	Are gates secured?		
114	Is fencing sufficient?		
115	Is the height of the fence sufficient (e.g., around utilities or the chiller area)?		
116	Were utility panels, gas mains, A/C units, and others properly fenced and gated?		
117	Is the height of the fence around these areas sufficient? Were gates locked?		
118	Describe the condition of the fencing—is it broken, falling down, or in need of replacement?		
	Vegetation/Groundskeeping		
119	Are shrubs and trees maintained properly to avoid creating hiding spaces or enabling access to the roof?		
120	Describe the condition of the school grounds.		
121	Were any holes or other trip hazards observed?		
122	Were rain gutters in good condition?		
123	Is there a drainage problem?		
	Building Ventilation Intake(s)		
124	Are outside air intakes located at least 15 feet above the ground?		
125	Are gas leaks, biological, and chemical detection systems in place?		
	Underground Access		
126	Is there underground access to facility?		
	Visibility/Possible Concealment		
127	Were any blind spots and hiding areas observed?		

	Area	Y/N	Description/Comments
	Alleyways and Service Drives		
128	Were alleyways and service drives properly secured?		
129	Were unauthorized vehicles parked in the area?		
130	Are protective barriers (e.g., bollards) needed to keep vehicles from hitting the building, curbs, dumpsters, or other along the service drives?		
131	Were all fenced-in areas secured in the alleyways and service drives?		
	Garbage Dumpster Area		
132	Is the garbage dumpster area secure?		
133	Are garbage dumpsters situated near the school building?		
134	Are vehicles parked near/in front of the dumpster(s)?		
	Exterior CCTV		
135	Does the school have an exterior CCTV system? Describe (# of cameras, digital vs. VHS, remote monitoring—Y/N, color/black-and–white, location of monitor(s), location of cameras)		
136	Are there any areas that need cameras that do not currently have them?		
137	Is there remote monitoring of the system from administrators' offices? Where is the main monitor located? Is it in an area that is consistently attended?		
138	Is the system VHS or digital? How often is backup?		
139	How long are tapes stored?		
140	Are there any cameras that do not work?		
141	Does the monitoring capability need improvement? Can all cameras be viewed at once?		
	Exterior Lighting		
142	Is night lighting sufficient?		
143	Were any broken lights observed?		

	Area	Y/N	Description/Comments
	Exterior Signage		
144	Are signs in good condition? Are there any outdated signs that are no longer applicable? Is there adequate signage around the facility regarding:		
145	parking areas (visitor vs. staff)		
146	speed limits		
147	proper drop-off/pick-up areas		
148	visitor policy		
149	location of the main office		
150	prohibiting the unauthorized use of school grounds (e.g., skateboarding, etc.)		
	Parking		
151	Are the parking lots clean and clear of litter and debris?		
152	Are the parking lots secured? Can they be, if needed?		
153	Are all parking areas covered by security cameras?		
154	Is parking allowed adjacent to the school building? How close to the facility can vehicles park?		
155	Is there designated visitor parking area that is separate from staff parking?		
156	Are designated parking spaces marked with personal names or titles (e.g., for the principal, SRO, secretary, etc.)?		
157	Are there sufficient designated handicapped parking spaces?		
158	Are designated handicapped parking spaces located near the sidewalk and ramp so that handicapped individuals do not need to navigate through traffic to access the ramp and sidewalk?		
159	Are parked vehicles blocking emergency egress routes or fire lanes? Are these areas adequately marked or signed?		
160	Is there enough parking?		
161	Is SRO parking space located in an area that is easily visible (e.g., in front parking areas near the main entrance)?		
162	Are the parking lots in good condition? Were any trip hazards from eroding asphalt observed?		
163	Are painted markings in parking lots (e.g., space markings, traffic flow patterns, fire lanes, etc.) worn or outdated?		

	Area	Y/N	Description/Comments
	Student Drop-off/Pick-up		
164	Is the student drop-off/pick-up area adequately signed?		
165	Are additional signs needed to deter speeding and to enforce proper traffic flow during drop-off and pick-up?		
166	Is there a problem with speeding during drop-off and pick-up, or in the parking lots in general?		
167	Does the drop-off/pick-up area allow for smooth traffic flow?		
168	Are there low curbs in the drop-off/pick-up zones?		
169	Is there adequate staff monitoring of drop-off and pick up?		
	Bike Racks		
170	Are bike racks fenced, gated, and secured to the school or pavement?		
171	Is there a sign indicating that the school is not responsible for bikes left after school hours?		
	Sidewalks		
172	Are sidewalks low enough that there is a potential for vehicles to accidentally drive up onto them?		
173	Were any trip hazards on the sidewalks observed?		
174	Are there adequate sidewalks around the campus?		
175	Are there adequate sidewalks in the school zone?		
	Exterior Access Control		
176	Are all exterior doors locked 24/7?		
177	Is there an access control system installed?		
178	Are there any exterior access points via gates, trees, etc.?		
	Exterior Roof Access		
179	Are there any roof hatches?		
180	If so, are they properly secured?		
181	Are there any doors on the roof?		
182	Is so, are they properly secured?		
183	Are there any skylights?		
184	If so, are they properly secured?		
185	Is there roof access from adjacent buildings, covered walkways, or low roofs?		
186	Is there roof access from tree branches?		

	Area	Y/N	Description/Comments
	Exterior Doors and Hardware		
187	Do doors shut and lock properly?		
188	Are panic bars installed on all exit doors?		
189	Are all panic bars working properly?		
190	Do exterior doors have protective film on them?		
191	Are all exterior doors marked?		
192	Describe the exterior doors (e.g., metal, glass, paneled, solid, etc.)		
	Exterior Windows		
193	Are first-floor windows adequately secured with grates, cages, or heavy-duty locks?		
194	Are all air conditioning units secured?		
195	Are there any broken, damaged, or leaky windows?		
196	Are there any problems with hurricane shutters?		
197	Do window need hurricane shutters?		
	Athletic Facilities		
198	What athletic facilities are on campus?		
199	Are all athletic facilities fenced?		
200	Is there any broken or damaged fencing?		
201	Are outdoor athletic facilities accessible to the public after hours?		
202	Do athletic facilities have adequate lighting?		
203	Are all fire exits in athletic facilities clearly accessible?		
204	Are there AEDs near the athletic facilities?		
205	Which staff members have AED training?		
	Playground		
206	Is the playground in good condition?		
207	Is the playground fenced?		
208	Is playground equipment in good condition?		
209	Do the steel I-beams in the covered play area have protective padding?		
210	Were any trip hazards observed in the play-ground area?		
211	Is there a fall protection substance underneath playground equipment? Is it sufficient?		

	Area	Y/N	Description/Comments
	Exterior Garbage Cans		
212	Are there freestanding exterior garbage cans located near the entrance of the building?		
213	Are they secured to the pavement?		
	INTERIOR		
	Main Office		
214	Does the main office have a safety barrier or door between the main area and the area where visitors enter?		
215	Is there a sally trap at the main entrance?		
216	Is there an operational weather radio in the main office?		
217	Were Bomb Threat Checklists observed near telephones?		
218	Are first-aid supplies and biohazard materials properly stored in the main office (if there is no clinic)?		
219	Is the school equipped with panic buttons at the front desk or other areas?		
	Nurse's Office/Clinic		
220	Are all medications and syringes secured at all times?		
221	Are all biohazardous materials properly stored and disposed of in accordance with district/local standards?		
	Public Address System		
222	Does the school have a PA system?		
223	Does it work properly?		
224	Doe the PA system have outdoor speakers?		
	Communications Devices		
225	Do all classrooms have two-way communication to the main office? List the ones that don't. What are the means of communication between classrooms and main office (e.g., PA, Phone, email, radio, panic button, etc)?		
226	Is there a battery back-up system for the telephones?		
227	Is there a secondary means of communication at the school (e.g. bullhorns, radios)? (Does the PA system work via the telephone? What happens if the phone lines are out?)		

	Area	Y/N	Description/Comments
	Alarm/Security System		
228	Is the school equipped with an alarm system? Are there motion detectors in the hallways, door detectors, window detectors, etc.?		
229	Does the alarm system have audible alarm sirens and flashing lights?		
230	Where is the alarm panel located?		
231	Who has access to alarm system codes? Do these individuals know what the zones are for the system?		
232	Are personalized access codes issued to individuals who are authorized to have access codes?		
233	Does the school have an external security monitoring system and if so who monitors the systems?		
234	Are there private security personnel assigned to the school?		
235	Have background checks been performed?		
	Interior CCTV		
236	Is there an interior CCTV system?		
	Fire/Life Safety		
237	Is the school equipped with sprinklers?		
238	Is the school equipped with smoke detectors?		
239	Are smoke detectors installed in restrooms and locker rooms?		
240	Is the school equipped with fire extinguishers?		
241	Are the extinguishers ABC-type?		
242	Are there any water-type extinguishers?		
243	Did all fire extinguisher boxes contain fire extinguishers?		
244	Are fire extinguishers inspected monthly?		
245	Is the school equipped with hoses?		
246	Are fire detection and suppression systems maintained to fire safety code?		
247	Do facility fire detection and suppression systems transmit an alarm to a communication center?		
248	Is the fire department capable of reaching the facility adequate/above average?		

	Area	Y/N	Description/Comments
	Interior Lighting		
249	Is the overall lighting in the interior of the facility adequate/above average?		
	Emergency Power and Lighting		
250	Is the school equipped with emergency back-up power in case of power failure?		
251	Are emergency lights checked monthly?		
252	Are there any defective emergency lights?		
253	Is the school a designated hurricane shelter?		
254	Does the school have a generator?		
255	Is the generator checked periodically?		
	Ceilings/Floors/Walls		
256	Were any missing or damaged ceiling tiles observed?		
257	Were classroom/hallway walls, floors and ceilings clear of excessive paper, storage items, and other obstructions?		
258	Were any holes in fire walls observed?		
	Interior Doors and Hardware		
259	Are interior doors secured at all times?		
260	Are the locks on classroom doors adequate in a lockdown situation and do not create a life safety hazard? (Can interior doors lock from the inside?)		
261	Are interior door knobs ADA-compliant?		
262	Are there access control systems on doors leading to sensitive areas or offices?		
	Interior Windows		
263	Are there any broken, damage, or inoperable windows?		
264	Is there a window or glass panel in doors/walls of administrative offices for visibility?		
	Interior Signage		
265	Is there universal evacuation and sheltering signage throughout the school? Does the signage highlight two means of egress?		
266	Are all exit signs illuminated?		
267	Do emergency exit signs point occupants in the correct direction(s) to exit the facility?		

	Area	Y/N	Description/Comments
	Hallways		
268	Are hallways clear of obstruction? Are items being stored in hallways?		
269	Are hallways adequately illuminated?		
270	Are there blind corners in hallways that need mirrors?		
271	Is there motion detector lighting installed in hallways?		
272	Are there signs above hallway fire extinguishers?		
273	Do all lockers have locks on them?		
	Classrooms		
274	Are classroom doors secured at all times, even when in use?		
275	Are classrooms exit doors and emergency egress windows free of obstruction and properly marked?		
276	Do emergency escape windows have visible, unobstructed signage?		
277	Are all bookshelves and cabinets secured to the walls or floor?		
278	Are all televisions fastened to stands with safety straps or other device?		
279	Is the outlet near the sink a GFCI outlet?		
280	Were any sharp objects observed lying around within reach of students?		
281	Were chemicals and cleaners found in cabinets under classroom sinks or other areas where children can reach them?		
282	Are there first aid kits or additional fire extinguishers in classrooms with tools or other equipment?		
283	Are items being stored on top of heating units?		
284	Are classrooms equipped with panic buttons?		
	Portable Classrooms		
285	Are portable walkways, handrails, and steps in good condition? Look for protruding nails, loose boards, rooting wood, etc.		
286	Are portables inspected for mold periodically?		
287	Are locks and doorknobs on portable exit doors ADA-compliant or have panic bars?		
288	Are portable doors and floors in good condition?		

	Area	Y/N	Description/Comments
	Library/Media Center		
289	Does the library have a security system in place to reduce the loss of books/items?		
290	Are mirrors needed in the media center to improve observation of hidden areas?		
291	Is the area where copiers and television routers are located properly ventilated?		
292	Are exit doors properly marked?		
	Art Room		
293	Is the ventilation system for the kiln adequate? Has it been approved by the fire marshal? Are there any complaints by the teacher regarding fumes or heat?		
294	Are there combustible materials stored within three feet of the kiln?		
295	Is linseed oil stored in a flammable liquids cabinet?		
296	Are oil-soaked rags properly disposed of?		
	Science Room		
297	Are science chemicals properly stored in a secure area?		
298	Are safety equipment (goggles, eye wash, shower, etc.) easily accessible in the science room?		
299	Are eye wash and shower stations inspected weekly?		
300	Were there old, unused, leaking, spilled, or unmarked chemicals observed in the science room? Does the school inventory and purge chemicals regularly?		
301	Do science rooms have a secondary means of egress?		
302	Are chemical or biohazards being stored in same refrigerators/freezers as food items?		
	Shop/Technology Room		
303	Are all tools secured when not in use?		
304	Are there emergency shut-off buttons in shop/technology classroom? Are they clearly accessible?		
	Restrooms		
305	Do restrooms have evacuation signage?		
306	Are the locks on bathroom stall doors working properly?		

	Area	Y/N	Description/Comments
	Restrooms (cont.)		
307	Are stall doors in good condition and working properly?		
308	Are there plumbing problems?		
	Stairways		
309	Do stairwells have non-slip surfaces to reduce chances of a slip-and-fall?		
	Computer Rooms		
310	Are computer rooms secured at all times?		
	Data/Server Room		
311	Is there an appropriate ventilation system in the server room(s)?		
312	Is the server room(s) being used for storage?		
	Kitchen/Cafeteria		
313	Is there a doorbell at the delivery door of the kitchen?		
314	Is there a peephole in the delivery door?		
315	Is the delivery door closed and locked at all times?		
316	Are all knives, box cutters, etc. stored securely when not in use? (e.g., locked in the pantry, locked in a separate drawer, etc.)		
317	Is the walk-in cooler equipped with a safety handle on the inside?		
318	Are there GFCI electrical outlets installed near sinks and water?		
319	Is there a sign above the activation button for the fire suppression system?		
320	Is the activation button for the fire suppression system within eight feet of the exhaust hood and frying area?		
321	Are cafeteria staff aware of students and staff with food allergies?		
322	Are cafeteria staff trained on basic procedures regarding handling choking situations, first aid, and how to recognize allergic reactions to food?		
323	Are there signs in cafeteria on how to handle choking and first aid situations?		

	Area	Y/N	Description/Comments
	Kitchen/Cafeteria (cont.)		
324	Are cafeteria staff trained in basic emergency management procedures (fire suppression, evacuation, shelter, and lockdown)?		
325	Is there an appropriate eye wash station near the chemical storage area and/or dishwashing area?		
326	Are all chemicals properly stored away from food items?		
327	Are MSDS forms properly maintained and accessible?		
328	Are kitchen fans working properly and not too loud to risk staff members being unable to hear the fire alarm or PA system?		
	Auditorium		
329	Is the auditorium secured when not in use?		
330	Are exits clearly marked?		
331	Is there reflective striping or low-level lighting at the edge of the stage and stairs?		
	Gym		
332	Is the school equipped with an automatic bleacher system? Is there a safety system installed?		
333	Are gym attendants properly trained on the use of the motorized bleacher system?		
334	Is the gym secured when not in use?		
335	Do bleachers have handrails at both ends?		
336	Is there a First Aid Kit and AED device in the gym area?		
337	Are illuminated exit signs installed in the gym?		
338	Are there grills to protect the lights and illuminated exit signs from flying objects?		
	Locker Rooms		
339	Are personal items left in unlocked lockers?		
340	Are mirrors needed in the locker rooms to improve visibility?		
341	Do exit doors have panic bars on them?		
342	Does the locker room have illuminated exit lights?		

	Area	Y/N	Description/Comments
	Weight Room		
343	Is weight room equipment properly maintained and are weights properly stored?		
	Mechanical and Custodial Rooms		
	Are the following equipment checked by the custodians on a regular basis?		
344	fire/life safety systems		
345	HVAC		
346	fire suppression		
347	fire extinguishers		
348	smoke/heat detectors		
349	generators		
350	security alarm		
351	Were mechanical, custodial, and electrical rooms found to be locked?		
352	Were all chemicals properly stored, labeled, and in their original containers?		
353	Are there any protruding metal beams that are not padded?		
354	Do custodial crews have portable weather alert scanners or other means to receive weather warnings?		
355	Do night custodians have an additional means of communication (e.g., radios) to communicate with each other in case of danger?		
356	Are gasoline and other flammables stored properly in a locked metal Flammables Storage cabinet?		
357	Is the gasoline/flammable storage area organized and free of clutter?		
358	Are there any bottle eye wash stations?		
359	Are outlets near sinks GFCI outlets?		
360	Is there at least three feet of clearance around all electrical and HVAC boxes?		
361	Are all electrical boxes (particularly in hallways) properly secured to prevent tampering?		
362	Were all physical operations rooms neat and organized?		

	Area	Y/N	Description/Comments
	Mechanical & Custodial Rooms (Cont.)		
363	Are administrators aware of the location of janitorial rooms, AHUs, and other physical operations rooms?		
364	Are they informed of proper shut-off procedures for the HVAC system?		
365	Is the HVAC shut off accessible remotely?		
	Elevators		
366	Are elevators inspected on a yearly basis or to code?		
367	Do students have access to elevators?		

* Retrieved from https://www.kycss.org/emp/SSVulnerabilityAssessment.doc

Appendix 11.2
Selected Handouts from School-Level Crisis Response Plan Model

Crisis Response Plan Table of Contents

Individual Responsibilities

Public Information Officer

- Determine, according to direction from the IC, any limits on information release.
- Develop accurate, accessible, and timely information for use in press/media briefings.
- Obtain IC's approval of news releases.
- Conduct periodic media briefings.
- Arrange for tours and other interviews or briefings that may be required.
- Monitor and forward media information that may be useful to incident planning.
- Maintain current information, summaries, and/or displays on the incident.
- Make information about the incident available to incident personnel.
- Participate in the planning meeting.

Safety Officer

- Identify and mitigate hazardous situations.
- Ensure safety messages and briefings are made.
- Exercise emergency authority to stop and prevent unsafe acts.
- Review the Incident Action Plan for safety implications.
- Assign assistants qualified to evaluate special hazards.
- Initiate preliminary investigation of accidents within the incident area.
- Review and approve the Medical Plan.
- Participate in planning meetings.

Drill Schedule and Log

Use the following worksheet to plan drills for your school. Submit a copy of the schedule with your school's plan, and use the original to document drills when they actually occur.

Fire Drills: **Two fire drills in the first month of school, and one per month each following month.**

Monthly Schedule	Date Conducted	Weather Conditions	Number of Occupants	Evacuation Time	Comments/ Notes
1st:					
2nd:					
3rd:					
4th:					
5th:					
6th:					
7th:					
8th:					
9th:					
10th:					
11th:					
12th:					

Emergency Team "Toolbox"

Each school's Emergency Response Team should consider developing a "toolbox" to have available for use during an emergency situation. Items in the toolbox should not be used for anything other than emergency preparedness training activities. A member of the Emergency Response Team should be assigned to keep the toolbox updated (change batteries, update phone numbers, etc.). The toolbox should be portable and readily accessible for use in an emergency.

- ☐ Copies of all forms completed in the development of the school or facility Emergency Response Plan (Chain of Command, Students Needing Assistance, etc.)
- ☐ Map of building(s) with location of Exits, Phones, First Aid Kits, Assembly Areas, AED
- ☐ Blueprints of school building(s), including utilities
- ☐ Videotape/DVD of inside and outside of the building and grounds
- ☐ Map of local streets with evacuation route (Alternate Building Location requiring transport)
- ☐ Flash lights (recommend the type that does not require batteries).
- ☐ First aid kit and latex gloves (and other types for latex-sensitive persons)
- ☐ Faculty/staff roster (including emergency contacts)
- ☐ Student roster (including emergency contacts for parents)
- ☐ Material Safety Data Sheet (MSDS)
- ☐ Two-way radios and/or cellular phones available
- ☐ Battery powered AM/FM radio and spare batteries (wind-up radios)
- ☐ Several legal pads and ball point pens
- ☐ Grease boards and markers (or dry erase boards)
- ☐ White peel-off stickers and markers for name tags
- ☐ Local telephone directory
- ☐ Lists of the district personnel's phone, fax, and beeper numbers
- ☐ Lists of other emergency phone numbers
- ☐ 5 Bullhorns
- ☐ Create a mini-toolbox for Library
- ☐ Other

Table of Contents for Crisis Response Protocols

Accident with Severe Injuries

PRINCIPAL

- Call 911.
- Notify the superintendent's office.
- Gather facts about the accident.
- Convene Crisis Team if warranted.
- Visit injured students, if possible.

TEACHERS

- Remove uninjured students from accident site.
- Refer distressed students to the counselor or Crisis Team.

OPERATIONS—CRISIS INTERVENTION & RESPONSE

- Counsel witnesses, friends and family.

ADMINISTRATION & FINANCE

- Log all activities and decisions.

SCHOOL NURSE

- Assess injuries.

PUBLIC INFORMATION OFFICIAL

- Prepare statement for the media.
- Provide accurate information to parents and the Community.

LOGISTICS—COMMUNICATIONS

- Notify Central Office.
- Notify parents or guardians.
- Inform teachers and students. (Do not use the PA system).

References

Bureau of Justice Statistics. (2012). *Guide for preventing and responding to school violence (2nd ed)*. Washington D.C.: United States Department of Justice and International Association of Chiefs of Police. Retrieved June 30, 2014 from https://www.bja.gov/publications/iacp_school_violence.pdf.

Fearn-Banks, K. (1996). *Crisis communications—A casebook approach*. New Jersey: Lawrence Erlbaum Assoc.

Federal Emergency Management Agency. (2014). *National incident management system*. Retrieved June 30, 2014 from http://www.fema.gov/national-incident-management-system.

Fink, S. (1986). *Crisis management: Planning for the inevitable*. New York: American Management Association.

Kentucky Center for School Safety. (2008). *Emergency management resource guide*. Richmond, KY: Author. Retrieved June 30, 2014 from http://www.kycss.org/emp/Home/EmerRevCol.pdf.

United States Department of Education. (2007). *Practical information on crisis planning: A guide for schools and communities*. Washington D.C.: Office of Safe and Drug Free Schools. Retrieved June 30, 2014 from http://rems.ed.gov/docs/PracticalInformationonCrisisPlanning.pdf.

Chapter 12

Tying it All Together

David C. May

I began this book as an attempt to provide a critical, data driven analysis of school safety in the United States. With the exception of Chapter 1 (the introductory chapter) and Chapter 11 (where limited reliable data exist), in each chapter my coauthors and I reviewed the literature around the particular topic, analyzed data about that topic, then used the results from those data analyses to present policy implications and suggestions for future research around that topic. Based on those analyses, a number of common themes emerged across a variety of topics. In this chapter, I will discuss those themes and present general recommendations to address those themes. I will then close this chapter with a discussion of ideas for future research in the area of school safety.

Common Themes Emerging from School Safety Research

The first theme from this book is the important influence the media and other popular (but not necessarily scholarly) texts have on public perceptions of school safety in the United States. In practically every chapter in this book, the data presented here contradict at least one common perception about school safety in that area of research. The most notable examples include the area of school homicides and parental aggression against teachers (where many members of the public believe these are almost daily occurrences when, in reality, these are very rare events).

Thus, the first and most important conclusion from this work is that some mechanism must be considered to encourage the media to present a more realistic picture of school safety. Schools, in reality, are safe havens for many students who suffer from physical or sexual abuse in their homes or who serve as "quasi-parents" for their younger siblings because their biological parents are incapable (through intent, mental or physical illness, or some other reason) for providing care for them. These students need schools as a place where they can interact with caring adults who offer them not only a safe and secure learning environment, but also provide them an educational opportunity to be successful in life upon their graduation.

Additionally, for every school shooting that occurs in the United States, there is some number (perhaps dozens) of potential shootings that are averted because a student found out about another student's plans to do harm (e.g., one student shows another student a weapon at school, another student warns his friends not to go to school on a particular day) and reported those plans to their parent, teacher, principal, or law enforcement authority. When these stories do occur, they should receive far more attention from the media than they currently do. This not only will present a piece of the puzzle that is rarely considered by current media presentations, thus giving the public a more objective view of school safety, but it may also embolden even more students to tell trusted adults when they are aware of plans to do harm. As we highlighted in chapter 3, the vast majority of students we surveyed responded that they would report another student if they were aware that student had a weapon (regardless of their relationship with that student or the weapon involved). This type of positive media attention will help turn students' words into action and may reduce the "culture of snitching" that is prevalent in some schools.

In addition to presenting a more realistic picture of student safety, more objective reporting by the media will likely encourage better-qualified teachers to consider education as a profession. Currently, there is a widespread perception that teachers are at an elevated risk of being physically assaulted by students and/or parents in the course of their daily activities. As the *Indicators of School Crime and Safety* report mentioned several times throughout this book suggests, and our work with Kentucky public school teachers in chapter 4 further confirms, public school teachers are at a very low risk of being assaulted physically. In fact, most of their confrontations will occur via email or phone. Thus, it is important to spread the message that, relative to many other professions, schools are safe places to work. Reports such as those conducted by the United States Department of Labor (2013) that present data about nonfatal and fatal occupational injuries should be used to advertise this relative safety on a much broader scale than they are currently being used.

A second theme that emerged across several topics is the importance of teachers in creating positive, safe learning environments for students and overall school safety. Teachers are essential for building rapport with students to give them an adult they trust at school in whom they can confide when they feel they need to. Thus, I would argue that the education curriculum taught at universities needs to be seriously revamped. Rather than being taught to be experts in developing lesson plans, which currently require hours of preparation during the university experience of the typical education major, teachers need to have far more training at the university in conflict management, social and emotional intelligence, empathy, cultural awareness, and classroom behavior management. Teachers need to learn in their university training that they are entering one of the safest professions in which they can work (a message they rarely receive from the media). However, there is a strong likelihood that they will experience verbal abuse from parents in their careers (e.g., being cursed at and perhaps even threatened by parents and students) and that likelihood is much greater at middle and high school levels. I teach in the area of criminology. I constantly remind my students (throughout every class I teach) that if they do not like conflict, and they cannot work in an environment where most people are not going to like them, then they should choose another major and another profession. Derivatives of this message also need to be delivered to teachers. Additionally, teachers need to receive university training on both how and when to discipline (since this is the leading cause of conflict with parents). They also need to enter the profession with their "eyes wide open" to the realities of the profession, rather than the current impression that they often have when graduating from universities.

One method to ensure that this occurs is to allow university professors to work more closely with local schools. My interviews with teachers and administrators in over a decade of work in this area reveal that both groups feel that too much time is spent on lesson plans and not enough time is spent on training teachers how to discipline and manage classroom behaviors, deal with conflict caused by clashing cultures, and learn how to encourage children to engage in positive behaviors through modeling and communication. The reality is that, in most areas of the United States, teachers are likely to be white, middle class females, serving populations that are not. It is essential that these teachers realize that the youths they are educating are simply not like them, and not likely to respond to things that have caused them to behave in their own experience. This realization needs to begin in the university, where students work closely with local schools as part of their education, and needs to be reinforced throughout their teaching careers.

However, this education does not need to stop upon graduation nor does it need to be limited to teachers. In local communities, school boards make important financial and planning decisions that have tremendous implications for school safety, often with little or no training about any of the topics just suggested as good topics to be covered in an education curriculum. Thus, it is essential that school board members receive similar training (although certainly much more condensed versions) as teachers in these areas. Additionally, many of the disciplinary actions that are used in the school setting (and at disproportionate rates among nonwhite students) are implemented because of board policy violations in the schools. Consequently, school board members should be exposed to "best practices" in considering and creating school board policy and implementing disciplinary actions to deal with those violations.

Currently, most states do not require professional development and training for school board members (Roberts & Sampson, 2011). School board members are generally elected individuals; at a minimum, as part of the requirement for taking office on a public school district board, state departments of education should require training around effective policy development in the area of school safety. This requirement would certainly not decrease school safety; there is a strong likelihood, at relatively little cost to the state, the requirement would improve school safety throughout the state.

Another theme that has evolved throughout the course of this book is the importance of good working relationships between school administrators, teachers, parents, and emergency responders to create the safest school environment possible. There are a number of benefits from these relationships. First, a good working relationship between a school administrator and the teachers in the school will lead to a situation where administrators will support (not undermine) teachers when they fairly enforce clear rules for classroom behavior among students. As we pointed out in Chapter 4, discipline is a frequent point of disagreement between parents and teachers. To reduce concern about this problem, teachers need to feel that they are being supported by the administrators in their schools.

One method through which these conflicts can be reduced is through the use of school-wide positive behavior interventions and supports (SWPBIS), a system that has been demonstrated to be effective in reducing misbehavior in schools and is currently being used in over 10,000 schools in the United States (Horner, Sugai, & Anderson, 2010). The goals of SWPBIS are to (1) prevent the development of problem behaviors,

(2) eliminate or decrease behavior problems among some students, and (3) increase positive behaviors among all students (Anderson & Kincaid, 2005). Although SWPBIS is not a "canned" approach, a number of common features are typically found in schools using this approach. These include: (1) using a team-driven approach to implement and sustain change into the school; (2) use of school data to identify recurring problem behaviors and the site-specific locations in which they are most likely to occur; (3) development of a set of school-wide expectations and rules based on that data analysis; (4) design of an incentive program to increase positive and appropriate behaviors; (5) development of a continuum of consequences for problem behaviors; (6) design and implementation of a curriculum to teach faculty, students, and staff about the rules, expectations, and rewards of the program; and (7) monitoring of school data to determine the effectiveness of the SWPBIS program (Anderson & Kincaid, 2005). Additional information about SWPBIS programs can be found at the Positive Behavioral Interventions and Supports Technical Assistance website (Positive Behavioral Interventions and Support, n.d.)

Implementation of SWPBIS has been demonstrated to decrease problem behaviors at school and, in doing so, is likely to reduce conflict with parents and increase school safety (Horner et al., 2010). SWPBIS also will help in dealing with other themes that were found throughout this book. First, a by-product of reducing problem behaviors is an improvement in the culture and climate of the school, which often helps student feel that adults in their school can be trusted. As Johnson, Burke, and Gielen (2012) argue, measures such as metal detectors, school resource officers, and security cameras are only "stop-gap" measures that treat symptoms of school violence rather than causes *unless* these measures are viewed by the students as part of a caring and supportive school climate. Encouraging students and adults to work together to make their school a positive environment, with shared ownership and good communication between all partners, is essential for making schools as safe as they can be. Additionally, students attending orderly schools are much more willing to do their part to maintain that orderly environment. Thus, it makes sense that improving school climate through SWPBIS has the potential to increase reporting of problem behaviors such as weapon carrying and bullying by reducing the stigma of snitching so often found in schools. Any effort that has the potential to improve reporting of misbehavior should definitely be considered.

Using SWPBIS as part of an overall effort to improve the culture and climate of schools may also improve school safety in other ways. Improving the culture and climate in schools by rewarding positive behaviors and reducing misbehavior also has the potential to reduce fear of crime at school. In Chapter 5, we highlighted the fact that if students' perceptions of risk of victimization are reduced, this will also reduce their fear of crime. The impact of an open reporting climate does not stop there, however.

As we discussed in Chapter 5, two of the most important causes of fear of crime at school are the shadow of sexual assault (particularly for females) and the shadow of powerlessness (particularly for males). By increasing the likelihood that students will report misbehaviors and rewarding them for doing so, schools will increase the likelihood of communication between students and adults about other topics as well. This avenue can lead to potentially powerful discussions between students and teachers about strategies to improve student empowerment and reduce their own likelihood of sexual assault. Universities regularly have training and programs targeted at female students that discuss strategies and behaviors in which they can engage to reduce their likelihood of sexual assault. These same programs often target males as well, and ask them to discuss the importance of controlling their own behaviors (and behaviors of their male friends) and intervening on behalf of their female friends when they are in situations that increase the likelihood of sexual assault (e.g., excessive drinking at parties). Programs modeled after these can be delivered in middle and high school settings as well; these programs are certain to stimulate discussion that adults delivering those programs can use to decrease fear and perceptions of risk.

Other components of SWPBIS are also important for increasing school safety. Schools that use SWPBIS typically use a team of school administrators, regular teachers, and special education teachers to develop a continuum of consequences for dealing with problem behaviors (Anderson & Kincaid, 2005). The use of this team increases the likelihood of school-wide implementation of this continuum of consequences. When a continuum of consequences is available, and all teachers and administrators are working from the same continuum, this should have a number of positive impacts that address themes uncovered in the course of this book. First, a continuum of punishments utilized by all teachers and administrators should reduce the number of students experiencing corporal punishment (Chapter 6) and/or out-of-school suspensions (Chapter 9), discipline strategies that have limited chance for reducing problem behaviors. Second, a consistently enforced continuum of punishments should reduce discretionary decision-making by teachers and administrators alike, which will likely reduce disproportionate suspensions of black students (Chapter 8). Thus, SWPBIS has the potential to address a number of themes that have emerged throughout this book.

Implementation of SWPBIS also has the potential to address other themes as well. Schools that implement SWPBIS, whether they know it or not, are using data-driven decision-making. As Johnson et al. (2012) argue, most schools collect data about misbehavior at school and culture and climate data each year. Nevertheless, my own experience is that these data are often turned into reports, but are ignored when decisions are made about school safety by the district or school administration. SWPBIS encourages schools to carefully consider the findings of these efforts and use those findings to assist with data driven decision-making.

For example, a culture and climate survey conducted at a school might find that only one in four students at School X felt comfortable reporting criminal behaviors of other children to an adult at their school. Thus, School X administrators should use this information to develop strategies to increase interaction between students and teachers so that this problem can be reduced. Analysis of school data may also uncover that one or two teachers are responsible for a disproportionate amount of office referrals; administrators can work with these teachers as they implement SWPBIS to ensure that their disciplinary strategies mirror those of other teachers in the school. An analysis of school data may also find that an inordinate number of problem behaviors occur at the lockers, or in the gym, or in the cafeteria. In each of these cases, strategies such as increased supervision at "peak" times of misbehavior or student traffic flow changes may also reduce these problem behaviors.

Another theme uncovered in the research conducted for this book is the importance of program fidelity for school-based programs. As we discussed in Chapter 7, the bullying prevention program that we evaluated lacked program fidelity—in other words, the people administering the program did not administer it as it was designed. Unfortunately, challenges facing programs delivered in school settings often lead to poor program fidelity, no matter what type of program is being delivered. SWPBIS provides one mechanism to reduce this problem. When schools use SWPBIS, programs such as bullying prevention programs (or drug resistance programs, anger management programs, or a host of many others) can be introduced by the team that is implanting SWPBIS strategies. These team members have often formed strong relationships with teachers and staff throughout the building; thus, teachers charged with delivering programming may be much more likely to do so in the way the program was designed because of their "buy-in" based on SWPBIS.

Nevertheless, SWPBIS alone will not solve all behavior problems in schools. Another important theme that has emerged through this book is the importance of parental involvement in decision-making processes at the school. Parental input is valuable on a number of levels.

Because discipline incidents are a primary cause of teacher-parent conflict (from the teachers' perspectives), disciplinary policy and practice should be procedurally clean, should involve parents, and should provide for transparency in its development, implementation, and monitoring. Additionally, concerted efforts should be made to involve a good number of nonwhite parents in these discussions, given that nonwhite students often are disproportionately impacted by school disciplinary actions. Schools can be proactive in preventing problems here by: (1) developing clear discipline codes, including consequences for specific infractions; (2) enforcing rules consistently and without favoritism; (3) communicating the rules to parents, students, and the community at large; and (4) creating and maintaining a process through which parents can address their concerns regarding discipline issues with the principal and, if needed, the superintendent and school board. Involving parents in the process of developing discipline codes can be a very effective approach (Sheldon & Epstein, 2002).

A clear disciplinary code and a process for addressing appeals and other issues should also be thoroughly explained in the student handbook. Recent research (National Center for Education Statistics, 2006) suggests that only 60% of schools have a formal process to obtain parent input on policies related to school crime and discipline, and only 19% of schools have a program that involves parents at school in helping to maintain school discipline. Moreover, data on disciplinary incidents should be assembled and published in a manner that is accessible to parents and other interested parties in the community. Schools should also be proactive in disseminating this information to parents at every opportunity and through a variety of media (e.g., print, electronic). Clearly and proactively communicating this information may reduce the number of potentially problematic situations that arise. While these strategies will certainly not completely eradicate parent-teacher conflicts, any strategy that reduces this conflict is a worthwhile strategy to explore.

Another theme emerging from this work is the important differences between middle/high school environments and elementary schools. Teachers and students in middle/high school are much more likely than teachers and students in elementary schools to experience conflict with parents (Chapter 4), work with SROs (Chapter 10), and experience fear and violence in their schools (Chapter 1 and Chapter 5). Thus, school districts should consider this reality and develop strategies to ensure retention of middle and high school teachers who both challenge students academically and manage student behavior effectively. Additionally, these teachers should serve as mentors for new middle and high school teachers who enter those environments. A variety of mechanisms could be used to do this, including incentive pay for teachers at this level, increased rewards and recognition for their efforts, and reduced district-level or community service expectations for those teachers working in these environments. A colleague who taught in a college of education at the first university where I was employed summed this phenomenon succinctly when he said "A good middle school teacher is worth their weight in gold. You will never pay them what they deserve or what they earn; you can only reward them when you can and pray that they never lose their passion for middle school students."

The next theme that emerged is the importance of including student voices in all efforts for school safety planning. Our research has demonstrated that most students will report weapons possession at school to adults (even when it is their best friend who has the weapon); my experience in crisis response planning suggests that students not only have ideas about school safety that adults have not considered, they are often energetic in their efforts to improve school safety. As mentioned earlier, improving the culture and climate in schools has the potential to touch a wide variety of groups. Asking students to help in that improvement is an often overlooked, but in my view, an essential step in the planning process.

There are several practical solutions that have emerged from this work as well. By now the reader understands the importance of clear, updated, crisis response plans and the importance of maintaining an active crisis response committee comprised of representatives from the community, school teachers, staff, and administrators, emergency responders, and student populations. Schools without school-specific crisis response plans need to develop them; this need can be communicated at the university level to prospective teachers and through training and professional development of school administrators and school board members.

In addition to an open reporting climate brought about through efforts to improve school climate, schools should also consider implementing methods through which students can anonymously report potential problem behaviors of other students, parents, school staff, and teachers. Students are often aware of problem behaviors among their fellow students and their teachers long before the adults working at the school become aware of these problems. Providing an anonymous reporting method (such as a drop-box or tipline) will certainly yield some false alarms; nevertheless, it is likely to yield information that other reporting mechanisms would not uncover. When students know that the school administrators and teachers care about their opinion, and respond to their requests, this is another step in improving the school climate. Just as importantly, the ability to anonymously report problem behaviors among parents can also improve school safety. Children that are abused (whether physically, psychologically, or sexually) or neglected often are afraid to report their own situation to adults at the school; other students, concerned about their well-being, are often more willing to report this suspected abuse. An anonymous reporting system will give them one more vehicle to help.

An additional theme that emerged in this book revolves around school resource officers (SROs). There is no convincing evidence that SROs reduce misbehavior in schools; on the other hand, there is no clear and convincing evidence they increase the number of youths entering the criminal justice system either, despite widespread media attention to a limited amount of evidence for this suggestion (Petteruti, 2011). Trained, utilized, and supervised properly, I suspect that SROs can be one tool in increasing school safety. However, as we demonstrated in chapter 10, school administrators do not always have a good understanding of the role of the SRO and SROs often perform duties that are not part of the law enforcement, counselor, or educator role they are designed to perform. For example, SROs may be an effective deterrent to reduce misbehavior of some children in the classroom setting; however, the presence of another adult to assist in that regard would probably be almost as effective.

Thus, a theme highlighted earlier in the discussion of crisis response applies here as well. Schools need to work closely with law enforcement to best utilize and supervise SROs when they are stationed in school. The presence of SROs in public schools in 2014 is a reality; whether their presence is a fortunate or unfortunate reality depends on the perception of the observer because the limited empirical evidence about SROs does not provide a definitive answer to that question. What we do know is that more attention to training and use of SROs is essential and schools and law enforcement should both be parts of that discussion.

A final theme involves use of disciplinary strategies other than out-of-school suspension. As we detailed in Chapter 9, at best, out-of-school suspensions have little impact on problem behaviors among students because they do not serve as a specific deterrent (the child who is receiving an out-of-school suspension for problem behavior may even consider time away from school as a reward) or a general deterrent (other students that witness a child receiving an out-of-school suspension will not be dissuaded from their own future misbehavior because of that punishment). More realistically, as we discussed in Chapter 8, out-of-school suspensions are disproportionately used against black students, thus increasing the likelihood that black students will be pushed out of schools into future problematic consequences at greater rates than white students (e.g., dropping out of school, being involved in crime, ending up in prison). Consequently, whenever possible, schools should seek to use punishments other than out-of-school suspension unless the presence of the student who misbehaved has a real potential for decreasing the safety of the teachers and students at the school. It is undoubtedly inconvenient for teachers when a student misbehaves in class; it is probably easier for a teacher to deliver a lecture from a lesson plan when disruptive students are not on the school campus. However, in the larger picture, using strategies other than suspension to avoid interfering with the educational process (while still controlling disruptive behavior) is essential to increasing chances of life success among students who misbehave in school, particularly black students. Community service is just one of a large number of strategies that work to do this.

Recommendations for Future Research

Despite the body of empirical evidence about school safety presented in this book, a number of questions remain that can only be addressed through future research efforts. These topics are discussed below.

First, more research is needed about parents' and students' concerns about safety in school settings. Chapter 5 reveals there is limited inferential and theoretical literature about fear of crime and perceptions of school safety among students. There is far less research about parental fear and concern for their children in school settings. We know that fear is potentially transmitted through parents (May, 2001); we need to explore the sorts of actions and situations that parents fear in the school setting to have a better understanding of student fear.

Additionally, there are a small number of efforts to examine perceptions of safety among students using nationally representative samples (for example, the School Crime Supplement of the National Crime Victimization Study and the often mentioned *Indicators of School Crime and Safety*). Nevertheless, the measures used in these studies have serious methodological problems (Lane, Rader, Henson, Fisher, & May, 2014). These limitations preclude serious theoretical investigation of why students are fearful at school. Future research efforts by the Bureau of Justice Statistics, the United States Department of Education, and the National Center for Education Statistics should seriously consider adding more valid measures of fear to these studies.

In addition to the aforementioned research about parental concerns about their children's safety at school, another important line of inquiry that is relatively unexplored is research about parental attitudes and strategies for their children around discipline, attendance, and other topics in the school setting. For example, we know that usage of corporal punishment in schools is more likely in areas with low social capital and of lower socioeconomic status. However, we do not know how parents in these areas feel about the use of corporal punishment and whether, given other disciplinary strategies, they would encourage schools to consider other forms of punishment. We also have little information from parents about their opinion of crisis response planning, bullying prevention programs, teachers' methods of implementing discipline strategies, or a wide variety of topics that might be considered that have implications for school safety. Future researchers should consider these topics as well.

A third important improvement to the research involves better tracking of school shootings. Each year, the Centers for Disease Control releases a report entitled *School Associated Violent Deaths* (2014), which suggests that they have data whereby further analysis could be conducted by interested researchers into this phenomenon. Nevertheless, these data are not publicly available nor are they necessarily timely; for example, the most recent data available in that report at the time of this writing in the summer of 2014 was for the year 2010. A dynamic, annual report and website, with known details about shooters and victims, would be helpful to researchers in this area but, perhaps more importantly, would present a current picture to the media interested in school violence that could adequately inform their presentations about school homicides and death. This website could easily compare the risk of a school-aged child dying in a school-related homicide with the overall risk of a school-aged child dying outside of school. Users of that website would thus be able to easily see that, among the wide variety of methods through which school-aged children die, school shootings are near the bottom.

Another line of inquiry that needs to be extended centers on the shadow of powerlessness discussed in Chapter 5. The research presented in that chapter suggests that an important determinant of fear among students is their perceptions of powerlessness. Nevertheless, little research has explored that phenomenon and none of which I am aware has attempted to differentiate between the various forms of powerlessness that children may experience (e.g., powerlessness to control academic outcomes, powerlessness to control victimization at school, powerlessness to control their peer relationships). Additional explorations in this area may prove to be fruitful as well.

As mentioned earlier, better research about the effectiveness of SROs in increasing school safety and reducing problem behaviors is also needed; enhanced knowledge about their training and their supervision is desperately needed as well. Nevertheless, there are other strategies to increase school safety not covered in this book that also need to be addressed. Preliminary evidence suggests that usage of metal detectors, security cameras, or school uniforms does not have a significant impact on school safety. Additional investigations into each of these school safety strategies (ideally using quasi-experimental strategies) are still needed.

Finally, as suggested in Chapter 11, research about implementation of crisis response plans and their effectiveness is also needed. Even if crisis response plans do not increase school safety, the process of their development (e.g., increased communication and concern about school safety among a wide variety of partners) is potentially beneficial. Consequently, researchers should examine both the process and the outcomes of crisis response planning in schools to determine their effectiveness.

Concluding Remarks

The journey to complete this book began over a decade ago when I was hired as the Kentucky Center for School Safety Research Fellow in 2001. Because of my activation for military service after the tragic events of September 11, 2001, I really didn't begin my school safety research in earnest until the summer of 2003. Eleven years later, there have been a number of changes in the area of school safety. Use of school-wide positive behaviors interventions and support systems has spread to more than 10,000 schools in the United States; school resource officers are in perhaps as many schools. Use of corporal punishment has declined; use of school-specific crisis response planning has dramatically increased.

Yet, as the French proverb states, "the more things change, the more they remain the same." We believe parents are just as concerned about their children's safety in schools as they were a decade ago (although better measures are needed to be sure of that fact). Yet another tragic school shooting occurred just last year (Newtown, Connecticut) and a number of other, less publicized shootings have occurred since. Students still face bullying as an omnipresent part of their daily school lives in many districts; a small proportion of children are afraid to go to school and live in fear throughout the school day.

Consequently, despite increased information (and, unfortunately, misinformation in some cases), school safety remains a current topic worthy of discussion and research throughout the United States and the world. My hope is not that the evidence and recommendations presented in this book will serve as a "cure" to increase school safety for every child and parent; I realize that goal is impossible. However, if the reader of this book walks away from that read with more informed knowledge about school safety than they had when they began, then this book was worth the effort. If that same reader now has a desire to make the schools in the local community safer, then this book has accomplished its goal. And, if the reader is willing to dispel myths about school safety that they hear from others, and is willing to work with school administrators, teachers, and students to make the schools in their community safer, then perhaps this book has played a small part in making one school, in one community, a little safer. That contribution makes the time, the energy, and the sacrifices to create this book worthwhile.

References

Anderson, C.M., & Kincaid, D. (2005). Applying behavior analysis to school violence and discipline problems: Schoolwide positive behavior support. *The Behavior Analyst, 28*, 49–63.

Centers for Disease Control. (2014). *School-associated violent death study*. Retrieved June 30, 2014 from http://www.cdc.gov/violenceprevention/youthviolence/schoolviolence/savd.html.

Horner, R.H., Sugai, G., & Anderson, C.M. (2010). Examining evidence base for school-wide positive behavior support. *Focus on Exceptional Children, 42*(8), 1–14.

Johnson, S., Burke, J., & Gielen, A. (2012). Urban students' perceptions of the school environment's influence on school violence. *Children & Schools, 34*(2), 92–102.

Lane, J., Rader, N., Henson, B., Fisher, B., & May, D.C. (2014). *Fear of crime in the United States: Causes, consequences, and contradictions*. Durham, NC: Carolina Academic Press.

May, D.C. (2001). *Adolescent fear of crime, perceptions of risk, and defensive behaviors: An alternate explanation of violent delinquency*. Lewiston, NY: Edwin Mellen Press.

National Center for Education Statistics. (2006). *Crime, violence, discipline, and safety in U.S. public schools: Findings from the school survey on crime and safety: 2003–04*. Washington, DC: Author.

Petteruti, A. (2011). *Education under arrest: The case against police in schools*. Washington D.C.: Justice Policy Institute.

Positive Behavioral Interventions and Support. (n.d.). https://www.pbis.org/school.

Roberts, K.L., & Sampson, P. (2011). School board member professional development and effects on student achievement. *International Journal of Educational Management, 25*(7), 701–713.

Sheldon, S., & Epstein, J. (2002). Improving student behavior and school discipline with family and community involvement. *Education and Urban Society, 35*(1), 4–26.

United States Department of Labor, Bureau of Labor Statistics. (2013). *Employer-reported workplace injuries and illnesses—2012*. Washington D.C.: Author. Retrieved June 29, 2014 from http://www.bls.gov/news.release/pdf/osh.pdf.

Index